Leeds Utd O V O AS Roma
2nd March 2000
Stadio Olim... ?0pm
1st leg

...ALL CLUB
P A86s
D
:00 P.M.

IMPORTANT - CONDITION OF SALE
TICKET UNLESS PRESENTED AT TURNSTILE

PRICE
0.00
0.00

GK Nigel Mo
RWB Gary Kell
LWB Ian Har
CB Lucas Radebe (C) 7½
CB Alfie Haaland 8

...rard proved a
...e as Leeds ba
...ously to keep Roma out. Lee
...could and should have take
...lead after 3mins, but Bakkes head
...was saved by Antonioli's leg. Ke...
...then went clean through but dela...
...and hit the side-netting. Apart ...
...that it was all Roma, with To...
...instrumental behind the 2 front ...

Celtic CHALLENGE MATCH
CELTIC V LEEDS UNITED
SAT 24 JUL 1999 03:00PM
THIS TICKET IS NOT VALID UNLESS
PRESENTED IN FULL
SOUTH EAST CORNER STAND

AREA	ROW	SEAT	PRICE
120	BB	024	15.00

ENTER VIA 66-67 ENTER BY K

IMPORTANT
TICKET NOT VALID
UNLESS PRESENTED
CURRENT MEMBER
GOALS

0141 551 8863

SOUTHAMPTON
THE DELL, MILTON ROAD, SOUTHAMPTON
THIS TICKET IS FOR THE SEAT STATED ONLY.
PLEASE TAKE UP YOUR POSITION AT LEAST 30 MINUTES PRIOR

THE FA CARLING PREMIERSHIP
...EEDS UNITED   A01648.
...ED 11 AUG 1999   KICK OFF 07:45
...URNSTILE 16,17 & 18
...OWER EAST STAND BLOCK L

...OW	SEAT	PRICE
	59	£19.00

...SITING SUPPORTERS ONLY
...STRUCTED VIEW

...RS TICKETLINE
703 - 337171
RETAIN THIS PORTION OF TICKET
FOR FUTURE APPLICATION

MEMBERSHIP CARD.

FIGC LEGA NAZIONALE
004 **as roma**
STADIO OLIMPICO
SETTORE OSPITI
...SETTORE FILA POSTO
...510   67   20
...ntero
...L. 35000   Euro 19,63

SERIE
1999-2000
IMA
Assital

1999/2000
stagione calcio...

WEST HAM UNITED
F.A. CARLING PREMIERSHIP CPL
LEEDS UNITED
SUN 14 MAY 2000 KICK-OFF:16:00P.M.
CENTENARY LOWER

AREA	ROW	SEAT	PRICE
NL3	X	112	£0.00 COMPLIMENTARY

ENTER VIA STILES:
1-7...
160

WEST HAM
Dr AirWair
Martens

LEEDS UNITED A.
UEFA CUP 4TH ROUND
's AS ROMA
HU 09 MAR 2000 KICK-OFF 2(
ORTH STAND UPPER
NTRANCE 8A

...OW	SEAT	PRICE
	128	£18.0

01200DEAN

LEEDS UNITED F
LEEDS UTD AWAY SEASON TKT
VALID SEASON 2000/01
Mon 25th DEC 2000 KICK OFF 3:0
AWAY AREA
20691

AREA	ROW	SEAT	PRICE
AW	6	0042	£475.0

Also available at all good book stores

9781785316470

9781785313929

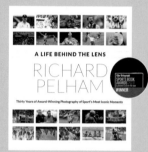

9781785315466

9781785319938

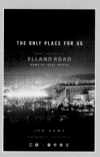

9781785318832

9781785318221

9781908051387

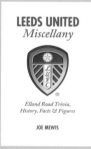

9781905411962

9781905411535

THE
O'LEARY
YEARS

THE
O'LEARY
YEARS

FOOTBALL'S GREATEST
BOOM AND BUST

ROCCO DEAN

First published by Pitch Publishing, 2022

Pitch Publishing
A2 Yeoman Gate
Yeoman Way
Worthing
Sussex
BN13 3QZ
www.pitchpublishing.co.uk
info@pitchpublishing.co.uk

A CIP catalogue record is available for this book
from the British Library.

ISBN 978 1 80150 053 1

Typesetting and origination by Pitch Publishing
Printed and bound in Great Britain by TJ Books, Padstow

Contents

For my mum and dad. Thanks for talking me out of a career in sports journalism. It's not turned out too badly I suppose.

And the families and friends of Christopher Loftus and Kevin Speight.

PROLOGUE

Sgt Wilko's Ten-Year Plan

IN 1996/97, while Leeds United were enduring quite possibly the dullest season in their history, something extraordinary was brewing at their Thorp Arch academy.

It had all started in October 1988, when Howard Wilkinson was appointed manager at Elland Road and set out a ten-year plan, with the aim of creating a production line of home-grown talent, feeding into the first team from a top-class academy. Eight years later, and Wilko's masterplan was coming together better than anyone could have expected. A state-of-the-art training complex had been opened in 1994, and the 1996/97 youth team was a sensation. With Paul Robinson, Jonathan Woodgate, Stephen McPhail, Matthew Jones, Alan Smith and Harry Kewell in the team they mullered the competition in the Northern Intermediate League, winning 28 of their 34 games, scoring 112 goals and conceding just 23. They also made it all the way to the FA Youth Cup Final, where they beat Crystal Palace 3-1 over two legs.

The youngsters made the step up into the reserves for the following season, men's football in the form of the Pontins League. Eddie Gray stepped up with them, promoted from youth team coach to reserve team manager, and there was no better man to prepare the starlets for their final leap into the first team. Gray was one of the great Leeds United legends. He had won almost every major honour for the club over a 20-year playing career and had managed the club too, bringing through a talented group of youth players in the early 80s; John Lukic, Denis Irwin, John Scales, Andy Linighan, Scott Sellars and John Sheridan, who all went on to enjoy careers at the top level. Under Eddie's guidance the youngsters of the 90s continued to thrive, adding to their medal collection by clinching the 1997/98 Pontins League title ahead of arch-rivals Manchester United, with a final day 5-0 thrashing of Blackburn Rovers.

Howard Wilkinson's ten-year plan was complete, and it was clear the club had a special crop of youngsters on their hands, yet the man who created the blueprint wasn't there to reap what he had sown. Sgt Wilko had been sacked in September 1996, with his ten-year plan just two years from fulfilment.

Wilkinson deserved better treatment. Leeds were struggling near the bottom of the old Second Division when he arrived – a hangover from the glorious Revie era had lasted longer than the era itself – but he dragged the club out of its stupor and within four years they were champions of England. However, the team that had won the title fell apart, metaphorically initially, finishing 17th as defending champions in the inaugural Premier League season; then, player by player, they left and were replaced inadequately, to put it mildly. Out went Eric Cantona, in came Frank Strandli. Out went David Batty, in came Carlton Palmer. Out went Gordon Strachan, in came David White. Out went Tony Dorigo, in came Nigel Worthington. Out went Gary Speed, in came Lee Sharpe. I could go on, but you get the picture. By the summer of 1996 the first team were stagnating, and with the club under new ownership, a humiliating 4-0 defeat at home to Manchester United was enough to bring the curtain down on Howard Wilkinson's tenure.

So back to summer 1998. The Thorp Arch products had conquered reserve team football at the first attempt, and both Eddie Gray and the first team's assistant manager, David O'Leary, believed they were ready to join the senior squad for the 1998/99 season. However, despite Harry Kewell thriving in his debut Premiership season, manager George Graham was adamant that the rest of the youngsters should continue to learn their trade in the reserves. It was an argument that he was used to having. The previous summer, Paul Hart, the youth team manager who had just won his second Youth Cup since joining Wilkinson's revolution in the early 90s, left abruptly after a falling-out with Graham over his reluctance to give youth a chance, specifically Jonathan Woodgate.

It's one thing winning arguments with the staff below you, quite another when it's the supporters that are on your case. Even in a pre-digital age, Graham was aware of the clamour from the supporters and used his first programme notes of the new season to emphasise his stance, 'We've invested heavily in our youth policy and I'm sure that will pay big dividends in the future. Obviously we have to nurture them and only bring them along when they are ready. Harry Kewell is something of an exception in that he came in and kept his place.' Jonathan Woodgate was taken on the first team's pre-season tour of Ireland, but when the season commenced, he was back in the reserves, along with the rest of his prodigious team-mates. None of them were deemed ready for top-flight football.

Everything changed when George Graham jumped ship just a month into the season. Graham had done an excellent job reinvigorating the first team and losing him to Tottenham Hotspur felt like the beginning of the end, but instead Leeds were elevated to the top of European football quicker than anybody could have imagined. It was a period of such prosperity for the club that 20 years later there is a common saying in South Korea, 'my Leeds years', which uses the rise of David

O'Leary's young side as a metaphor for the best years of your life. Ironic really, because as Leeds excelled on the pitch with scintillating football and euphoric highs, they were constantly tempered by bad luck, bad decisions, and the darkest times any football club could ever face. There really isn't another football story quite like the goings-on at Elland Road over the turn of the 21st century: a modern-day Greek tragedy.

ACT I

1998/99 – O'Leary's Babies

Tottenham Hotspur 3-3 Leeds United

Leeds United 0-1 Leicester City

Leeds United 2-1 Sheffield Wednesday

Leicester City 2-1 Leeds United

Liverpool 1-3 Leeds United

Manchester United 3-2 Leeds United

Leeds United 4-0 West Ham United

Newcastle United 0-3 Leeds United

Leeds United 1-1 Tottenham Hotspur

Aston Villa 1-2 Leeds United

Leeds United 0-0 Liverpool

Leeds United 1-1 Manchester United

Leeds United 1-0 Arsenal

Tottenham Hotspur 3-3 Leeds United
Saturday, 26 September 1998
White Hart Lane – 3pm
FA Carling Premiership

George Graham was our idol. My dad loved him from the moment he arrived, and I did too. He called for 'Yorkshire Grit' in an irresistible Scottish accent and boasted a proud managerial record, having led Arsenal to two league championships, an FA Cup, a League Cup and the UEFA Cup Winners' Cup. Not so proud was his departure from Arsenal in 1995. George was accused of accepting a 'bung' from his agent, Rune Hauge, and was sacked even before he was found guilty and banned from football for 12 months. In his autobiography, George claimed the £425k was just a thank you present, not a 'bung', but as defences go it was even weaker than the recurring joke on the hit comedy of the time, *Father Ted* ('The money was just resting in my account').

George was left devastated at the way he was treated by his beloved Arsenal. He believed they should have stood by him, in fact he believed there should have been a bust of him in Highbury's famous marble halls (he was probably right on the second count). He spent his exile scouring the European market in preparation for building his next great team, wherever that would be, and two months after his sentence was served George Graham replaced Howard Wilkinson in the Elland Road hotseat. Leeds United had ambitious new owners and a rich history; a top club for a top manager, and vice versa.

Graham did little to endear himself to the Leeds faithful in his first season, which turned into a war of attrition against relegation. The war was won despite Leeds scoring just 28 goals. The manager was keen to explain that great teams are built from the back (and his Leeds team kept a whopping 20 clean sheets), but he didn't help his relationship with the Leeds fans by decimating the attack. The club's record signing, Tomas Brolin, refused to turn up for training under Graham, while his poor treatment of legendary striker Tony Yeboah drew derision from the terraces and resulted in the Ghanaian hurling his shirt at the manager when substituted at Spurs. An acrimonious end for an unforgettable player. Nevertheless, the Leeds fans accepted the dismal season as a necessary evil and eventually made light of the dire football on show, singing 'We'll score again, don't know where, don't know when, but I know we'll score again some sunny day!'

Mine and my dad's faith never waned, and the following season Leeds enjoyed their best campaign since winning the league title in 1992. The hands of time have been cruel to the team George built, their reputation tarnished by the hideous 28-goal season that preceded it, and the electrifying era that followed. Leeds finished fifth and were mesmeric going forward at times, with Jimmy Floyd Hasselbaink and Rodney Wallace striking up a terrific partnership, and teenage sensation Harry Kewell in support. They had a world-class goalkeeper in Nigel Martyn, while in defence the newly appointed captain, Lucas Radebe, was emerging as one of the best centre-backs in the country and Gary Kelly was already one of the best right-backs. Leeds also had Britain's most expensive teenager, having paid £2.7m to win the race for Lee Bowyer, a box-to-box midfielder with an eye for goal. Alongside the star players were the bargains Graham had scouted during his exile: Robert Molenaar, Bruno Ribeiro and Martin Hiden from the continent (the aforementioned Hasselbaink could join this list too, having cost only £2m from Boavista in Portugal), plus Gunnar Halle, Alfie Haaland and David Hopkin, who were picked up from struggling English clubs.

I had such faith in George's expertise that I expected him to guide Leeds all the way to European Cup glory, but the man we loved didn't share the same vision – he was using us all along. George saw Leeds only as a stepping-stone back to London, and with the 1998/99 season only six games old and Leeds still undefeated, George's head was well and truly turned when Christian Gross was sacked by Tottenham Hotspur.

Research will tell you that Graham believed Spurs were a bigger club with more potential, yet Leeds United had a bigger stadium, a bigger fan base, a richer history and were already in Europe. When talking of the season ahead George had listed Spurs as 'one of the wealthy clubs', while referring to 'clubs like us' needing to develop their own players, yet in the five years since the Premiership had been formed, Leeds United had a net spend of £23.4m (the fifth most in the division) while Spurs had a net spend of just £4.7m (the fifth least). Plus, George was also leaving behind the best group of youngsters in the country. All this led me to an alternative theory, that George's broken heart was ruling his head, and the opportunity to serve up his revenge on Arsenal from the home of their bitterest rivals was just too sweet to pass up.

For a while the Leeds fans fought for their manager by singing their support from the terraces, but amid growing speculation their patience snapped when Graham refused to deny that he'd like the opportunity to speak with Tottenham. It was a stab in the back for the supporters, and a stab in the heart for me and my dad. An ironic twist of fate offered some consolation – Leeds were heading to Tottenham in their next fixture, the perfect venue to give George Graham the send-off he deserved.

I loved away games. My dad had started taking me the previous season, though initially he wouldn't allow us to sit with the Leeds fans; 'too dangerous' he said. Our third away trip was to Villa Park, where we had tickets in the Holte End. What a horrible experience that was, having to stand, clap and pretend to be happy when Dwight Yorke scored the only goal of the game. We were low down and right behind the goal, and I could almost feel the ball being sucked into Nigel Martyn's net. Thankfully my dad realised that football was safe enough for a 14-year-old, even surrounded by his own supporters, and we were in with the Leeds fans thereafter. It was such a thrill being amongst the travelling army, singing our hearts out and humiliating home fans up and down the country.

I loved getting tickets for away games too. They would go on sale on a Saturday morning a few weeks before the game, and my dad and I would set off at 6am to get to the ticket office nice and early. I'd join the queue and my dad would go to *The Cracked Egg* to get the hot sandwiches; Bacon-Egg-Sausage for me, Full House for my dad. We would then stand and wait patiently, exposed to the elements for two hours, plus another half-hour or so depending on how close we were to the front of the queue. I loved the camaraderie between the early-morning queuers, watching the line grow as the sun came up, the excitement of the ticket office lights coming on, the thrill of the shutters going up, and finally the joy of having the tickets in your hands. Ah, them were t'days.

The journeys to away games were not so great, though we would always try and start with a hot sandwich from *The Cracked Egg*, if logistics allowed. I would clock-watch from the passenger seat while my dad listened to Radio Two, until 1pm, when 5Live Sport would finally come on, though the pre-match chitter-chatter never lived up to the brilliance of the opening theme tune. Once off the motorway it was map duties for me. My mission wasn't precise, I just needed to find the vicinity of the ground. Once we saw fans walking we would park up and join the herd, knowing it must be a walkable distance, and the sooner you parked the more of the traffic you would avoid after the game.

I was a bit of a saddo really: I loved football grounds (I still do I suppose, the old ones anyway), so it was always a thrill to see a stadium in real life for the first time. White Hart Lane was impressive, right in the heart of the community, surrounded by homes, shops and life, just as it should be. Inside was even more impressive, an enclosed two-tiered structure all the way round. It felt modern, the stands behind the goal were quite new at least, and right on top of the pitch. The Leeds fans were housed in the corner of the ground and me and my dad were in the top tier, while my friends, Lewis and Joe, were in the bottom tier. I'd been friends with Lewis since primary school and he came with us to all the home games, but for away games he would go on the supporters' coach with Joe, to practically every game. Joe was in the year above us at school and new on the scene, but he would become a friend for life. These were the days before mobile phones, but we were all at the ground so early that we were able to have a little chat by shouting between tiers.

Having spent all day waiting for kick-off (all week actually, if not longer), now came the hard yards. The clock would tick so slowly during the wait for the game to begin. I passed the time by reading the programme while ticking off all the little milestones. Out came the goalkeepers first, for a bit of kicking and catching with their coach, soon followed by the players, individually or in little clusters, each getting their own little ovation on to the pitch from the growing travelling army. After a kick-about and a few sprinting drills they would all head back to the dressing room together to get ready for the match, accompanied by the first meaningful chant of the day, always 'We are Leeds'. As the clock inevitably ticked around to 3pm the anticipation grew, and by the time the teams re-emerged it was a white-hot atmosphere at White Hart Lane.

Straight from the kick-off Spurs started up their anti-George Graham chants. They hated the man, not only for his Arsenal links but also for his reputation as a shrewd tactician, which contrasted with the Tottenham ideology of free-flowing, attacking football. The home fans were doing all they could to let Graham know he wasn't welcome at their club and the away fans were on the same page, chanting, 'You can stick George

Graham up your arse, you can stick George Graham up your arse, you can stick George Graham, stick George Graham, stick George Graham up your arse. SIDEWAYS!' Just four minutes later the Leeds fans were asking, 'Georgie, Georgie, what's the score?' as utility man Gunnar Halle headed their team into the lead. Spurs soon equalised with a carbon copy goal by Ramon Vega, a Swiss defender who had chosen Spurs over Leeds earlier in the year, just as John Scales had done the year before, and just as George Graham was about to do. The Leeds fans found other ways to abuse their manager while they were unable to goad him about the scoreline; however, just before half-time Hasselbaink restored the lead, and the joyful travelling fans enquired once more, 'Georgie, Georgie, what's the score?'

At half-time, chairman Peter Ridsdale made his way from the directors' box over to the away end to appeal for calm, pleading with the fans to stop abusing the manager. We were having none of it. In the second half it was as you were, abuse for George Graham from all corners of the ground, with a Spurs fan even invading the pitch and sitting in silent protest in front of the Leeds dugout, until he was dragged away by the stewards.

The second half turned into a real ding-dong battle. Clyde Wijnhard extended the lead, before Steffen Iversen's unstoppable half-volley set up a frantic last 20 minutes. In the last of those minutes Leeds were still hanging on to a 3-2 lead that would send them second in the table, but Spurs hadn't given up. It was a horrible sight when Nigel Martyn failed to gather the last high ball pumped into the penalty area, a horrible sound when the excitement rose around the stadium as the ball bounced loose in the box, and a horrible feeling when Sol Campbell headed it past the green flash of Martyn's desperate dive. The net bulged and White Hart Lane erupted. I was devastated. It was a long journey home, and the pantomime of George Graham's protracted move to Spurs dominated the airwaves.

The million-dollar question that George couldn't answer, 'Was that a point gained, or two points dropped?'

After the match Graham confirmed to Peter Ridsdale that he wanted to go to Tottenham, citing family reasons; they were all in London, including his soon-to-be wife, and soon-to-arrive first grandchild. In a last-ditch attempt to keep him at the club, Ridsdale offered George a director of football role, so that he could still move to London but continue his work at Elland Road. The offer was rejected. Within days a £3m compensation fee had been agreed with Spurs, and George Graham was heading back to the capital (and straight to the top of my blacklist, even ahead of Eric Cantona). Everyone expected Graham to take his young assistant with him, but David O'Leary had just bought a lovely house in Harrogate and remained at Leeds United, in temporary charge of the first team.

Leeds United 0-1 Leicester City
Saturday, 3 October 1998
Elland Road – 3pm
FA Carling Premiership

If it wasn't ironic enough that Leeds had just played the team that was trying to steal their manager, next up in the Premiership was the team whose manager they were trying to steal. Peter Ridsdale drew up a three-man shortlist to replace George Graham: former Leeds captain Gordon Strachan was believed to be one candidate, caretaker manager David O'Leary was another, but top of the list was Leicester City's Martin O'Neill. Having angrily accused Alan Sugar of 'tapping up' George Graham, Ridsdale was adamant he would go about his pursuit of O'Neill 'in the right way', so Leeds politely requested Leicester's permission to speak with their manager, and Leicester politely refused.

Meanwhile, David O'Leary was preparing George Graham's Leeds team for his first match in management. Lee Sharpe was dragged from the wilderness into the first 11, perhaps an indication of O'Leary's deepest desires to add flair to the side, but otherwise this was George's line-up. It was a poor performance. Leeds looked lethargic and flat. With the headmaster gone their application and commitment seemed to desert them and Martin O'Neill pulled off an impressive 1-0 away victory, thanks to Tony Cottee's second-half strike.

As a 'George Graham man', David O'Leary had expected to be jeered by the Elland Road crowd, so he was deeply moved by the hero's reception he received despite the disappointing defeat. He shouldn't have been too surprised. Only six months earlier, after an away defeat to West Ham, Leeds United's chartered flight back to Yorkshire crash landed moments after take-off, a fall of 150 feet. The pilot was the hero of the hour, his snap decision to pull the plane back down to earth when the engine exploded saving all 44 lives on board, but O'Leary was lauded as a hero too. The Irishman had barged open the emergency doors to get everyone off the plane, with the wing on fire and the flames spreading.

O'Leary had initially ruled himself out of the running for the manager's job but receiving such backing from the Elland Road faithful gave him a hunger for it, although in reality the fans were just respectfully wishing him a fond farewell. Everyone presumed Martin O'Neill would be back at Elland Road, in the home dugout, after the first international break of the season.

When the domestic season resumed the managerial saga was still deadlocked. The boot was firmly on the other foot but Leeds were still on the receiving end of a kicking. Where George Graham had a clause that enabled him to speak with other clubs, O'Neill only had a gentlemen's agreement, which his chairman John Elsom refused to honour, against his manager's wishes. In his desperation, Ridsdale reached out to the Premier League and League Managers' Association to try and find a solution, but they couldn't help. The chairman's hands were tied.

Leicester's next game was live on Sky, at home against, yep, you've guessed it, George Graham's Spurs. The home fans spent the whole match showering loving adulation on their manager, begging him to stay with thousands of 'Don't Go Martin' banners. Leicester grabbed a late 2-1 victory on an emotionally charged evening, and an emotionally charged manager announced afterwards that he had decided to stay, as a thank you to the wonderful fans. Maybe if Leicester hadn't scored late O'Neill would have given a goodbye speech, maybe if he'd slept on it, he would have seen sense, but it was done now and Leeds had lost out again.

Out of the ashes came a knight in shining armour. In David O'Leary's second match, at Nottingham Forest, he thought, 'ah bollocks to it', and brought two 18-year-olds into the team; Jonathan Woodgate and Stephen McPhail. The two debutants didn't just improve the team, they looked like the best players. Woodgate was so commanding at the back, McPhail so composed in midfield, and despite playing with ten men for most of the match it took a late goal to deny Leeds victory.

Then came Roma away in the UEFA Cup second round, on the night after Leicester's victory over Spurs. The mighty Italians were building a team that would win the Scudetto in two years' time but were already formidable opponents, with the legendary Francesco Totti alongside Marco Delvecchio up front, and World Cup winners Cafu and Candela patrolling the wings. O'Leary's young team were magnificent. They conceded early and had Bruno Ribeiro sent off, but they hit the post twice, rattling the frame of the goal as much as their glamorous opponents. Delvecchio's goal was enough to win the game, but it was a moral victory for O'Leary, and with Martin O'Neill now out of the picture there was only one man for the job.

Leeds United 2-1 Sheffield Wednesday
Sunday, 8 November 1998
Elland Road – 4pm
FA Carling Premiership

David O'Leary was thrilled when he landed the Leeds job and was setting his sights high. He expected European qualification year after year and he wanted to do it in style, with a team that always played on the front foot, with freedom and without fear. This was in stark contrast to his predecessor, and his vision didn't stop there. O'Leary wanted to transform the whole culture of the club and turn Leeds United into everybody's second team. Leeds United had never been anybody's second team. For over 30 years they had been the most loathed team in the country, starting when Don Revie's young upstarts hijacked the top flight in 1965 with an uncompromising style of never-say-die football. But O'Leary's dream didn't seem so crazy based on the snippet we had seen in his time as caretaker.

The new manager also talked up the young talent in the squad, reiterating that he would not be afraid to give them a chance, having himself been thrown into the Arsenal team at 17 years old, yet his overriding message was that the board would need to get 'better quality players' into the club if they wanted to progress to the next level. It was a point O'Leary felt so strongly about that he only accepted the job once assurances over transfer funds were given.

His chairman was happy to oblige. Peter Ridsdale was a huge Leeds fan, whose teenage years had been spent watching Don Revie's team dominate English football. Ridsdale was determined to bring the good times back to Elland Road and passionately believed in the potential of the club; after all, he had seen for himself the heights that Leeds could hit. He was sold on O'Leary's philosophy and vision, and hailed his new manager's integrity, honesty and enthusiasm, and also his decision to promote Eddie Gray to assistant manager, where he could continue to nurture the young players as they made the final step into first-team football.

Two draws in the league preceded a 0-0 draw in the second leg against Roma, a result that brought an early but dignified exit from the UEFA Cup. Despite the defeat it was a fantastic night at Elland Road, and I was completely intoxicated by the electric atmosphere, especially as it was my first big game in the Kop. I had always sat in the East Stand – the family stand – since it was completed in 1993, but I was now deemed old enough to join the ranters and chanters behind the goal. I was thrilled when my dad authorised the move – it completely revolutionised the matchday experience.

Roma was also my first classic 'European night' at Elland Road. I suppose you could call the 1992 'Battle of Britain' against Rangers a classic European night, but it didn't feel like that with Leeds whimpering out of the first ever Champions League before the group stages commenced. There was nothing whimperish about Leeds against Roma, they were desperately unlucky to be held to a goalless draw. The closest they came to levelling the tie was a chance akin to Gazza vs Germany in Euro '96; Kewell sliding in at the back post was unable to reach the low cross. Wijnhard behind him could reach it, but Kewell's momentum caused him to inadvertently block the ball before Wijnhard's effort could cross the line. Leeds had done themselves proud, but the result brought a very odd juxtaposition. O'Leary had only won once in his first seven games as a manager – a 1-0 victory over Bradford City in the League Cup – yet he was already being lauded as the new messiah. Talk about a knowledgeable crowd.

Next up was the Yorkshire derby with Sheffield Wednesday, live on *Super Sunday*. The Roma games had been televised on BBC, but this was the grand unveiling of 'O'Leary's Babies' to the Premiership audience and felt like an occasion in itself. It was also the day that my dad, Lewis and I moved into our new season ticket seats. The seats we initially selected in the Kop looked great on paper – low down and right behind the goal – but in reality they were a nightmare. You had to watch the whole match through the net, worse still, the crossbar blocked almost the whole goal at the other end. We requested a move, so the ticket office stuck us on trial on the very back row of the Kop, to the left of the goal in block N11.

It was brilliant. The atmosphere didn't sound quite as loud as you were behind all the shouting, but I loved being able to see the whole Kop in front of me, and from higher up we had a much better view of the action; you could actually see what was going on at the other end. Being on the back row also meant we could stand up for the whole game, which had not yet become standard practice throughout the stand. The three blokes in front of us were a hoot too, amazing characters led by the enigmatic Gerry, who once took such offence at a Tony Adams foul that he launched himself forward, clambering over people to get all the way down to the pitch. He only made it down about five rows, but every contentious incident thereafter had the people in front nervously peering over their shoulders, and us trying to control our laughter. I was worried what my dad would think of me being surrounded by their crude banter, but he loved it too, and there we would stay throughout the O'Leary years.

The match itself was no classic, but Leeds took all three points thanks to a gangly teenager with peroxide blond hair, Jonathan Woodgate. Woodgate was impeccable in defence and scored the winning goal too with a lovely looping header over Kevin Pressman, thus receiving the man of the match champagne he was barely old enough to drink. 'We were worthy winners,' proclaimed David O'Leary for the first time. They were words we would hear almost as often as his go-to filler, 'as I say'.

Leicester City 2-1 Leeds United
Wednesday, 11 November 1998
Filbert Street – 7.45pm
League Cup, Fourth Round

It was my 15th birthday and I got exactly what I wanted, a trip to Filbert Street for the League Cup fourth round. These were the days when the domestic cups meant something, a good cup run could keep a manager in his job, and if you actually won a cup the manager would be bullet-proof. With fewer spots available through the league, the cups were also an important route into Europe, and English clubs had recently voted in favour of the League Cup winners retaining UEFA Cup qualification. Martin O'Neill praised the decision in his programme notes, though his reasoning was quite unique – he felt it would have been unfair to block one of only two routes into Europe for lower league clubs.

The domestic cups also presented players and fans with the opportunity to visit the most iconic stadium in the world. I'd never been to Wembley and I was desperate to go with Leeds, but the clock was ticking on its existence, with only four more cup finals before the Twin Towers would be scandalously demolished. There were only three rounds to navigate before O'Leary could lead his babies out at Wembley, but this would be a tough tie. Leicester were a dangerous team under Martin O'Neill, and only behind Leeds on goal difference in the Premiership. Matt Elliott was a man-mountain at the back and Emile Heskey a man-mountain up front, but their real strength was the midfield quartet of Robbie Savage, Muzzy Izzet, Neil Lennon and Steve Guppy.

Filbert Street was a funny old stadium. The away fans were given a tiny shed of a stand that stretched down the touchline, adjoined to terraced housing which you had to go through to access the ground. My first visit had been one of the worst games of my life; it was on the 40th anniversary of the Munich

Air Disaster and there was a minute's silence before the game. Well, that was the plan, but the Leeds fans dishonoured it, and they continued to mock the dead throughout the game. It was as toxic an atmosphere as I had experienced, and to top it all off Jimmy Floyd Hasselbaink fired a 90th-minute penalty wide. Such was the behaviour of the Leeds fans it almost felt like justice had been done, but I still felt desolate on the way home. Surely tonight couldn't be worse than that, could it? Sadly, it could.

O'Leary's babies were terrific, dominating the match with slick passing that left Leicester chasing shadows all night. Harry Kewell was imperious going forward, and with two minutes remaining it looked like the Australian's first-half header would be enough to seal a quarter-final spot. Then, out of nothing, Leeds crumbled. A long clearance enticed Nigel Martyn into racing out of his box. He reached the ball ahead of the attacker but headed it straight to Muzzy Izzet, who lobbed home from 40 yards. Filbert Street was rocking, and I was reeling. Then, three minutes later, 'Big Bob' Molenaar gave away a penalty and suddenly it was all over, Leeds were out. I couldn't believe what I'd witnessed. The Leicester fans were going crazy, and Martin O'Neill's name was ringing around Filbert Street as the dejected Leeds players trudged off the pitch. Football had been nothing but cruel to me all my life, and now this, on my birthday. Brutal.

That wasn't even the end of it. On the way back to the car we stopped off for a kebab to cheer up the birthday boy, and as we waited for our order some meathead confronted my dad, 'Are you a Leeds fan?' Cool as a cucumber, my dad turned and pointed to his heartbroken son, 'He is.' I was gobsmacked, thankfully only metaphorically. It was out-the-box thinking and it did the trick. The neanderthal wouldn't reduce himself to attacking a child so there were no further birthday bumps. I'd already had my lot.

Liverpool 1-3 Leeds United

Saturday, 14 November 1998

Anfield – 3pm

FA Carling Premiership

As a one-club city, Leeds fans will never experience a true local rivalry, the type that splits families in Liverpool, Manchester, Sheffield and Glasgow. However, growing up I was able to sample the feeling as Liverpool were Leeds's local rival in my house. My brother, Gianni, is a die-hard red and our childhood was spent arguing over who was better, Liverpool or Leeds. It didn't stop at whose team was better, everything was up for debate: the managers, the coaches, the fans, the chants, the kits, the dugouts, the nets, the stadiums, even the stadium announcers. The arguments were perpetual, nobody could ever win, so when Leeds played Liverpool the unambiguous bragging rights were like gold-dust.

As with Leeds, Liverpool had gone stale since last winning the title at the start of the decade, and this match marked the start of a new era for them. It was Gerard Houllier's first match in sole charge; the ill-fated managerial partnership with Roy Evans had lasted no longer than most anticipated. Liverpool may have been in transition, but they still had many top-quality players and were clear favourites to win this match, and although I would never admit it to Gianni, I fully expected a defeat.

'You'll Never Walk Alone' greeted the players on to the pitch and the 4,000 Leeds fans did their best to drown out the 40,000 Scousers, though by the time of the rousing chorus we had given up. The Kop weren't having it all their own way though. Scottish heart-throb David Hopkin won the toss and turned Liverpool around, forcing them to attack the Kop in the first half. It was a bitter-sweet victory for the travelling fans, as you always want your team attacking your end in the second half, but this was a necessary evil; the Kop was famed for sucking the ball into the net during late onslaughts. Thus, when the teams trudged off at half-time locked at 0-0, I was delighted, despite a disappointing performance by Leeds. Their only effort of note was Harry Kewell's long-range drive that dipped just over the bar, but they were rarely threatened by an equally poor Liverpool performance. The second half brought much the same, until the deadlock was broken with 20 minutes remaining. Nigel Martyn clattered into Karl-Heinz Riedle in the box, the referee pointed to the penalty spot in front of us and Robbie Fowler duly converted with ease. The game was panning out just as expected.

The last 15 minutes couldn't have been more unexpected, starting with possibly the most unexpected thing of all, Leeds bringing on a player I'd never heard of. It had only happened once in my life, when Imre Varadi came on at home to Sheffield Wednesday in the inaugural Premier League season and scored with his first touch in a 3-1 victory. This good omen went unnoticed at the time. I only remember thinking, 'Alan Smith, who the hell is that?' His name wasn't even on the back of the programme, even though it listed 36 Leeds players all the way down to number 38, Damien Lynch (who I had heard of). A scrawny, blond-haired teenager jogged up front and I assumed he was a striker.

Smith shouldn't even have been in the country, let alone on the pitch. He should have been in Israel with England Under-18s but the trip had been cancelled at the very last minute, two days before the Liverpool game, due to political unrest in the region. Jonathan Woodgate would have been on that trip too, and five minutes after Smith's introduction Woodgate made a magnificent sliding tackle in the box, his big toe taking the ball off the attacker's foot. The referee correctly ignored the Liverpool players and fans, who howled for a penalty as Leeds charged upfield on the counter-attack. Smart play from Kewell set up a chance for Hopkin, whose shot was blocked and the ball fell kindly to the 18-year-old substitute who was loitering on the edge of the box, still waiting for his first touch in professional football. With the coolness of a striker twice his age, Smith stroked a beautiful side-footed finish past David James and into the corner of the net, sending the Leeds fans potty. We couldn't believe it, and our delight was amplified when Gianni's favourite stadium announcer confirmed what we thought we'd just seen, 'Goalscorer for Leeds, number 39, Alan Smith.' What a moment at the Kop end for Smith, and what a moment for O'Leary too. Had he unearthed another gem?

Amid the wild celebrations I spotted Lewis and Joe who were standing on the very back row, where there was apparently plenty of space for me and my dad (deduced from Lewis's frenetic hand signals). We joined them for the last ten minutes, and seconds after completing our greetings Jimmy Floyd Hasselbaink picked up the ball on the halfway line. Jimmy started running towards goal and as he got closer I kept screaming, 'Shoot!', but each time I did he skipped past another defender. After zig-zagging past two challenges, and side-stepping a third, Hasselbaink finally pulled the trigger, firing Leeds into a 2-1 lead. What a goal! My dad turned and bolted, head down, finger pointing in the air, while Lewis, Joe and I threw ourselves around deliriously. If you're wondering why you don't remember this spectacular goal it's because you weren't at Anfield. The cameras missed nearly all of Hasselbaink's dribble, cutting away from an altercation between Hopkin and Oyvind Leonhardsen just in time to catch the finish at the end; the best Leeds goal you've never seen.

My word, was the adrenaline pumping now. Two goals in two minutes had turned the game on its head, and five minutes later Harry Kewell's fantastic long ball sent Hasselbaink away again, this time with only one defender to beat. Some nifty footwork left Vegard Heggem on the floor, and a powerful low drive gave David James no chance. 3-1, Leeds had won it!

What an amazing feeling it was to beat Liverpool at Anfield, especially with a late flurry of fantastic goals. I was on cloud nine all week! In these days I would write match reports after all away games (and the best home games), and three days after describing Leicester as 'the cruellest defeat I have ever experienced', today's match report described 'the best feeling of my life'. That's football for you.

Manchester United 3-2 Leeds United
Sunday, 29 November 1998
Old Trafford – 2pm
FA Carling Premiership

Alan Smith followed up his dream debut with a dream home debut, coming off the bench and scoring with his first touch again in a 4-1 demolition of Charlton Athletic. It was another crisp finish into the bottom corner, this time struck with power from just outside the box. Leeds had registered three successive Premiership wins, 2-1, 3-1 and 4-1, with the increasing margin of victory reflecting the surge in the team's confidence. But there was little chance of continuing the sequence as O'Leary's babies headed to Old Trafford, the formidable home of our bitterest rivals.

I never thought for one second that I'd be going to this game. I'm not even sure if I bothered asking my dad; he would obviously deem it too dangerous. It would be a hostile atmosphere, the car would get smashed up and we might too. Three days before the Manchester United game, tickets for Arsenal away went on sale and, as I was at school, my dad went to the ticket office alone. Once at the window he asked on the off-chance if there were any tickets left for Old Trafford and, incredibly, there were. Some had been sent back and my dad couldn't turn down the opportunity in front of him. I still vividly remember him standing in the hall when I arrived home from school, holding the golden tickets in his hand (well, red and golden to be precise). I couldn't believe they were real, I was astounded, and I've never loved him more! The added bonus was not needing to wait too long for the match. At this age Leeds United was the only interest in my life. I was absolutely obsessed, and when there was an away game coming up it would be all I could think about for weeks. Thankfully it was just days in this case.

We arrived at Old Trafford very early, before large crowds could gather. As we approached the ground, I felt like a soldier heading into battle, and when we snuck through the away turnstiles I had invaded enemy lines. The echoey stairs led us to the concourse, and while my dad went to the loo, I went for a peek at the stadium. It was magnificent, though I wouldn't have admitted it back then. It was a bit like Elland Road, in that three sides of the ground were a similar height, with a big stand down one side. This was a lot more polished, though. The roof joined up, unlike Elland Road, and it was clearly much bigger – a capacity of 55,000 made it the biggest ground I'd ever been to.

I hated Manchester United; as far as I was concerned, Beckham was a spice boy, Keane was a thug, Giggs was overrated, Cole was a pillock, Yorke was a prat, the Neville brothers were rats and Alex Ferguson was the worst of the lot. Yet Ferguson had some very kind words to say about Leeds in his programme notes, especially their new manager: 'It's already clear that he [O'Leary] is intent on bringing his own ideals to bear at Elland Road.' Ferguson continued, 'It's refreshing to see because he is doing the game a service and I hope his beliefs work out. I have seen young coaches trying to change football, only to find the realities of the game changing them, which is always a shame. There is no doubt the game can change you, let's hope not in the case of David O'Leary.'

My hatred for our rivals was so severe that I had never touched any Manchester United memorabilia (except the match ticket, which I was completely in love with), so I was repulsed when my dad bought me a drink and it was in a Manchester United cup; that evil combination of red, black and white, with their horrible badge plastered all over it. I felt so dirty that a couple of sips were as much as I could muster. As the ground filled up, the excitement and anxiety rose. There was a marked difference in the atmosphere of the travelling Leeds fans – it was much less jovial and much more intense. This was war.

Straight from the kick-off Leeds were under intense pressure and should have fallen behind within minutes, but Nigel Martyn came to the rescue in denying Andy Cole what looked a certain goal. Martyn was at it again when he pulled off a superhuman save to claw Nicky Butt's header out of the top corner. It was the greatest save I have ever seen, partly because we were adjacent to Martyn and had a perfect view of the arch in his back as he strained every nerve and muscle to reach the ball. Little by little the visitors worked their way into the game, and on the half-hour mark Hasselbaink picked up the ball out on the left wing. Phil Neville allowed the powerhouse striker to meander into the box, where he unleashed a rocket towards Schmeichel's near post. The Leeds fans at the opposite end of the ground drew a breath as the ball cannoned off the inside of the post, flew across goal, and before we could groan in disappointment it had rippled the net inside the far post. Hasselbaink wheeled away in wild celebration and the Leeds fans followed suit. What a moment, I couldn't believe it, Leeds were beating 'the scum' at Old Trafford!

The home team turned it up a notch but Leeds were playing out of their skins, and Harry Kewell missed a golden opportunity to double the lead when he raced clear but lobbed wide of goal with Schmeichel stranded. Then, right on half-time, Nigel Martyn could only stand and watch as Ole Gunnar Solskjaer drilled home the equaliser. It was a cruel blow for the visitors, crueller still because Martyn was only helpless due to an injury picked up when making the wonder-save from Butt's header, and to compound our misery he didn't make it out for the second half.

Replacing him was Paul Robinson, a 19-year-old who had been man of the match on his debut a month earlier, when he had kept a clean sheet against Chelsea at Elland Road. Robinson's immaculate record lasted barely another minute. His first job at Old Trafford was to pick Roy Keane's shot out of the net. I feared the worst, but the players redoubled their efforts and ten minutes later Harry Kewell was sent one-on-one with Peter Schmeichel again. Kewell had just turned 20 years old, and was blossoming into one of the stars of the Premiership. A year earlier he had silenced 120,000 Iranian fans by scoring for Australia in a World Cup qualification play-off, and now he silenced Old Trafford by lifting a beautifully cool finish over the legendary Danish goalkeeper. Being adjacent to the action, we knew before Schmeichel that Kewell's chip had the required elevation, but we were the last to know that it had landed between the posts. It was magical when the ball settled in the net, causing mayhem in the away end. Leeds were going toe-to-toe with the best in the country. United were back!

For the next 15 minutes Leeds's youngsters took the game to Manchester United. I'd never seen my team play so well. The midfield trio were bossing the match; McPhail dictating from the middle, never losing the ball, Haaland to the right of him, flying from box to box, and Ribeiro to the left, playing like a young Johnny Giles, according to my dad. For a split second the Leeds fans were celebrating a winning goal when Kewell agonisingly hit the side netting when sent clean through for a third time, but when the winner came it was the home side who scored it, a typically late goal (if not quite in 'Fergie Time', as additional time would soon become known). Leeds had tired in the closing stages, but their lagging defence didn't need to do much wrong. Allowing Nicky Butt a yard of space on the edge of the box was their only sin and Butt fired the best goal of his career past Robinson. Old Trafford exploded, but just as the Leeds fans couldn't revel in glory after the opening goal, the home fans couldn't revel after the last goal. Leeds piled forward, desperate for the equaliser they so richly deserved, but it was not to be.

After the final whistle we were made to wait in the ground for 45 minutes while the police cleared the home fans to prevent any trouble, which was standard practice at the time. My dad was concerned it would leave us exposed when walking back to the car but all I could think about was the great game I had just witnessed, as 'We're Leeds, and we're proud of it' echoed around the empty stadium on repeat.

The record books will always suggest that the 3-1 victory at Anfield was the moment O'Leary's babies announced themselves, and I suppose it was, but this defeat was more significant. Anfield had been a poor performance against a struggling team, coupled with a late turnaround; anyone could do that. At Old Trafford Leeds took the game to the best team in the country in their own back yard; only the cream of Europe could do that. After the match O'Leary spoke of his pride in the team, and of his ambition to one day 'kick Alex Ferguson's butt', but today it was Alex Ferguson's Butt that kicked O'Leary's likely lads.

Leeds United 4-0 West Ham United
Saturday, 5 December 1998
Elland Road – 3pm
FA Carling Premiership

Match of the Day used to be great, I never missed it, ever. In the mid-90s it was on past my bedtime so my dad would record it for me, and I'd be so excited that I'd creep downstairs at six o'clock on Sunday morning (if not earlier) to watch it. Oddly, it always seemed to be on at different times. Sometimes it didn't start until nearly 11pm and once I was old enough to stay up that just made it more exciting; the later the better! There used to be a pre-selected main game with in-depth analysis which would take up half the programme, a second game with extended highlights, then a third game just with brief highlights before they quickly ran through the rest of the goals. It was magical seeing the action you'd only read or heard about come to life and, in the days when sports reporting was a service not a business, when a big incident dominated the airwaves you were rarely left underwhelmed.

On this particular day, Leeds v West Ham would be *Match of the Day*'s main match, which always amplified the pre-match buzz; you knew the whole country would be watching, and you wanted to be excited about watching the highlights later. And boy, was I excited about watching this later! Leeds produced an incredible display with a team featuring seven players that were 21 or younger, six of them academy products from Thorp Arch: Robinson, Woodgate, Harte, McPhail, Kewell and Smith. It could have been 10-0, and this against a West Ham side who were third in the league with some top young talent of their own: Rio Ferdinand, Frank Lampard, Michael Carrick and Joe Cole, ably assisted by the experience of Ian Wright, Paolo Di Canio, Neil Ruddock and Julian Dicks.

O'Leary went man-for-man with Harry Redknapp's 3-5-2 formation, with captain Lucas Radebe alongside Woodgate and Molenaar in a rock-solid back three. West Ham couldn't penetrate the defence, and they couldn't contain the midfield dynamo Lee Bowyer who, like his big pal Harry Kewell, was blossoming into a top Premiership player. Against the team he supported as a boy, Bowyer put in the best performance of his young career and opened the scoring with a lovely 20-yard curler. Leeds created chance after chance but didn't double their lead until the second half, when Bowyer started a counter-attack deep in his own half then sprinted 70 yards to bury Hasselbaink's pass, first time into the top corner; a brilliant goal that typified his afternoon. Molenaar added a third and Hasselbaink completed the rout, leading Harry Redknapp to praise Leeds as the best team West Ham had faced. On *Match of the Day* they went even further, comparing O'Leary's young Leeds side to Manchester United's famous 'Busby Babes' and tipping them to hold on to the third and final Champions League spot which they now occupied.

Despite my tender age I knew this was a special time and so did my dad, who hadn't seen anything like it since the Revie years. The feel-good factor went through the Elland Road roof a few days later with the news that the prodigal son had returned. Prior to the game at Old Trafford, Newcastle midfielder David Batty had handed in a transfer request, prompting a few renditions of 'Batty's coming home' from the away fans. Two weeks of tough negotiations followed, and Leeds finally got their man for £4.4m, reportedly because Batty waived a payment due to him from Newcastle in order to break the deadlock. Batty was a straight-talking, no-nonsense Yorkshireman, who played his football in the same vein. He came through Leeds's academy in the late 80s but, just 18 months after winning the First Division title, the Leeds fans were left shell-shocked as Batty was sold to Blackburn, where he won the league again before moving to Newcastle and nearly won it a third time. At the age of 30 he was ready to come home, and David O'Leary saw him as the perfect addition to his inexperienced squad.

There was nobody happier than Peter Ridsdale to get the Batty signing over the line. Having failed in three attempts to land a striker in recent weeks (Dion Dublin, Pierre van Hooijdonk and Ashley Ward), the chairman was delighted to prove to the fans that the club had the money to support O'Leary's ambitious plans: 'This signing blows out of the water, once and for all, the myth that we are not prepared to pay the right transfer fees for the right quality players.' Ridsdale also stressed that player valuations were the manager's field, that it was O'Leary who hadn't been willing to stretch to £6m for van Hooijdonk, while Barnsley's asking price for Ashley Ward was also deemed too expensive by the manager. Ridsdale continued, 'We have to make sure that our spending is at the right level so that we can continue to invest in the future.' The manager and his chairman seemed perfectly aligned; they would be patient in the transfer market to ensure the club would grow at a sustainable rate.

The good times kept rolling as Nigel Martyn and Lucas Radebe signed new long-term contracts before the week was out, tying them to Elland Road for the rest of their careers. O'Leary explained that Martyn, Radebe and Batty would be the three experienced rocks he would build his squad around, with the aim of blending new signings with the young talent already at the club to form a squad of 20 top-quality players. Leeds were certainly building on solid foundations. Batty and Martyn were both seasoned England internationals, while Lucas Radebe wasn't only an exceptional defender but also an inspirational captain. He was an icon in his native South Africa, where in a national poll he had come second only to Nelson Mandela as the person who best epitomised the spirit of their nation. Mandela himself would later name Radebe as his hero.

Leeds celebrated the prodigal son's homecoming with a 2-0 home win over Coventry City, broadcast live on *Monday Night Football*. Batty's second debut included a booking after five minutes (to the delight of the Leeds fans) and was cut short by a broken rib. The hour he was on the pitch was enough to show that Batty was returning to the club a much more accomplished player than when he left; nevertheless, O'Leary had immediately been robbed of the experience and grit he'd added to his midfield. Lucas Radebe was also injured in the Coventry victory, and having recently lost experienced defenders Molenaar and Hiden to season-ending knee injuries, O'Leary's babies would have to keep doing it themselves.

Newcastle United 0-3 Leeds United
Saturday, 26 December 1998
St James' Park – 3pm
FA Carling Premiership

If you were to ask me what game I'd most looked forward to in my life, I would have to say it was this Boxing Day trip to Newcastle. There have been many bigger games of course, but as you get older the feeling becomes normalised. This game hit the sweet spot. I couldn't wait to experience the famous Geordie Roar, see St James' Park in the flesh, and hopefully see this vibrant young Leeds team rip Newcastle to shreds. Furthermore, we had missed out on getting tickets the normal way so my dad bought a special package that included a tour of Sunderland's Stadium of Light en route. For me, an inside look at a brand-new stadium was almost as exciting as going to the match!

My older brother had also been going to away games for a couple of years and, with Liverpool at Middlesbrough, between us we would tick off all three North East grounds on one day. In those days we shared a bedroom and must have whipped each other up into a frenzy. While most kids are too excited to sleep on Christmas Eve, this year Christmas was just a warm-up act for the main event. I remember lying in bed on Christmas night, unable to think about anything else but the next day, realising that I'd probably be going on no sleep at all.

New stadiums were a novelty for me, and everyone, I suppose. Most Football League clubs had managed for over 100 years by upgrading their existing stadiums, but Sky had promised to broadcast 'a whole new ball game' and football was moving into different times. Decrepit facilities meant less corporate income so building new stadiums made business sense, thus a wave of new stadiums would be built over the coming years. The bowls that would become ten-a-penny in the 21st century were still exotic, at least to a 15-year-old saddo, although the Reebok Stadium at Bolton was quite unique and blew my mind at the time; it was as if a spaceship had landed on the M61. The Stadium of Light was similar to the other new-build I'd been to (the Riverside Stadium, Middlesbrough), but it was bigger and felt like it had a lot more character. I loved it. We had a walk around the pitch, sat in the manager's seat, and had a Christmas Dinner in the executive suite. I was in my element: what an experience.

Fast-forward 20 years and the gentrification of football grounds in this country has robbed clubs of so much individuality. The Premier League is becoming dominated by two types of stadium – elite bowls flooded with corporate boxes, and non-elite bowls with fewer corporate boxes – but the lack of variation goes deeper than that. All the pitches are now pristine, whereas some used to be mud-baths, others just had muddy goalmouths, others had large patches of sand in the middle, and a certain few were kept like carpets nearly all year round. Pitches also changed with the seasons, and it was a source of interest to see what the pitch would be like on any given day. In the modern game the substitutes' benches must all be of an exact standard too, whereas in the past you had the really low dugouts at Anfield, the ridiculous little greenhouses at Highbury, and plenty more in between. Even the nets are all the same now, compared to the past where some were tight, some were baggy, some were deep, some were shallow, some stanchions were hooped, some had bars down to the ground, and each brought extra individuality to every goal scored. All this might seem pedantic, but to me the standardisation just makes the whole game that bit less interesting!

Just a fortnight after his Elland Road homecoming this should have been David Batty's return to St James' Park, and in the matchday programme Batty explained how he wouldn't have left Newcastle for anybody else except his home-town club. 'It was just too dear to my heart to resist, a bit like Alan

Shearer felt when he signed for Newcastle.' A 3-1 defeat against the reigning champions at Highbury had knocked Leeds down to size somewhat, and Newcastle would pose another tough challenge. Under Ruud Gullit the Toon Army may not have been the force they were under Kevin Keegan, but they still had a squad brimming with quality. Stuart Pearce and John Barnes were past their best, but Shay Given, Rob Lee, Gary Speed, Didi Hamann and Nolberto Solano were top Premiership players, and then there was Alan Shearer up front, who always scored against Leeds, alongside the towering head-case Duncan Ferguson. It was an intimidating prospect for 18-year-old Jonathan Woodgate – this would be his sternest test yet.

The scoreline would suggest Woodgate passed the test with flying colours, yet the reality was very different. Roared on by a passionate home crowd, Newcastle bombarded Leeds from the off. The Whites looked nervous and an error from Woodgate presented a glorious early chance for Shearer; incredibly he missed from just eight yards. Leeds were under pressure for almost the whole first half, but took the lead courtesy of Harry Kewell, who hammered Hasselbaink's cut-back into the bottom corner after a rare foray towards the Gallowgate End.

It was a great relief to hear the half-time whistle – finally some respite from the Geordie bombardment – but once the second half resumed so did the torture. Leeds couldn't get out of their own half and only Nigel Martyn was keeping the lead intact. He made three fantastic saves in ten minutes, parrying wide from Shearer, tipping over a Ferguson header, then getting his fingertips to Rob Lee's volley into the top corner. When another Ferguson header finally did beat Martyn, Leeds had a defender on the line to save them. Then they delivered a sucker-punch on the counter-attack.

Harry Kewell was improving every week and was well on his way to becoming a world-class forward. His touch was impeccable and he could glide past players with just a dip of his shoulder, and at the end of a flowing move he combined both those skills before unleashing a low drive that was too hot for Given to hold, allowing Bowyer to slide in ahead of the defender on the goal line to make it 2-0. The celebrations were elevated as Bowyer had quickly become my favourite player. I would always 'be Bowyer' for 'Knockout Wembley' during lunch break at school; I loved running around like a man possessed and I loved scoring goals, two things Bowyer was making his name for.

With the Geordies well and truly silenced, or already heading home, Hasselbaink sealed a flattering 3-0 win when he collected McPhail's cute backheel, brilliantly spun Steve Howey and fired past Given, before firing imaginary pistols at the Newcastle fans who had bothered to stay to the end. Finally, the Leeds fans could relax and enjoy the closing moments, and there was no better way to see out the game than belting out the seasonal classic, 'Jingle bells, jingle bells, jingle all the way, oh what fun it is to see United win away, hey!'

Leeds United 1-1 Tottenham Hotspur
Saturday, 13 February 1999
Elland Road – 3pm
FA Cup Fifth Round

'Revie Revisited?' asked the front page of the Christmas issue of Leeds United fanzine, *The Square Ball*. It reflected the mood within a fanbase who were now counting their lucky stars that George Graham upped and left for Tottenham, and wondering just how far David O'Leary could take their club. The comparisons with the man who put Leeds United on the map were centred around the emphasis on youth, the signature of an influential midfielder to guide them (for David Batty see Bobby Collins), and the fact neither O'Leary nor Revie had any previous managerial experience. A new golden era was just around the corner!

The big difference between the two was their reputation with the mainstream media. Don was often lambasted in the press and his team was hated by many, while O'Leary was the media darling and his young side were now everyone's second team. Being liked was a strange feeling for those fans who had followed the club through the 60s and 70s, and even through the doldrums of the 80s their club was constantly bad-mouthed, but I was loving the Leeds love-in. I loved how everyone appreciated our great young manager, his refreshing approach and his wonderful team.

Amid all the adulation, Leeds suffered a real hangover after Christmas. Injuries were piling up and the babies were tired. No fewer than seven first-team defenders were unavailable, with Gary Kelly the latest to be ruled out for the season after his shin splints flared up on his return to reserve team action. The Whites signed off 1998 with a disappointing 2-2 draw at home to Wimbledon and started 1999 by drawing with non-league Rushden & Diamonds in the FA Cup, and a 2-0 victory over Middlesbrough at Elland Road was sandwiched by defeats at Blackburn and Southampton. Thus, despite a stunning 5-1 victory at Portsmouth, a 1-0 home defeat to Newcastle had me fretting that the past few months had just been an extended honeymoon period.

Nevertheless, it was during this spell that my best friend, Paul, who'd previously had no interest in football, finally caught the bug, while Lewis and Joe clocked up nearly 2,000 miles in January by making the trips to Rushden, Blackburn, Southampton and Portsmouth. O'Leary's revolution was the crest of a wave that fans old and new were riding upon, and attendances at Elland Road had sky-rocketed. Every match was selling out; even the FA Cup replay with non-league Rushden & Diamonds attracted a crowd of 39,159, which was just two fans fewer (my dad and I) than Italian giants Roma had attracted. The supporters were clamouring to see O'Leary's young whippersnappers in action; who they were playing against was immaterial, with the odd exception...

I had been waiting all season for George Graham's return and the FA Cup fifth round draw ended the wait prematurely, pitting Graham's Spurs against O'Leary's Leeds; the master vs the pupil. The Spurs team that Graham brought to Elland Road was bang average. Sol Campbell, Darren Anderton, Les Ferdinand, Tim Sherwood and Steven Carr were the better players in the squad. The rest were dross, with one exception: David Ginola. The French winger had lit up the Premiership at Newcastle but at Spurs he had found his 'home from home', prospering against expectations under his new manager, a strict disciplinarian. The same couldn't be said of his team-mates. Spurs were on a run of six draws out of seven, but they were solid at the back and had the flair of Ginola so, despite turgid football and a disgruntled fanbase, they were not easy opposition.

The FA Cup was the most famous cup competition in the world because it was the oldest, with a unique selling point that no other country could offer: a Wembley final. Thus, the big FA Cup ties always brought a special atmosphere. The away fans would fill the South Stand, which wasn't uncommon for league games but the feel for a cup game was totally different. It was win or bust, do or die. The atmosphere would be buzzing even before the players came out, and it always seemed a more colourful occasion too, with away fans often bringing balloons and flags. Everyone was desperate to reach Wembley, though I was almost as desperate just to go to a semi-final. I'd always wanted to experience the neutral ground element, heading to Villa Park, or Anfield or Old Trafford with over 20,000 Leeds fans: what an experience it would be.

A quarter-final place was up for grabs and Elland Road was rocking, with the crowd's hatred for George Graham adding plenty of extra spice. In the pre-match build-up O'Leary, Ridsdale and the Leeds players all spoke of their gratitude for the job Graham had done at Elland Road, while Graham himself spoke of how much he had enjoyed his time in Yorkshire and his admiration for the job O'Leary was doing at the club. Such respect was never going to be reciprocated from the terraces. An eight-man police escort led Graham out of the tunnel and abuse rained down on him throughout. O'Leary, on the other hand, was praised as a high god. This wasn't done to send a message to 'Judas Graham', it was standard practice. Every time the manager emerged into his technical area the Kop would burst into song, 'O'LEARY! O'LEARY! O'LEARY! O'LEARY!' until their hero waved back. He always did, and often threw in a 'Leeds Salute' to boot (a horizontal forearm pump that Leeds fans use to greet each other, one that hadn't been seen on the pitch since Howard Wilkinson's early days).

When the game got underway Leeds struggled to get the better of a tense battle. Spurs were awkward opposition from the moment they won the toss; they forced Leeds to attack the Kop in the first half and kept them at bay with relative comfort. In the second half Tim Sherwood scored a lucky goal at the Kop end and I feared the worst. Going out of the FA Cup would be bad enough, but going out to George Graham would be a catastrophic double-whammy. Thankfully our goalscoring left-back came to the rescue. Defenders were so scared of the wicked deliveries from Ian Harte's left foot that he would always get shown inside, and often Harte would happily oblige, as he did with 15 minutes left that day. He wasn't too bad with his right foot either you see, and unleashed a low drive beyond the reach of Ian Walker, into the corner of the South Stand net. Elland Road erupted. The home team couldn't force a winner, so it was yet another draw for Spurs and a difficult replay at White Hart Lane for Leeds.

The quarter-final draw paired Leeds or Tottenham with second-tier strugglers Barnsley, which made the replay even bigger; the winners would be nailed-on for a semi-final spot.

As I settled in front of Sky Sports, I remember thinking to myself that I'd never wanted to win a game more in my life. Unfortunately, it wasn't to be for O'Leary's babies, who dominated a pulsating first half but succumbed to two stunning goals midway through the second. A scorching 35-yard drive from Darren Anderton flew past the outstretched glove of Nigel Martyn into the top corner, then eight minutes later David Ginola met a high looping ball in mid-air, with a spectacular 25-yard volley that flew past Martyn into the bottom corner. George Graham shook his fists like a macho-man, O'Leary had a look of bemused acceptance – you just can't legislate for two goals like that. Leeds received the post-match plaudits but it was scant consolation. I was devastated.

Ginola scored another wonder-goal to beat Barnsley in the quarter-final, slaloming through their defence before slotting home one of the great FA Cup goals. Thankfully Graham's cup run was ended by Newcastle in the semi-final at Old Trafford, a semi-final that should have been ours, and victory would have set up the dream FA Cup Final vs Manchester United. Oh, what could have been!

Aston Villa 1-2 Leeds United

Tuesday, 17 February 1999
Villa Park – 7.45pm
FA Carling Premiership

With only one league win since Boxing Day, Leeds had slid down the league. David Batty was still recovering from his broken rib, one of 11 first-team injuries, so O'Leary reinforced the squad by adding an attacking midfielder on loan from Holland, Willem Korsten. At 6ft 4in, 'Big Willy' was an unconventional playmaker, and at Villa Park he made his first start.

Aston Villa had been the Premiership's pace-setters: they raced into an early-season lead then added quality from their position of strength. Having sold their star striker, Dwight

Yorke, to Manchester United in August, they wasted little time in re-investing the money, and more on top. They signed Paul Merson in September, right-back Steve Watson in October, and beat Leeds to the signing of Dion Dublin in November. Villa already had Stan Collymore in attack, Alan Thompson and Lee Hendrie feeding the front line, a solid back three of Gareth Southgate, Ugo Ehiogu and a 17-year-old Gareth Barry, and Mark Bosnich in goal. This was a top team. However, since their maverick manager, John Gregory, made one of his trademark sweeping statements – 'If we don't win the title from here it's my fault' – Villa had stuttered and were now at a crossroads. A victory over Leeds would reignite their season, moving them within four points of leaders Manchester United, but with a defeat the hunters would become the hunted. Villa currently occupied the fourth and final European spot, and the chasing pack of West Ham, Liverpool, Leeds and Derby were closing in. As big a game as this was for the hosts, it was just as big for the visitors. Leeds trailed Villa by seven points at kick-off so defeat would effectively end their chase for European football.

This was the first time I'd been to an away game without my dad, in fact it may well have been the first time I'd been to any game without my dad. Lewis, Joe, Paul and I went on the supporters' bus and had a right laugh. We befriended an older boy with whom we got on like a house on fire; he was built like a beanpole and we christened him The BFG. I had been to Villa Park the previous season but this was my first time in the away end, which was one of my least favourites in the league (still a marked improvement on being in the Holte End, mind). We had the full bottom tier behind the goal, but it was only a shallow section of a tall stand so the acoustics were rubbish. The Leeds contingent sounded half the size it was, and often wasn't even chanting in unison. Leeds away ends are a free-for-all, nobody sticks to their allocated seat, so we were able to stand with The BFG on the back row, right in front of the executive boxes, which were always fun to goad.

Aston Villa flew out of the blocks, and without the injured Woodgate the Leeds defence struggled to cope. But cope they did, and despite all the injuries O'Leary still had two of the best forwards in the league; Hasselbaink and Kewell. Hasselbaink opened the scoring on the counter-attack and made it 2-0 with a delightful free kick into the top corner. In my memory, Lewis, Joe, Paul and I bounced around while The BFG wrapped his long arms around us all, although I'm sure it wasn't quite that wholesome. Hasselbaink was then denied a first-half hat-trick by the inside of the post, but at half-time we were overjoyed with the two-goal lead.

Similar to the Newcastle game, the second half was terrifying. It was all Villa as the Holte End roared their team on. Dublin, Collymore and Joachim all went close, then with 15 minutes remaining an Alan Thompson corner was headed home and Villa were back in the game. However, the more desperately the home team attacked, the more dangerous the visitors became on the counter, and Leeds's best chance to wrap the game up fell to the impressive Willem Korsten. Big Willy carried the ball almost the full length of the pitch, twisted Gareth Southgate inside out, before firing a disappointing finish straight at Bosnich. Thus, there was to be no comfortable finish, which made the final whistle all the more delightful. O'Leary's babies had secured a huge three points and the travelling fans lauded their heroes. The chase for Europe was alive again.

The mood in the camp was further improved on the way out of the ground, when we noticed a promotional stall giving away free Yorkies. We filled our boots, well actually it was a Leeds United beanie that we filled, chock-a-block with chocolate. Once back on the coach we counted our takings; precisely 50 Yorkie bars, to add to the two goals, three points and new friend, who we never saw again. Looking back on this episode makes me wonder whether The BFG was just a figment of our imaginations, or a guardian angel for the schoolboys off the leash.

After the win at Villa Park, Leeds went from strength to strength. Korsten scored the only goal in a home win over Everton, and the following week the Filbert Street hoodoo was ended (or put on hiatus) with a 2-1 victory on *Monday Night Football*. Lucas Radebe walked away with the man of the match champagne that night, his rock-solid performance even more impressive considering he had just played for South Africa two days earlier and missed his flight home. 'The Chief' didn't arrive back in the UK until Monday lunchtime, just hours before kick-off.

After a much-needed ten-day break, Leeds finally welcomed David Batty back into the side, and gained some revenge on George Graham by dispatching Spurs 2-0 under the lights at Elland Road. Unfortunately, the result was inconsequential for George. His team was already destined for a bottom-half finish, and ten days later they were parading silverware around Wembley having overcome Martin O'Neill's Leicester City in the League Cup Final, who had conquered Leeds so cruelly on my birthday. Had fate not conspired against us it might have been our dream final, O'Leary vs Graham at Wembley. Oh, what could have been!

Leeds United 0-0 Liverpool
Monday, 12 April 1999
Elland Road – 7.45pm
FA Carling Premiership

With David Batty anchoring the midfield, the youngsters were given even more freedom to express themselves. Alan Smith became an automatic pick alongside Hasselbaink in attack, Harry Kewell had licence to roam behind them, and Bowyer and Korsten had licence to join them in the box at every opportunity. Coupled with a settled defence – Haaland, Woodgate, Radebe and Harte – O'Leary's young upstarts turned into the real deal. They rattled off seven consecutive Premiership victories as their confidence soared, catapulting themselves into the title race.

The winning run was packed with great goals as Leeds swept aside their opponents with ease. In nearly every game Ian Harte or Jimmy Hasselbaink were scoring from scorching free kicks, and our enthusiastic youngsters seemed to come up with inventive new corner routines every week, which never led to a goal but always added to the excitement. Even their kick-off routines were exciting, if less inventive. The ball would immediately be played to Kewell, who would attempt to dribble his way to goal. As with the corner routines, this approach never worked but it was wonderful to see. The innocence of youth.

O'Leary had equalled the feat of the great Don Revie, and standing in the way of a club-record-breaking eighth straight top-flight victory were Liverpool, and the curse of the manager of the month award. It was O'Leary's first award in management and he thanked his players for winning him the matches, his chairman and fans for their support, and also his mentor George Graham, for the players he left and the lessons he taught. With the game televised on *Monday Night Football*, Leeds knew exactly where a victory would leave them; three points behind Arsenal and Chelsea, and four behind leaders Manchester United, who were next up at Elland Road. With all three title-chasers still to be faced in the final six games, O'Leary's young team found themselves in a mouth-watering position. They were showing the form of champions, and if they kept winning, they would almost certainly be champions at the end of the season.

It was an emotional evening at Elland Road as the Liverpool fans, my elder brother Gianni among them, marked the tenth anniversary of the Hillsborough disaster. They packed out the South Stand and called for justice throughout the game, before which there was an impeccably observed minute's silence, which drew commentator Alan Parry to describe the fans as 'brothers in arms'. It was a huge night for Leeds, but the team could not produce the magic required to beat a stubborn Liverpool side, despite Gerard Houllier naming three young academy graduates in the back four; Dom Matteo, Jamie Carragher and 18-year-old Steven Gerrard, who impressively kept Harry Kewell under lock and key. Hasselbaink had a certain goal blocked on the line by Matteo in the first half, but after that Leeds struggled to cause the visitors any problems as the game fizzled out into an underwhelming 0-0 draw. Injuries had forced O'Leary into fielding three young academy graduates in defence himself, so a clean sheet was no mean feat against the Premiership's top-scoring strike pairing, Robbie Fowler and Michael Owen, who were backed up by one of England's brightest creative talents, Steve McManaman.

The following week brought another draw, a disappointing 1-1 at relegation-threatened Charlton which ended any realistic hopes of a late surge to the title, but there was better news around the corner. David O'Leary had been given a pay rise but not a contract extension when he was appointed manager, and with the club preparing new long-term contracts for all the youngsters, Peter Ridsdale felt it was appropriate to tie the manager down too. Ridsdale declared he'd like O'Leary to remain in charge of Leeds for 20 years, but the Irishman was eventually offered the industry standard maximum of five years and everyone at Elland Road was delighted when O'Leary put pen to paper. Nobody had expected him to leave, but his contractual situation had been rumbling on for a number of months and was threatening to turn into a saga. Putting this to bed was the perfect way to head into the 'War of the Roses'.

Leeds United 1-1 Manchester United
Sunday, 25 April 1999
Elland Road – 1pm
FA Carling Premiership

This was the big one for all Leeds fans, and a fixture we had prospered in with three wins in the last four years. The Red Devils were dominating English football, but their young team couldn't seem to cope with the verve of Elland Road. That said, Ferguson's fledglings were now coming of age and heading to Elland Road on the back of a historic victory in Turin, which earned them a place in the Champions League Final at the expense of the mighty Juventus: Zidane, Davids, Deschamps, et al. Regardless of our rivals' success, this was the first time in my life that I felt we were facing Manchester United as equals.

'Down to da bare bones' had become as big a catchphrase for O'Leary as 'wordy winners' and 'long may dat continue'. Injuries forced him into fielding six under-21s from the Thorp Arch academy against the treble-chasers from Old Trafford, four of them teenagers, but you wouldn't have known. Leeds dominated the opening stages of a rip-roaring match, played in a cauldron of noise and hate, and after half an hour the pressure told. Harry Kewell ran at the heart of a petrified Manchester United defence, which backed off while bunching together to nullify the threat of the Australian. It didn't work. Kewell took advantage of the disarray he had caused by sliding a perfectly timed, and perfectly weighted, diagonal through-ball to the unmarked Hasselbaink, who converted via Schmeichel's near post for the second time in the season. Lewis had recorded the Radio Leeds commentary so we could listen back to the atmosphere after the game, and it proved to be a masterstroke. What a noise it was when the goal went in, so much more authentic on the radio, with the microphones in the rafters of the West Stand, compared to the heavily managed TV audio. We must have listened to that goal 20 times, and the Geordie tones of Norman Hunter are ingrained in my head to this day, 'Elland Road is going absolutely potty!'

In the second half Ferguson's team fought back well, and even I couldn't begrudge their equaliser when Nigel Martyn's save landed in the goalmouth and Andy Cole reacted a split second quicker than Woodgate to prod home. With the very last attack Dwight Yorke could have snatched all three points, but he blasted a golden opportunity high and wide from eight yards out, a miss that helped negate the disappointment of failing to beat our most hated of rivals. The point gained took Leeds to ten games unbeaten and provided more evidence that O'Leary's babies were already a force to be reckoned with. It also took the title race out of Manchester United's hands, with Arsenal taking top spot after a 6-1 thrashing of Middlesbrough at the Riverside (Nwankwo Kanu's fantastic back-heel provided icing worthy of any cake).

The most challenging of run-ins continued the following Saturday with a trip to West Ham, who were fifth in the table and looking to move within three points of Leeds. With no place in Europe for finishing fifth, and with games against Chelsea and Arsenal still to come, UEFA Cup qualification was far from a done deal. This was a crunch six-pointer, and it couldn't have gone any better for Leeds. Hasselbaink opened the scoring after just one minute, Ian Wright was sent off after just 13 minutes and Alan Smith doubled the lead right on half-time. Paolo Di Canio pulled a goal back for the Hammers just after the break, but when Shaka Hislop was sent off it was as good as over, especially with Harte converting the resulting penalty. Bowyer and Haaland got in on the act as Leeds ran riot, and West Ham's day got even worse as Steve Lomas's red card reduced them to eight men for the final minutes. With a stunning 5-1 victory, David O'Leary had achieved his season's goal – UEFA Cup qualification was secured.

'But we don't want to give you that!' Chris Tarrant's catchphrase on the hit new gameshow *Who Wants To Be A*

Millionaire would be applicable here, as qualification for the Champions League was still up for grabs. Just four days later, Leeds headed to Stamford Bridge for another crunch six-pointer, looking to cut the gap on Chelsea to two points with two games remaining. For Chelsea, a draw would all but secure their Champions League spot, but only a win would keep their title challenge alive. Such a huge game, yet it wasn't televised. We could only listen on the radio as Leeds fell to a tight 1-0 defeat, Gus Poyet's goal enough to defeat O'Leary's defiant young team and confirm their fourth-place finish. Leeds's season may have effectively been over, but they would still have a big say in where the Premiership title would go.

Leeds United 1-0 Arsenal
Tuesday, 11 May 1999
Elland Road – 8pm
FA Carling Premiership

There was a carnival atmosphere at Elland Road for the last home game of the season, a celebration of the joy and excitement we had been treated to by a team which promised there was so much more to come. 'And now you're gonna believe us …' chanted the Kop, 'We're gonna win the league, NEXT YEAR!'

Amid the jauntiness there remained a big-game feeling, and how could there not? With Arsenal and Manchester United both having straightforward home games on the last day, this match was practically the title decider. Arsene Wenger's defending champions had their destiny in their own hands and could have been forgiven for expecting Leeds to roll over. After all, their manager had played for Arsenal for 18 years and their fans wouldn't want to aid their hated arch-rivals in their pursuit of a historic treble.

Nobody at Elland Road got the memo. Leeds had nothing to play for except pride, but they played like pride was the be-all and end-all, while on the terraces the support was as partisan as ever. Arsenal right-back, Lee Dixon, would later describe Elland Road as the loudest football stadium he experienced in his career, at home or abroad, and he can only have been pointing to this night. Arsenal won the toss, so in the first half Leeds would be attacking the Kop, who were treated to an earlier and more boisterous meeting with David Seaman than normal. A born and bred Yorkshireman and massive Leeds fan, Seaman was always subjected to playful abuse from the Kop, and he wasn't shy at giving it back either. As he trotted towards us from the South Stand, the Kop broke into song, 'England's No.2, England's, England's No.2' declaring their sincere belief that Nigel Martyn was the country's best goalkeeper. Seaman clapped, laughed, and slyly flicked us 'the Vs'.

Then it was down to business, and Arsenal must have wished they'd lost the toss as Leeds incessantly laid siege to Seaman's goal. David Batty's long-range volley beat Seaman and would have blown the roof off Elland Road had it not sailed inches wide of the top corner, then Kewell's rasping drive did find the top corner but didn't beat Seaman. The Gunners were visibly rattled. This was a team filled with experienced, trophy-laden, powerhouse players, in stature and physicality – Seaman, Adams, Keown, Petit and Vieira – but they were being bullied by Leeds's teenage whippersnappers. Alan Smith, fresh from squaring up to Peter Schmeichel a couple of weeks earlier, was scrapping throughout with the Gunners' two stalwart centre-backs, who just couldn't handle the intensity and were constantly being caught in possession. At the end of the first half Smith's non-stop harrying forced Keown into another mistake, a poor header that didn't find his keeper. Smith pounced on the loose ball and Keown lost his head, flying into a tackle and scything down the teenager in the box. The referee pointed to the spot, but due to my pathological hatred of Manchester United I was relieved when Ian Harte blasted a penalty against the underside of David Seaman's bar, and Hasselbaink's follow-up stuck in Seaman's midriff.

In the second half Arsenal were becoming desperate. The title was on the line but any chances they managed to create were repelled on the goal line by Nigel Martyn or Jonathan Woodgate. Batty once more almost blew the roof off Elland Road with a 40-yard lob that again sailed just wide. Finally, in the 86th minute Leeds landed the knockout blow. Harry Kewell got half a yard on Lee Dixon and whipped in a wicked cross that evaded the legendary Arsenal defence, leaving Hasselbaink with a simple diving header to win Leeds the match and hand the title on a plate to Manchester United. Elland Road exploded, but I felt empty. I jumped up and down with Lewis so as not to dampen his moment, though deep down I was gutted. After good draws or heroic defeats home and away against Manchester United, Chelsea and Roma, O'Leary's babies had managed to claim their first major scalp when it mattered the least, and when Alex Ferguson needed it the most. Bloody typical. The rest of Elland Road didn't seem to mind at all, their heroes had signed off the season with a brilliant win and a statement of intent; Leeds were as good as anyone, and all the pundits agreed that next year they would have a great chance of pushing Manchester United and Arsenal all the way.

Having fallen short in the race for the domestic trophies, there was a similar tale at the PFA player of the year awards. Alan Smith, Lee Bowyer and Harry Kewell made up half of the young player of the year shortlist, but all three went home empty-handed. Nevertheless, a failure to win honours was not the headline of season 1998/99. Leeds hadn't only jumped one place in the table – from fifth to fourth – they had jumped into the Premiership's top bracket, mixing it with the best teams in the country, rather than scrapping to be the best of the rest. The club had progressed much faster than anybody had anticipated, and the foundations were in place for great success; but O'Leary warned that his squad would need more quality adding to it in order to live up to the hype.

1999/00 – Coming of Age

Pre-Season

Southampton 0-3 Leeds United

Manchester United 2-0 Leeds United

Tottenham Hotspur 1-2 Leeds United

Coventry City 3-4 Leeds United

Everton 4-4 Leeds United

Derby County 0-1 Leeds United

Leeds United 1-0 Spartak Moscow

Chelsea 0-2 Leeds United

Manchester City 2-5 Leeds United

Sunderland 1-2 Leeds United

Liverpool 3-1 Leeds United

Leeds United 0-1 Manchester United

AS Roma 0-0 Leeds United

Leicester City 2-1 Leeds United

Leeds United 2-2 Galatasaray

Sheffield Wednesday 0-3 Leeds United

West Ham United 0-0 Leeds United

Pre-Season

IN A time before the internet created a wealth of football content and all the footage you could wish to see, pre-season was like torture for 15-year-old football fanatics. The summer was basically spent glued to teletext for transfer news, waiting for the fixture list to be released and re-watching old season review videos, while waiting for the latest season review to come out. The season review wouldn't quench the thirst though; in fact it just made me even more desperate for the start of the new season, so one day during the school summer holidays, Lewis and I got the bus to Elland Road, just to see the place again.

When the bus arrived, we shielded our eyes from the bounty before us and headed up Beeston Hill without looking back; we wanted our first glance to be from the top of the hill, as it would be on matchday. Once back at the bottom of the hill we began a lap of the stadium. We headed around the back of the West Stand towards the Kop turnstiles and noticed that the first aid tunnel in the north-west corner was open, so Lewis and I just wandered in. It was a dream come true, we had Elland Road all to ourselves! First stop was our season ticket seats, then we headed over to the 'Cheese Wedge' in the south-east corner that housed the away fans, eager to imagine what it would be like to come to Leeds away. With no sign of any adults, our initial caution disappeared and we darted across the hallowed turf to the substitutes' bench, while curling imaginary balls into imaginary nets along the way (the goals were not in situ during pre-season). After a little sit down, we climbed the West Stand all the way up to the gantry, the best seats in the house, then it was back down the stairs and into the directors' box, where we made imaginary phone calls on the telephone that O'Leary would use to communicate with the bench, on the occasions when he spent the first half in the stands for a better view (a practice lost from the modern game).

An angry shout from beneath us brought an abrupt end to our adventure, or so we thought! The man who collared us was not best pleased, and as we headed pitch-side we were worried about the punishment that would lie in store for us. A police charge for trespassing? Worse still they could ban us from Elland Road! We needn't have worried; our punishment was a continuation of our stadium tour! We were led down the players' tunnel, past the changing rooms and into Elland Road's main entrance, where we stood with our tails between our legs in front of the famous honours board, awaiting our fate. After a slap on the wrists we were on our merry way. On such a high we could have flown home, but we already had return bus tickets.

The over-excitement that drew us to Elland Road can't have been helped by a summer of real intent from Leeds United. There was money to spend and David O'Leary wanted four top-quality additions to build a squad that could handle injuries and loss of form, a squad that could be rotated for freshness, like Ferguson and Wenger were able to do. O'Leary made no secret of his strategy either; invest in young British talent who had the right attitude to slip into the social dynamic of the squad, as well as the team itself.

The first signing of the summer didn't completely fit that mould, nor did the man who should have been first. Leeds had agreed a deal for the permanent transfer of Willem Korsten, but George Graham also liked Big Willy and swooped to steal the

Dutchman from under O'Leary's nose. Apart from increasing the fans' animosity towards their former manager, this drove a huge wedge between two former friends. 'I am not happy with George,' said O'Leary. 'In fact, I'm disgusted.'

So, Leeds's first signing turned out to be a young Norwegian midfielder called Eirik Bakke, joining for £1.5m from his home-town club, Sogndal. Danny Mills was the next arrival, a powerful young right-back signed from relegated Charlton for £4m. O'Leary's third signing was Michael Duberry, a highly rated young centre-back costing £4.5m from Chelsea, where he wasn't getting a look-in ahead of Marcel Desailly and Frank Leboeuf. I wondered why Duberry expected to have more chance competing against Radebe and Woodgate, but that was his problem. The fourth and final signing was Michael Bridges, with Leeds beating off competition from George Graham for the Geordie striker's signature; some welcome retribution for the Korsten saga, amongst other things. The £5m fee was an eyebrow-raising amount for a youngster who couldn't force his way into newly promoted Sunderland's team, although they did boast a strike force most Premiership clubs would envy: Niall Quinn and Kevin Phillips.

O'Leary had his four signings, but with Bakke considered 'one for the future' it suggested Leeds had missed out on a fourth 'top player', who appeared to be Kieron Dyer. The prodigious Ipswich midfielder instead signed for Newcastle, with Leeds reportedly refusing to stretch to the £6m asking price. It was another example of the club's conservative and patient transfer strategy.

Leeds had enhanced the quality in the squad but not the depth, following six first-team departures. Gunnar Halle, David Wetherall and Lee Sharpe all moved to newly promoted neighbours, Bradford City, and Wijnhard, Ribeiro and Danny Granville moved to First Division neighbours Huddersfield, Sheffield United, and Manchester City respectively. A thin squad was boosted by the return of right-back Gary Kelly, who hadn't kicked a ball last season due to injury. Kelly was another product of Leeds's youth system, though a few years older than the new crop of players, who looked upon him like an older brother. Except for Ian Harte, who I suspect looked upon him as an uncle, considering he was Kelly's nephew.

It had been an exciting summer, but rumbling on all the while was speculation over the future of the Premiership's golden boot holder, Jimmy Floyd Hasselbaink. Peter Ridsdale had extended the contracts of ten players over the summer and was working hard on improved terms for the club's star striker, but Atletico Madrid were sniffing around and Leeds could not match the reported £40k per week wages being offered by the Spanish giants.

Hasselbaink was still a Leeds player when pre-season training got underway and scored a hat-trick in the first game of the traditional Scandinavian tour; a 15-0 rout of Byske CF. Leeds returned home and beat Celtic 2-1 at Parkhead, a magnificent performance and one of the best away games I'd ever been to, followed by a 5-0 demolition of local rivals Huddersfield. Optimism was at an all-time high with Leeds winning all six pre-season games, scoring 28 goals and conceding only one, but prior to the last warm-up game at Birmingham, O'Leary's preparations for the season were thrown into disarray as Hasselbaink handed in a transfer request.

I was on holiday with my parents in Lanzarote at the time and Hasselbaink's future was all I cared about, but keeping abreast of developments was almost impossible. Being abroad stripped me of the most up-to-date news source available, teletext, and phoning Clubcall was completely out of the question too. My dad had only ever authorised that once, when the headline coaxed us in by declaring Leeds were signing an 'England Star'. I still remember it vividly. My dad was on the downstairs phone (landline) and I was on the upstairs phone, listening in as my over-excited dad screamed down the phone 'IT'S CHRIS SUTTON!' He was convinced Leeds had pipped Blackburn to the British record signature, but the England star turned out to be Carlton Palmer and we vowed never to call again.

All I could do was wait for the morning newspapers, which told me Hasselbaink had played at Birmingham and was booed by his own supporters. His departure was now inevitable, and on the eve of the season Atletico Madrid got their man for £12m. The fee was hefty, but this was a hammer blow to United's title chances before a ball had even been kicked. Jimmy entered my black book, and chairman Peter Ridsdale's comments on the matter were refreshingly scathing, 'When a player feels that his heart is in his wallet and not in the club, it is time to draw a line under things. Jimmy made it absolutely clear that he had no wish to stay here.'

I had been convinced Leeds could win the Premiership but the squad looked far less fearsome with Hasselbaink taken out of the attack, with the reliance for goals now falling on Alan Smith, still only 18 years old, and Michael Bridges, a 21-year-old who was unproven even in the second tier. David O'Leary's target for the season didn't change, but in the wake of Hasselbaink's departure his cautious optimism now just sounded like optimism, 'It will be a magnificent achievement if we can move into one of the Champions League places and combine that with a good run in a cup.'

The gaping hole in the squad was there for all to see in the opening game of the season, a lacklustre 0-0 draw at home to Derby County. Leeds were as toothless in practice as they looked on paper, and O'Leary used the result to ridicule the fans like me who had been shooting for the stars: 'Anyone who thinks we will win the Premiership this year and the European Cup next, is not living in the real world.' Those in the real world would be shocked at how close O'Leary's team would come.

Southampton 0-3 Leeds United

Wednesday, 11 August 1999

The Dell – 7.45pm

FA Carling Premiership

For the start of the 1999/00 season Leeds introduced a new system for away match applications. Gone were the days of queuing outside the West Stand Ticket Office. We were moving into the 21st century, so now it would all be done by post. Radical!

The applications were done in batches, and my dad and I applied for three of the four games initially available. We passed on the Southampton game as it was considered too far to travel for a midweek fixture, but on the Monday after the opening day bore-draw, reports emerged that Leeds were about to sign Darren Huckerby, and my dad was so excited he became desperate to make the trip to the south coast. So, he concocted a cunning plan in the hope of capitalising on any chaos caused by the new postal system, cheekily phoning the ticket office in a pretend panic, explaining that we'd applied for all the games and wondering why our Southampton tickets hadn't arrived yet. It was a stroke of genius. The ticket office wilted, and our tickets would be available to collect from the Southampton ticket office on matchday.

It was a real thrill heading down to Southampton, the furthest venue from home, especially on a Wednesday night as you knew that everybody in the away end lived and breathed Leeds United. The travelling contingent were split over two tiers in the corner of the ground, next to the most boisterous home fans behind the goal. My dad and I were in the lower tier, as were Lewis and Joe, who were delighted to see that my dad's masterplan had paid off. The Dell was an old ground that had always intrigued me when seeing it on telly; it was small, tight, and nonsensical. The stand behind the goal at the far end was

63

less than ten rows deep at one corner flag, but the highest point of the ground at the other.

The transfer of Huckerby had been completed in the morning and, even though he wasn't in the matchday squad, there was a great buzz in the away end; this signing had completely overshadowed the disappointing opening day stalemate. For £4m O'Leary had signed a forward whose lightning pace had been the scourge of Leeds many times in his short career, and at 23 he was the perfect age. Better still, Huckerby was not the replacement for Hasselbaink. O'Leary had wanted another forward even if Hasselbaink had stayed, so Leeds remained in the market to fill their vacant number nine shirt.

Once again, the manager was urging patience and caution: 'I'd do it tomorrow if I could get the right man, but I'm not going to throw away £12m and then find at the end of the season we've bought the wrong player.' O'Leary confirmed that the whole lot had been offered for two different players, reportedly Tore Andre Flo and Emile Heskey, though both bids had been rejected. In the end Leeds's search for a striker went no further, because their new number eight turned out to be all the number nine they needed.

Southampton boasted an excellent home record in the Premiership in the previous season, but that was a distant memory as Michael Bridges announced himself to the Leeds fans in spectacular style. He opened the scoring after 11 minutes with the type of goal The Dell had become accustomed to, though usually from the boot of their favourite son, Matt Le Tissier. Harte's dinked free kick into the box was headed clear but straight to Bridges on the edge of the box, who flicked the ball into the air before lofting a brilliant volley over Paul Jones and into the top corner. What a start!

Leeds then survived an almighty let-off right in front of us. A deep Southampton corner found Mark Hughes free at the back post, and the so-called 'king of volleys' unleashed a strike that was so ferocious it apparently bounced in and out of the goal off the advertising boards behind the net, without the officials noticing. The Southampton players and fans appealed furiously for the goal, but it was not awarded. Being adjacent to the Leeds goal line we had the perfect view of this incident, and although my match report stated that the ball bounced out of the goal, I'm still not convinced it was possible. To this day Lewis is adamant it was a goal, but the BBC report attributed Bridges with a goal-line clearance, while the footage on YouTube is too grainy to tell conclusively.

The Leeds fans took great delight in Mark Hughes's disappointment, made sweeter due to his Manchester United connections. All ex-Manchester United players were regularly booed by Leeds fans, even ex-academy players who had never played for their first team (I was always impressed by the knowledge and memory of my comrades). However, the more notorious 'ex-scummers' would get their own personalised chant to accompany the boos, and 'Useless, Useless, Useless' rang out from the away end, a play on his 'Hughesy' chant, with the words sounding fairly similar. This was a pretty tame berating compared to some others, especially the abuse dished out to David Beckham and his wife and kids.

In the second half, Leeds capitalised on their good fortune. Bridges swept home his second goal after a surging run and cross from Danny Mills, then he completed his hat-trick by heading home another Ian Harte free kick. We were in dreamland! 'Who the fuck, who the fuck, who the fuck is Hasselbaink?' asked the Leeds fans. Bridges had a fourth goal ruled out for offside but nobody cared, and our new hero came over to salute the travelling army at the final whistle, with the match ball safely tucked under his Lazio-themed away shirt like a foetus. The fans chanted his name adoringly and Leeds's season was up and running.

Manchester United 2-0 Leeds United
Saturday, 14 August 1999
Old Trafford – 12pm
FA Carling Premiership

Facing their cross-Pennine rivals would always be the most hotly anticipated clash of Leeds's season, but there was an extra dimension added this time as O'Leary's babies were facing the European champions. Manchester United had gone on to win the treble after Hasselbaink's goal snatched the title out of Arsenal's hands. They won the Premiership with a 2-1 victory over Spurs (as if George Graham was going to do Arsenal a favour!), the FA Cup with a 2-0 victory over Newcastle, and completed the set with the most fortuitous of victories in the European Cup Final against Bayern Munich.

Ferguson's team were as lucky against the Germans as Leeds had been unlucky against the same opponents in the infamous 1975 final, a game that was effectively refereed by Bayern's legendary captain Franz Beckenbauer. In the 1999 final, Manchester United were outplayed from minute one to 89, with Bayern hitting the post and the crossbar before two injury-time deflections turned the game on its head; the most dramatic final in history. It was all too much for me to take. I was in floods of tears after the match, and that's no exaggeration. My dad must have thought I was crazy. It was a rage of jealousy and self-pity. They had been so lucky, as they always were, the exact opposite of Leeds. I couldn't believe what I had seen.

In order to combat such formidably fortunate opponents, David O'Leary made a tactical alteration and gave two new signings their debuts. Michael Duberry was added to the defence to form a back three, while Darren Huckerby was added to the attack to form a front three, and the changes seemed to work well as Leeds silenced a rowdy and boisterous Old Trafford with a superb first-half display. Bowyer and Kewell missed Leeds's best chances, but despite all their pressure it was the home side who should have taken the lead when Denis Irwin fired over the bar from six yards.

At the break the teams were locked at 0-0, and throughout half-time bare-chested Leeds fans swung their tops around their heads, singing, 'We are champions, champions of Europe'. It was a practice carried out routinely at every away game, but never had it been delivered with such verve and impetus; Don Revie's Leeds team were worthy European champions, Ferguson's Manchester United weren't.

When the teams re-emerged, the clouds descended on Old Trafford, bringing conditions that were so gloomy the floodlights were required despite this being a high-noon kick-off in the middle of summer. Welcome to Manchester. The weather was befitting of the situation as the home side took control but, similar to the first half, it was the team on the back foot who created the clearest opening. The world seemed to stop still when Harry Kewell was sent clean through on goal midway through the second half. My dad, Lewis, Joe and I were on the back row of the away end and I grabbed on to Joe and held my breath; this was it, the moment I'd dreamt of was about to happen. Kewell didn't even have Schmeichel to beat, he had left in the summer so his former understudy, Raimond van der Gouw, was in goal, and Kewell duly beat him with a low right-footed drive that left the keeper with no chance. Kewell had hit the side netting the previous season when faced with an identical chance in an identical situation, and he went one better this time as his finish rebounded off the inside of the near post and out to safety. Here we go again.

Minutes later the heavens opened, and as the rain came down a Phil Neville cross found Dwight Yorke free in the box, and he nodded the ball into the corner of the net and sent Old Trafford into raptures. Minutes after that, Yorke met a Beckham corner with the same result, and in the blink of an eye the game was over. The feeling of total deflation in the Leeds end was not shared by their players, who refused to give up and continued to carve out openings, but couldn't force the ball into the net. The Manchester United fans didn't seem at all concerned about any fightback and taunted us with glee, '2-0 in your cup final!' They were in such buoyant mood that they even taunted David Beckham for a long-range shot that almost ended up in the Stretford End's newly completed upper tier, 'What the fucking hell was that?' Beckham held his hand up in apology to the home fans, a very different response to the taunts he'd received from the away fans in the first half, when he had flicked us 'the Vs' while waiting to take a free kick in front of us.

After the final whistle the clouds cleared and the sun came out, but the mood in the Leeds end during the inevitable lock-in was sombre, in total contrast to last season when we had been exhilarated even in defeat. The excellent performance was no consolation this time; this was a bitterly disappointing defeat against a title rival, a game Leeds were the width of a post away from winning.

Tottenham Hotspur 1-2 Leeds United
Saturday, 28 August 1999
White Hart Lane – 3pm
FA Carling Premiership

While Manchester United will always be the big one for Leeds fans, coming up against George Graham ranked a close second for me and my dad. George's decision to leave Leeds for Spurs would always be scrutinised considering the strides O'Leary had made, but his decision could be considered vindicated with silverware already in the White Hart Lane trophy cabinet. Three successive victories had briefly sent Spurs to the top of the early Premiership table, yet their fans still couldn't warm to the Arsenal legend in their dugout, even though last season's cautious style had now given way to a more attacking approach. Chants of, 'The man in the raincoat's barmy army' was as close as they could bring themselves to showing him affection. George spoke very fondly of his time in Yorkshire in his programme notes, praising the great work of O'Leary and his young team and wishing them all the best for the season ahead, which he was sure would be another great success. His words did nothing to soften the ill feeling that I, the rest of the Leeds fans, and now David O'Leary himself felt towards his former mentor.

It was a boiling hot day in London, but that didn't seem to affect the players in a high-intensity first half. O'Leary once again adopted a three-man defence, but neither Radebe, Woodgate nor Duberry could get to grips with the physicality of Les Ferdinand or the flair of David Ginola, and Spurs controlled proceedings from the off. Ginola was always mocked by the Leeds fans, 'Fell-over, fell-over, fell-over!' they chanted to the Frenchman, who spent as much time rolling around on the floor as he did dribbling around defenders. Midway through the half Tim Sherwood opened the scoring with a clinical volley, and Steffen Iversen could have doubled the lead if it weren't for the heroics of Nigel Martyn. At half-time it was a relief that Tottenham weren't out of sight.

For the second half O'Leary made a double substitution and switched back to 4-4-2, while Les Ferdinand never re-appeared, having failed to recover fully from a clash of heads with Lucas Radebe. Leeds instantly looked more comfortable and began to dominate, yet they were again thankful to Nigel Martyn for a flying save to deny Ginola. Moments later came the equaliser, when Alan Smith received the ball in the box with his back to goal, turned his defender, and hit a crisp, low shot past Ian Walker and into the far corner of the net. The Leeds fans went ballistic, bursting into songs of praise not for the goalscorer, but for their beloved manager, 'O'LEARY! O'LEARY! O'LEARY! O'LEARY!'

The Leeds players were feeding off the buzz in the away end, especially David Hopkin, whose uncharacteristically flamboyant turn by the corner flag in front of us left two defenders in his wake and presented Lee Bowyer with the chance to win the game. What a goal it would have been, but Bowyer fired agonisingly over from six yards. While the fans rued the miss, the players set about putting it right, and in the 84th minute won a free kick on the edge of the Spurs box. Anticipation rose in the away end as Ian Harte sprinted towards the ball and let fly with his hammer of a left boot, and in the blink of an eye it bulged the roof of the net, sending the away fans into pandemonium. Again, the fans ignored the goalscorer, this time focusing their energy on the manager that deserted them, 'Georgie, Georgie, what's the score?' The song was belted out in delight, though my delight was overpowered by aggression. They say you can't hate someone if you haven't loved them first, and the majority of Leeds fans never loved George like I had. Thus, my chants had more of a 'fuck you, George!' kind of vibe.

Despite the searing heat, the Leeds end was bouncing. My dad kept asking me to touch his back to feel how sweaty he was but I didn't need to, I could see his white shirt was completely saturated. He looked like he'd been for a dip in the Thames. In the closing stages the atmosphere threatened to boil over as a melee broke out by the corner flag in front of us (it was all happening in our corner today). Out of nothing, Argentinian left-back Mauricio Taricco hit the deck holding his face, bringing outrage from the away end, which was amplified when the referee steamed over and brandished his red card in Alan Smith's direction. Smith had developed a reputation for being a hothead and I was sure he had been sent off on reputation alone (footage would later confirm Smith had headbutted the Argentine in the stomach). The away fans were absolutely livid, as were their players, but the perceived injustice only strengthened their resolve and Leeds saw out the victory safely, leapfrogging George Graham's team in the table in the process.

After the final whistle special praise was reserved for O'Leary, as the players and coaching staff lapped up the applause of the travelling contingent, but they left the pitch to the sound of my favourite song echoing around White Hart Lane, 'You can stick George Graham up your arse. You can stick George Graham up your arse. You can stick George Graham, stick George Graham, stick George Graham up your arse. SIDEWAYS!'

Coventry City 3-4 Leeds United
Saturday, 11 September 1999
Highfield Road – 3pm
FA Carling Premiership

After a two-week international break, Leeds returned to action with another away game, on another boiling hot afternoon in what could now be described as an Indian summer. My dad and I drove down, meeting Lewis and Joe in one of the larger away ends in the Premiership. With half of a decent-sized stand down the touchline allocated to the visitors, there must have been nearly 5,000 Leeds fans in attendance. While United's travelling contingent was never out-sung, the home fans usually had the power to drown us out when they really got going, but with such a large allocation we took delight in overwhelming the hosts each time they had the audacity to try and support their team.

It was back to 4-4-2 for O'Leary, no surprise considering the second-half performance at Spurs, although it wouldn't have been a straightforward decision as Coventry were a dangerous side. Their attack included the flair of Moroccan pair Youssef Chippo and Mustapha Hadji, and teenage Irish sensation Robbie Keane, with Gary McAllister pulling the strings in the middle of the park. Despite winning the title with Leeds in 1992, McAllister was now considered a villain by the Leeds fans, who were still furious that their captain had left for a payrise at Coventry. However, you have to wonder who the bad guy was if Coventry were offering more money than Leeds, a point lost on me at the time.

Within 40 seconds of kick-off, McAllister was handed the chance to silence the boo-boys as Coventry were awarded a penalty for an innocuous-looking handball. McAllister never missed penalties unless Uri Geller was involved, and duly converted to give the hosts the perfect start. A frenetic half ensued. Just three minutes later Leeds thought they were level, but the linesman's flag denied Michael Bridges. Three minutes after that there would be no denying Bowyer, despite the best efforts of Magnus Hedman who saved the midfielder's initial shot. Leeds were looking dangerous with every attack, but Coventry were scoring with every attack and soon regained the lead through a glancing John Aloisi header.

McAllister wasn't the only pantomime villain on show today; there was one in a Leeds shirt too. Just a month after leaving Coventry, Darren Huckerby started the game in place of the suspended Smith and repeated McAllister's trick, sprinting clear of the defence and poking Batty's lovely through-ball beyond the keeper to silence the boo-boys. The sight of Huckerby reeling off towards us with arm aloft told us it was a goal before the ball had reached the net, and the travelling fans saluted their new hero by mimicking the abusive chants from the home end, who had sung his name with a slight alteration of the first letter. I was delighted for Huckerby; where better for him to open his Leeds account than at his old stomping ground.

Although David Batty was still a defensive midfielder, he was far more cultured than I had ever given him credit for. His first season back at the club had started too late to get a true understanding of his brilliance, but now that he was embedded into the team his class was shining through. His long- and short-range passing was always pitch perfect, and he always chose the right option. When needed he could burst forward too, as he did in the 33rd minute at Highfield Road before being bundled to the floor and winning a penalty. Up stepped Ian Harte, who blasted into the corner to send the Leeds fans wild, and send his team-mates into the half-time break with a 3-2 lead.

Stoked up by their fiery, flame-haired manager Gordon Strachan (another legend of Leeds's 1992 title-winning side), Coventry equalised early in the second half when a swift counter-attack ended with a spectacular volley into the top corner by Chippo. We had a great view of it, and it had to be great to beat Nigel Martyn at full stretch. Back came Leeds. Everything was going through Kewell, the Australian was running the show, and it was his shot which rebounded off the post into the path of Michael Bridges, who couldn't miss. 4-3! There was a frantic last ten minutes as Coventry threw everything at Leeds, with the visitors happy to sit back and look to kill the game on the counter. Huckerby, Kewell and Bridges all missed chances to do so, but Nigel Martyn ensured that four goals would be enough with a couple of vital saves as the clock ticked down.

This was a great win for Leeds – now they were rocking and rolling. Home wins over three of their northern neighbours followed – Middlesbrough, Newcastle and Sheffield Wednesday – and an away win at Watford sent O'Leary's babies to the top of the Premiership for the first time. It hadn't been a vintage performance at Vicarage Road as Leeds relied upon a goalkeeping error to take all three points, but being top of the league made for a great coach journey home. Not as good as the coach journey down mind, when we had listened in disbelief as Manchester United were humiliated 5-0 by Chelsea at Stamford Bridge.

Including victories in the League Cup and UEFA Cup, Leeds were on a club-record ten-match winning run, while off the pitch O'Leary's coffers continued to grow. The Hasselbaink money was still burning a hole in his pocket, and now a further £14m was added by BSkyB, who bought a ten per cent stake in the club. Leeds also signed a £6m three-year sponsorship deal with Strongbow, having already signed a deal with Nike for next season's kit. Leeds United were growing stronger by the week.

Everton 4-4 Leeds United

Sunday, 24 October 1999
Goodison Park – 3pm
FA Carling Premiership

Thanks to Thursday night UEFA Cup duty – a thumping 4-1 victory over Lokomotiv Moscow – the trip to Everton was moved to Sunday, and thanks to George Graham's 3-1 victory over Manchester United the previous day, Leeds remained top of the league with the chance to pull three points clear. Arsenal were level on points with Leeds after a stunning Nwankwo Kanu hat-trick grabbed them a late 3-2 victory at Chelsea, but the main threat to the leaders came from Sunderland, who were playing West Ham simultaneously with the Leeds game. Peter Reid's team were enjoying a great start to life in the Premiership, with Kevin Phillips and Niall Quinn proving too hot to handle for nearly all defences, and a victory at Upton Park would send the Mackems top if Leeds slipped up at Goodison Park.

I loved Goodison, an old-school ground that was as atmospheric as it was historic. I also loved the away end, despite it splitting the travelling fans into two tiers which is never ideal. It was a rickety old stand with great acoustics, in the corner of the ground next to the only modern stand behind the goal, which always seemed even louder than the more famous Gwladys Street end.

The day started badly. My dad overestimated the light Sunday traffic, leaving later than normal and getting caught in awful congestion on the M62. After a brief internal deliberation, he took the plunge and pulled off the motorway, choosing a 'round-the-houses' route in pursuit of making the game on time. My dad was convinced we would still make kick-off, I was convinced we wouldn't, and in the end it was a photo finish.

Impressively, he got us there on time, only to be thwarted by big queues at the turnstiles, with the Leeds fans characteristically late in dragging themselves from the pub.

The rain was pouring down on a gloomy afternoon as autumn turned to winter, and with the conditions making defending and goalkeeping difficult, a goal-fest ensued. We took our place in the stand three minutes after kick-off, just in time to see Kevin Campbell curl a beauty past Nigel Martyn at the far end of the ground. The explosion of noise was something else when the ball hit the net, unbearable at the time but unforgettable after the event. It didn't take long for Leeds to equalise, Michael Bridges diverting Kewell's superb run and cross into the net, but Everton quickly regained the lead, Campbell again putting Leeds to the sword. 'Super, Super Kev, Super Kevin Campbell' bellowed the Goodison faithful.

Leeds went searching for another equaliser and found it when Harry Kewell's deep cross floated over Paul Gerrard into the top corner. Such was the Australian's reputation that pundits argued over whether it was deliberate, but the celebrations happened in front of us and the cameras missed Stephen McPhail asking Kewell if he meant it, to which Kewell smiled and shook his head. Two minutes later the smiles were wiped from all our faces as Don Hutchison pounced on a loose ball to prod home Everton's third, with the Leeds defence in disarray. There was still time for Leeds to equalise for a third time – in fact there was still time for Jonathan Woodgate to grab a first-half hat-trick – but his three headers from a late flurry of corners all failed to find the net and the Whites trudged off at half-time, 3-2 down.

In the second half there were fewer goals but no less action. It was a pulsating, end-to-end affair. Hutchison missed a close-range volley before Harry Kewell glided past two Everton defenders and curled a sumptuous 30-yard effort inches past the post. What a goal that would have been, and what a goal it was when Leeds did equalise for a third time. Bridges produced a replica of his first goal at The Dell, looping a beautifully controlled volley over the keeper and into the net. The away end were loving it, 'Let's go fucking mental, let's go fucking mental, na naa naa naa, LEEDS! Na naa naa naa, LEEDS!' The chant was still in full flow when Woodgate met yet another corner, and this time guided his header in off the underside of the bar, sending the Leeds fans even more fucking mental. United finally had the lead, 4-3.

There were still 18 minutes left, plenty of time for more goals. Darren Huckerby had been introduced and his pace was proving a great weapon on the counter; both he and Bridges could have sealed the win but instead we were made to suffer an excruciating end to the game. Deep into injury time, with time almost up, Everton won a free kick in front of us on the left wing. Lewis climbed on to the railings above the exit, 'I'm gonna end it, die a happy man.' His joke lifted the tension for a moment, but seconds later David Unsworth's deep cross evaded the defence and goalkeeper, and David Weir powered home the equaliser. What a gut-wrenching way to end a ten-match winning run.

Once back in the car we received a nice consolation prize – Trevor Sinclair had scored an 89th minute equaliser for West Ham, denying Sunderland a 1-0 victory which would have stolen top spot from Leeds. The following week West Ham did succumb to a 1-0 defeat, at Elland Road. It was a tight and tense game, but Ian Harte's right-footed thunderbolt secured three points, and top spot for another week.

Whenever Leeds were top of the league, Lewis and I would take great pride in marking the feat in our school planners. The letters 'WATOTL' were appearing every day, and the ritual lost none of its appeal as the weeks flew by. Defeat at Wimbledon ended a run of five weeks at the top, but Leeds immediately bounced back by beating Bradford 2-1 in the first West Yorkshire derby in top-flight history, and the following week an injury time stunner by Michael Bridges scraped a 1-0 victory over Southampton to send Leeds back into first place.

What a season Leeds were having. I was on cloud nine, despite O'Leary's best attempts at keeping everyone's feet on the ground. He insisted his team was too young and inexperienced to challenge the big boys, and his 18-man squad was too small to cope with a four-pronged trophy hunt, but nobody was buying it. Leeds were playing some spectacular football, and even when they weren't, they were finding a way to win; the true mark of champions.

Derby County 0-1 Leeds United
Sunday, 5 December 1999
Pride Park – 3pm
FA Carling Premiership

After his heroics in getting us to Goodison Park practically on time, my dad was feeling bullish and planned another late start to our journey based on his expected light Sunday traffic. I felt uneasy after the panic of Everton and we struck a sportsman's bet, my dad saying we would be in Derby an hour before kick-off, pessimistic old me saying we wouldn't. As 2pm approached we were still some way off, 30 miles according to the signposts (remember this was before the days of sat-nav), but the next signpost offered an exit for Derby and my dad seized his opportunity, pulling off the motorway and desperately claiming victory. It was ridiculous, and could have resulted in us missing kick-off again, but thankfully there were no further shenanigans and we met Lewis and Joe on the back row of a generous away end in good time for kick-off. I was a big fan of Pride Park, the novelty of new stadiums hadn't yet worn off, and with the Leeds fans packing out the whole stand behind the goal, the atmosphere was fantastic.

Despite some excellent free-flowing football, Leeds's surge to the top of the league had been largely thanks to a solid foundation. Gary Kelly had reclaimed the right-back spot from Danny Mills, having quickly recaptured his top form after a long absence, while his prolific nephew, Ian Harte, continued to blossom at left-back. Radebe and Woodgate were a Rolls-Royce partnership in the middle, and with Nigel Martyn behind them and David Batty sitting in front, O'Leary had moulded a defensive unit that was perfectly balanced and of the highest quality. Due to the adventurous nature of the Leeds team, they didn't have the best defensive record, but the rocks at the back ensured most matches were dominated.

However, today there was no David Batty: he had sustained an injury that was expected to keep him out for a number of weeks (a number that was much less than the 58 weeks he actually missed), so in came Eirik Bakke to partner Stephen McPhail in midfield. McPhail was often described as the most gifted of Leeds's youngsters and had now nailed down his place in the team.

'He has a terrible habit of keeping possession,' was the go-to compliment that his manager used time and again, while others would often compare him to an iconic Irish midfielder from yesteryear, Liam Brady. Bakke, meanwhile, had made a highly impressive start to his career in England, slotting in seamlessly, either in Bowyer's new role on the right of midfield or in the centre where he was more comfortable. Tall and commanding, and effective in possession, Bakke earned the label 'The White Vieira' from me, which might have been going a bit far, but he was proving to be a superb addition to the squad. This was a midfield duo that could shine at Leeds for years to come.

Needing three points to return to the top of the league, United dominated proceedings at Pride Park, but their first-half performance lacked spark. There were no goals and no clear openings as Derby coped with Huckerby and Bridges with relative comfort. In the second half the Rams grew in confidence, and it was Leeds's turn to withstand periods of heavy pressure. Derby almost took the lead when the mercurial Georgi Kinkladze jinked through a sea of yellow shirts, only to be denied by the outstretched leg of Nigel Martyn. Leeds were tiring as the game entered its final stages, and in the end resorted to simply giving the ball to Harry Kewell and seeing what he could conjure up. The Aussie was doing all he could, but nothing was quite coming off. He ran half the length of the pitch but fired wide, and another great run culminated in a sitter for Huckerby, who could only hit the bar.

It was looking like a frustrating 0-0 draw, but with seconds remaining Kewell picked up the ball and drove at the Derby defence one last time. Having been untouchable for 45 minutes, what happened next was quite ironic; Kewell entered the box, knocked the ball past the defender, and threw himself to the floor without being touched. The Leeds end screamed for a penalty, and astonishingly the referee obliged. The players and fans celebrated fervently before realising the penalty still needed scoring; now we were awash with nerves. With top spot up for grabs I'd never been so nervous, and the Derby protests made the long wait even more painful. Could Ian Harte hold his nerve? Whether he did or not is debateable. His penalty was drilled low and hard down the middle – a hit and hope, if you will – but the ball flashed between Mart Poom's diving legs and into the net. Leeds had snatched all three points! The celebrations were as wild and chaotic as I could ever remember; people were rolling around their seats, down the gangways, screaming in delirious delight.

It was later revealed that the players had just as much fun as the fans after the game, singing and celebrating on the coach journey home, and the camaraderie in the camp seemed to be reaching an all-time high. Leeds were bulldozing their way through the season and fighting on four fronts, although over the next ten days four had the potential to become one.

Leeds United 1-0 Spartak Moscow
Thursday, 9 December 1999
Elland Road – 7.45pm
UEFA Cup Third Round, Second Leg

What made the late victory at Pride Park all the more impressive was the fact that it came three days after a draining 2-1 defeat away to Spartak Moscow. The European campaign had been a tiring experience through every round, but somehow Leeds kept registering victory after victory in the Premiership, despite a huge number of miles travelled.

The main challenges in the early rounds of the UEFA Cup had been off-field issues. In the first round Leeds were drawn against Bosnian champions Partizan Belgrade, but UEFA were eventually forced to relocate the away leg to a neutral venue, Heerenveen, where Lucas Radebe brought a whole new meaning to the term 'sitter'. 'The Chief' scored the first goal of a 4-1 aggregate victory by hooking a brilliant volley into the top corner while sat on his backside in the penalty box – some way to open his account for the club after over 150 games. Next up was a long trip to Moscow, where Lokomotiv were disposed of comfortably – 7-1 on aggregate – but returning to Moscow to face Spartak in round three was always going to be a much sterner test. This was a classy team packed with internationals, the champions of Russia.

On arrival in Moscow the temperature had dropped to minus 22, and Leeds's training session on the day before the game had to be postponed because Spartak had 'forgotten' to turn the under-soil heating on, leaving the pitch frozen and unplayable. Their 'mistake' had further consequences. The pitch was frozen so solid that it failed to thaw the following day and the referee had no option but to call the game off. Incredibly, Spartak kicked up a right fuss, claiming Leeds had connived to get the match postponed! Why Leeds would want to travel all the way to a freezing cold Moscow, for no reason, remains a mystery. The wasted trip caused havoc to an already congested schedule, which threatened to derail a small and inexperienced squad's challenge for the Premiership title.

There was more fury from the Russians when UEFA announced that the re-arranged tie would be played in Sofia, and they were even more furious when UEFA refused to move the second leg to a neutral venue too. When the football finally took place, Spartak recovered from falling behind to a Harry Kewell opener to win the first leg 2-1, though heading into the second leg Leeds were in confident mood; they knew the importance of their away goal.

It was another electric atmosphere inside Elland Road. The off-field wrangling and disrespectful conduct of the Russians made for a frosty atmosphere in the directors' box, and the tensions transmitted to the terraces and the pitch. A high-intensity battle ensued, and after Spartak's Brazilian striker, Robson, was denied a crucial early away goal by Nigel Martyn it was all Leeds. Harry Kewell was central to all their good work as always, yet the ball just wouldn't go in the net. Russian international goalkeeper, Aleksandr Filimonov, was proving a real nuisance – only Michael Bridges managed to beat him but prodded Harte's wicked free kick against the upright. It may have appeared a blessing when Filimonov was stretchered off in the 38th minute, but his replacement proved just as stubborn, denying Leeds time and time again as his goal was bombarded by shots.

The Leeds fans were doing everything to suck the ball into the net and, although time was running out, as the clock ticked down Leeds's task became clearer; one goal would send them through on away goals. With three minutes remaining the Russians finally wilted. McPhail's deep corner left the keeper stranded and Lucas Radebe arrived at the back post to nod home what would surely be the winning goal. It was a goal that would have sent the Leeds fans crazy whoever scored it, but because it was our much-loved captain's first goal at Elland Road the moment was even more thrilling. By the end of a scintillating battle there had been over 40 attempts between the sides, and the last of those brought an almighty scare as Spartak rattled the underside of the crossbar in the dying seconds. But when the final whistle blew Leeds were through, and neither players nor fans were more jubilant than David O'Leary, who ran on to the pitch to hug his players in what would become a trademark celebration on European nights.

Once the euphoria subsided O'Leary stood stoically by his claim that Leeds weren't ready to challenge for trophies this season, but actions speak louder than words and his team's results made his words sound like ironic humour. This 'young and naïve squad with a young and naïve manager' had safely navigated their way through the early rounds of the UEFA Cup, while maintaining their position on top of the Premiership. The European campaign would now be placed on the back-burner until it resumed in February, but with three domestic trophies still to play for there was to be no let-up in Leeds's incessant schedule.

Chelsea 0-2 Leeds United

Sunday, 19 December 1999
Stamford Bridge – 4pm
FA Carling Premiership

Three days after the heroic victory against Spartak came the FA Cup third round. It was the first time it had been played prior to Christmas, an attempt to ease pressure on the fixture list and supposedly help England's chances in Euro 2000. O'Leary fielded a full-strength side, who overcame Port Vale 2-0 with a brace from Eirik Bakke. Next up was a midweek trip to Filbert Street to take on Martin O'Neill's Leicester City in the League Cup, with a quarter-final against second-tier Fulham awaiting the winners. Leeds were at full strength again, and after last year's heartbreak in the same round, at the same ground, I could have been forgiven for expecting a kinder outcome this time around. It wasn't to be.

The teams battled out a 0-0 draw, taking the game into extra time, which was the last thing Leeds's weary players needed. Actually, the last thing they needed was to play extra-time with ten men, and that's what happened with Lucas Radebe sent off in the 90th minute. Our heroes battled on, and the supporters matched them for effort by singing 'Champions of Europe' all the way through extra time, but after a gruelling 120 minutes Leeds succumbed 4-2 on penalties. At least I didn't have to experience the Leicester celebrations in person this time, though the pain of the defeat would linger on as Leicester ended up reaching Wembley again, facing second-tier Tranmere Rovers in the final, and beating them of course. Oh, what could have been!

It wasn't all bad news. Leeds were afforded an extended break in order to recover from the physical and mental torment at Filbert Street, a whole extra day thanks to Sky televising the weekend trip to Stamford Bridge. Gianluca Vialli's team were languishing in mid-table, but with the quality at his disposal everyone expected Chelsea to make a dash up the league eventually. Their squad was oozing quality; French World Cup winners Marcel Desailly, Didier Deschamps and Frank Leboeuf, Italians Roberto Di Matteo and Gianfranco Zola, and some pretty decent Englishmen too in Dennis Wise, Graeme Le Saux and Chris Sutton. A victory for Leeds would ensure they spent Christmas Day on top of the Premiership, but this would be a formidable challenge for a young team that must surely have been running on empty by now.

David O'Leary had managed to add some strength to the squad at least, with a signing that initially looked underwhelming but turned out to be extremely astute. Jason Wilcox was a quick and direct left-winger, joining for £3m from

Blackburn Rovers where he had won the league in 1995. After spending his whole career up to that point at Ewood Park, he was ready for a new challenge, and landed the biggest challenge of them all, battling with Harry Kewell for a place in the most exciting team in the country. However, O'Leary had other ideas up his sleeve. Adding Wilcox to the squad gave him the option of using Kewell in a more central role behind Michael Bridges, where he would have the freedom to express himself and be more difficult to mark out of a game. Wilcox's arrival also added some much-needed experience and nous to the midfield. With David Batty and David Hopkin both sidelined with long-term injuries, O'Leary only had five midfielders to choose from, all aged 22 and under.

With two London fixtures over the festive period, my dad made me choose between going to Chelsea or Arsenal, as we couldn't get away with going to both. I chose Arsenal, so watched this one at home with my dad and Paul, whose family didn't like football so didn't have Sky. Chelsea were rampant in the first half, but Leeds managed to survive until half-time, and shortly after the break Wilcox was introduced in place of the hobbling Bridges, freeing Harry Kewell from the shackles of the left wing.

After Nigel Martyn denied Dennis Wise with a terrific reaction save, Leeds started to work their way into the game, and on 66 minutes a long, high clearance landed on the head of Harry Kewell midway inside the Chelsea half. With a manoeuvre Diego Maradona would have been proud of, Kewell cushioned the ball into the air with his head before turning his marker and beating Frank Leboeuf by flicking the ball over his head. As he approached the box Kewell jinked back inside the two defenders chasing him and was hacked to the floor by the frustrated Leboeuf. The referee played a superb advantage as the ball ran into the path of Lee Bowyer, who pulled it back for Stephen McPhail, arriving late in the box to slide a beautiful finish past Ed de Goey. Paul and I charged around the living room, we couldn't believe it!

Ten minutes later Chelsea imploded, or more specifically, Frank Leboeuf imploded. You could sympathise with Leboeuf for being sick of the sight of Harry Kewell, and when the Australian stole the ball from him in midfield and accelerated away once again, the Frenchman could take no more. Already on a booking, Leboeuf cynically tripped Kewell, before stamping on his foot for good measure as he lay on the floor. There was only one possible outcome – Chelsea were down to ten men and Leeds had three points in the palm of their hand. After waiting 20 months for his first Leeds goal, McPhail only had to wait 20 minutes for his next, sealing a fantastic victory when his in-swinging free kick bounced through a crowded box and inside the far post. The exuberant players celebrated with a pile-on in the corner – the Christmas number one spot was theirs.

In Italy the leaders at the halfway point are declared 'Winter Champions', and for O'Leary to achieve this with an 18-man squad that contained nine players under the age of 22, while playing the maximum number of cup games, plus a wasted trip to Moscow, was a tremendous achievement. In fact, it was so impressive that it forced a change of tack from the manager, who finally accepted that his team had a chance to be 'Summer Champions' too. 'I think they're strong mentally, but only time will tell whether we're strong enough to handle the last ten games of a season, when every game is like a cup final.' A pumped-up O'Leary continued, 'I don't know if we can win the Premiership this season, but what I do know is that we will give it a real go.'

I was a bit gutted to have missed such a significant victory, and the subsequent trip to Highbury only compounded my misery; it proved to be the day everything caught up with Leeds. It was men against boys from start to finish as the leaders were outclassed in every department. Petit and Vieira ran the match from midfield, Freddie Ljungberg and Thierry Henry provided the goals in the 2-0 win, and Leeds were lucky not to lose more heavily. Lucky too that Manchester United were held at Sunderland to ensure O'Leary's babies still ended the year, decade, century and millennium on top of the Premiership.

Manchester City 2-5 Leeds United
Sunday, 9 January 2000
Maine Road – 2pm
FA Cup Fourth Round

O'Leary's babies started the year, decade, century and millennium with a surprise defeat at home to Aston Villa; Gareth Southgate's brace rendering a stunning 40-yard Harry Kewell goal irrelevant. Still, with Manchester United jetting off to play in the inaugural World Club Championship in Brazil, Leeds stayed top, and next up was a trip to Manchester for an FA Cup clash with the leaders of Division One. The FA Cup brought Leeds United's final chance of playing one more time at Wembley before the Twin Towers were demolished, giving this game, and this cup campaign, added significance.

I was thrilled when the draw paired us with Man City. Maine Road was another iconic British stadium that I had always wanted to visit, and like Wembley it would soon be demolished, with City due to move into the new stadium being built for the 2002 Commonwealth Games. A 'War of the Roses' and a clash of league leaders, this was the tie of the round and caught the imagination of the whole country. Except for my dad, who couldn't be bothered going, so Paul, Lewis, Joe and I went on the supporters' coach. The coach always got us to the ground before the turnstiles opened, and on this occasion, there was nothing else for four 16-year-old lads to do other than have a wander around the ground and the surrounding area, the notorious Moss Side.

At the start of the season my brother had given me a book to read, *The Geezer's Guide to Football*, written by a Watford fan who explained how football 'casuals' should behave. Casuals are not hooligans, they are a step down from that, but they are still expected to dress in the infamous expensive clobber on a matchday. I'd love to read the book again, I can imagine it would be a cringe-fest, but as impressionable teenagers it became our bible. Thus, we were strutting around Moss Side dressed head-to-toe in a mash-up of Burberry, Rockport, Henri Lloyd, Paul Smith, Fred Perry and Lacoste (we couldn't afford the likes of Stone Island). I remember buying my Rockport boots from the McArthur Glenn designer outlet in York. It was love at first sight, but they only had size 12 and I was just a size ten. My heart ruled my head and I bought them regardless; it wasn't like they were going to fall off my feet, I thought. Better to be too big than too small, I reasoned. Would anyone even notice?

It was quite a job affording clobber like that too. I only earned £10 per week in my role as garage manager for the family business (washing and drying towels, filling water containers, tidying equipment), although I was able to earn a little extra from washing the vans, and in school holidays I'd be able to do a proper day's work that paid £15 per day. I didn't have any outgoings either, as my dad would buy all my match tickets as long as I was getting good reports at school. Lewis and Paul had paper rounds to feed their habits, although Paul was notorious for getting his poor mum to drive him around his route, and even deliver the Sunday papers herself once we started drinking on Saturday nights. Anyway, our expensive clobber almost got us in a spot of bother as we wandered aimlessly around one of the roughest areas in one of the roughest inner-cities in England. 'Fancy a little rumble, lads?' The invitation came from a group that looked even younger than us. Nevertheless, we continued on our merry way without even responding, and headed straight for the safety of the turnstiles, where we waited patiently for them to open without ever discussing our cowardice.

When the match got under way, we were treated to an FA Cup classic. Within a minute Shaun Goater had given City the ideal start, but Leeds made the perfect response, equalising through Eirik Bakke. Ian Bishop put the hosts 2-1 up with a fine strike from the edge of the box but again the lead didn't last, Smith equalising less than ten minutes later. Leeds were playing magnificently. The goals they conceded could have rocked a young team playing in a partisan atmosphere on the back of successive defeats, but if anything it was spurring them on. Nicky Weaver in the City goal was called into action time and time again, and by half-time Leeds had managed to get their noses in front thanks to superb wing-play from Jason Wilcox, which left Harry Kewell with a tap-in. City's resolve was broken.

The second half was all Leeds, and when Bowyer rifled an unstoppable half-volley into the top corner it was a question of how many the visitors would get. It could have been ten, but they settled for five. Huckerby skinned the defence to lay another tap-in on a plate for Harry Kewell, who almost completed a memorable hat-trick, but after dribbling through half of the City team he was denied by the inside of the post.

O'Leary's team had bounced back with perhaps their best performance of the season, a performance that drew a one-word description from opposing manager Joe Royle, 'Awesome'. Leeds had scored five goals in their title rivals' back yard, and Manchester United would have been next on the fixture list themselves if they weren't lapping it up on the Copacabana. Instead, Leeds were treated to a well-earned two-week break. Lucas Radebe headed off to captain South Africa in the African Nations Cup, while the rest of the squad were told to let their hair down. And the O'Leary era would never be the same again.

Sunderland 1-2 Leeds United

Sunday, 23 January 2000

Stadium of Light – 4pm

FA Carling Premiership

If England hadn't been bidding to host the 2006 World Cup, Manchester United would not have been put under such pressure to compete in the inaugural World Club Championship. It was seen as a 'Mickey Mouse' tournament, a theory that rang true as it was cancelled the following year and not seen again for half a decade. Alex Ferguson's team had already been crowned Intercontinental champions and felt they had nothing to prove, so treated this tournament like a mid-season break and were eliminated in the group stages.

They shouldn't even have qualified for the tournament in the first place having been the luckiest European Cup winners of all time. That statement doesn't just relate to the final, the most miraculous victory I'd ever witnessed. In the semi-final first leg they were completely outclassed by Juventus at Old Trafford, but a 92nd-minute Ryan Giggs equaliser gave them hope, and although I can give them credit for a remarkable comeback in Turin, they really should have been dead and buried (maybe they would have been if Juve's star striker, Alessandro Del Piero, hadn't been injured for both legs). They didn't win their group either – a group won by losing finalists Bayern Munich – but qualified as one of the two best runners-up from the six groups. They were the first 'non-champions' to be crowned champions of Europe (this was only the second season of allowing domestic runners-up to enter the Champions League), and they had only won five matches throughout their Champions League campaign: no team has ever won it with so few wins. But win it they did, and go to Brazil they did, and at odds of 19/1 it was Leeds who were the team to have their league fixture cancelled in mid-January.

As a result of all this, the Leeds players were able to go on a big night out on the Tuesday after the win at Maine Road; the night Leeds would have hosted Fulham in the League Cup quarter-final had they won the penalty shoot-out at Filbert Street (you couldn't make it up). During this night out there was an altercation, a very serious one, during which a student, Sarfraz Najeib, was beaten to within an inch of his life. In the following days and weeks the police were a regular presence at the Thorp Arch training ground, interviewing a number of players who were at the Majestik nightclub in Leeds city centre on the night of the attack. Bowyer, Woodgate and reserve team player, Tony Hackworth, were eventually charged with grievous bodily harm with intent, while Michael Duberry was charged with perverting the course of justice.

It was a lightning bolt through the whole club. Just when Leeds United were at their height of popularity in the whole of the club's history, suddenly that status plummeted. Leeds's name was being dragged through the mud. The club stood by their players, but while 'innocent until proven guilty' was an understandable stance, the seriousness of the crime meant this stance was under severe scrutiny. The governing bodies allowed the players to remain available for selection for their club, but the FA banned them from being selected for England, when both Bowyer and Woodgate had looked certainties to make Kevin Keegan's Euro 2000 squad.

The next match was Sunderland away, a real test for O'Leary's rocked team. The Mackems hadn't won a game since Christmas but could still move within three points of table-topping Leeds with a win on *Super Sunday*. Bowyer, Woodgate and Duberry all started, and just two minutes into the game Bowyer was sent clean through but screwed his shot wide of the far post. Sunderland responded well and Nigel Martyn was forced into a miraculous save to deny Kevin Phillips, but it was Leeds who took the lead when Wilcox continued his impressive form by firing his first Leeds goal into the roof of the net after Stephen McPhail split the defence.

It was a red-hot atmosphere in the Leeds end, one that I wouldn't quite describe as toxic, but with their club under attack there was a real sense of defiance in the air. It must have been no coincidence that this was the day I had my first taste of violence at a football match. At half-time I nipped to the little boys' room but walked into a stand-off on the concourse between a swarm of Leeds fans and the police. The fans were angry, the police were angry, and soon the police took action and started swinging their truncheons. Mesmerised, I stuck around, but as the fearless fans at the back surged forwards, and the concerned fans at the front somehow departed, I found myself being pushed closer and closer to the firing line. It was pretty scary, but quite a rush for a 16-year-old, and somehow, when I was almost at the point of being confronted with the firing squad, I managed to squirm away to safety.

It was a great relief to make it back to my seat in one piece, and straight after the restart Wilcox's brilliant cross was flicked home by Bridges. The former Mackem didn't hold back on his celebrations – respecting your former employers wasn't a thing back then – and the Leeds fans saluted the goalscorer with a bespoke chant for the occasion, 'Thank you very much for Michael Bridges, thank you very much, thank you very, very, very much.' The smiles were wiped from our faces two minutes later when a Woodgate mistake was pounced on by Phillips, who scored his 20th goal of the season. Amid severe pressure and many goalmouth scrambles, Leeds managed to hold on and open up a three-point lead at the top of the Premiership.

It had been an intoxicating afternoon, and on the way home we listened as man of the match Michael Bridges gave an assessment that must rank as one of the most inaccurate in the club's history, 'The commotion of the past week has all been forgotten.' Maybe O'Leary was right all along regarding the naivety of his players.

Liverpool 3-1 Leeds United
Saturday, 5 February 2000
Anfield – 3pm
FA Carling Premiership

The two weeks following the Sunderland victory were gut-wrenching. Well, the day after wasn't bad, Manchester United returned from Brazil and scraped a 1-1 draw at Old Trafford against Arsenal, so still trailed Leeds by three points. The following Saturday they hosted Middlesbrough, a match I listened to while playing cards all day with my mates after a wild Friday night out at Trotters Bar in Harrogate. I only needed a £10 note to get blathered from four pints of Tetley's, with enough left over for a pack of bacon fries and a kebab. It may have been a cheap night out, but I paid for it in the morning with a stinking hangover.

My hangover was exacerbated by what developed at Old Trafford. In the second half Middlesbrough were awarded a penalty, a blatant penalty, the first penalty awarded to an away side at Old Trafford for seven years. The Manchester United players were aghast at the brawn of the young referee, Andy D'Urso, and furiously rounded upon him. This incident is the most diabolical scene I have witnessed in 30 years of watching English football (YouTube: 'Manchester United players protest to referee'). D'Urso was backed from the penalty spot right over to the corner flag, with the Manchester United players almost fighting amongst themselves to join Roy Keane and Jaap Stam on the front line. They were behaving like wild animals, furiously screaming in the face of the referee, who was too scared to book any of them. Incredibly there were no retrospective bans handed out by the FA. They should have all been banned, they could even have been docked points!

And it gets worse. After all the commotion Juninho missed the penalty, then 'Boro left-back Christian Ziege was sent off, and in the 87th minute David Beckham scored the winning goal. I was absolutely furious. I still am to this day, in case you can't tell!

Even worse was to come, as the next day the Wembley dream died forever. Leeds put in a wonderful first-half performance and led 2-1 in the FA Cup fifth round clash at Villa Park, but Benito Carbone had the game of his life, scoring a hat-trick to turn the game around. My clearest memory of the day comes from the last minute, when Leeds won a throw-in by the corner flag in front of us. It was the final chance, but Danny Mills planted his foot half a yard over the touchline as he launched the ball into the box: foul throw. I was livid (I still am). Once again our conquerors went all the way to the final, where they played Chelsea. It should have been us. The last FA Cup Final at Wembley would have been a re-run of that classic final of 1970. Oh, what could have been!

Three days later, Manchester United played their final game in hand at Hillsborough and prevailed 1-0 with yet another late goal to establish a three-point lead at the top. At the weekend three points turned to six as they beat Coventry 3-2 while Leeds were turned over by Liverpool at a raucous Anfield. Liverpool were progressing nicely under Gerard Houllier and on this day they were the better side, but it was still an unfortunate and controversial defeat for Leeds. A 30-yard free kick from Dietmar Hamann deflected past Martyn to give the hosts a 1-0 half-time lead, but after the break Leeds were much improved and deserved their equaliser when a great move and cross was bundled in at the back post by the head of Lee Bowyer. There were jubilant scenes in the Anfield Road end, and Leeds had the bit between their teeth.

Into the fray came referee, Mike Reed. Bowyer was clattered when clean through ... play on said the ref. Kewell was clattered when clean through ... play on said the ref. Kewell was sandwiched in the box ... play on said the ref. If those incidents weren't controversial enough, what came next was truly astonishing, although I only found out about it listening to 606 on the way home. Ironically this incident started when a Liverpool player was fouled and the ref waved play on. Moments later Patrik Berger hit a 30-yard piledriver that screamed past Martyn into the top corner, and the referee punched the air in delight! It was caught on camera and Reed was forced to admit he did celebrate the goal, but only because the advantage he had played had come to fruition. His excuse was accepted by the FA and no further action was taken. Liverpool sealed the win in injury time with another 30-yard screamer, this time from Danny Murphy. Anfield went crazy, it was as loud a noise as I had ever heard and supporters from the Main Stand spilled on to the pitch in celebration. Amid the pandemonium it was a wonder the referee managed to keep his composure.

Outside the ground there was more trouble as a group of Leeds fans confronted a group of Liverpool fans who they felt shouldn't be so happy to have 'won Scum the title'. When the squabbling progressed into argy-bargy my dad whisked us out of harm's way, but the tensions were reflective of the mood in the Leeds camp: it had been a nightmare start to the year. Some supporters may have been ready to concede the title, but O'Leary's babies weren't spitting their dummies out just yet.

Leeds United 0-1 Manchester United
Sunday, 20 February 2000
Elland Road – 11.30am
FA Carling Premiership
A week before one of the biggest 'Wars of the Roses' in 500 years, Leeds cut the gap at the top from six points down to three with an ill-tempered 1-0 victory over George Graham's struggling

Spurs team, coupled with Manchester United's 3-0 defeat at Newcastle. It was quite the afternoon at Elland Road, a day when injury-cursed Willem Korsten finally made his first start for Spurs after his controversial U-turn on a move to Yorkshire. As with his manager, Leeds could consider themselves fortunate to have been rejected by Korsten, and regardless of the injuries it was probably worth all the heartache to be able to chant, 'You can stick Big Willy up your arse'. I was thrilled Korsten's season had been ravaged – he was on my blacklist after all, and the first on the list to receive their comeuppance (cruelly, Korsten would be forced into retirement within two years).

Things were not working out for George Graham at Spurs, in fact his first full season had been as bad for him as it had for Korsten. Tottenham had been knocked out of all three cup competitions early and were languishing in the bottom half of the table when they arrived at Elland Road. They looked bereft of confidence but at least put up a fight, and it took a beautiful goal from Harry Kewell to settle the match. Kewell latched on to a through-ball ahead of Neil Sullivan and headed over the onrushing keeper before a little shimmy left Sol Campbell on the floor, and the Kop goal wide open to pass into.

By now the rivalry with Spurs had extended beyond George Graham. There was plenty of needle every time the sides met and this game was no exception, with stamps, elbows, punches and malicious tackles flying in left, right and centre. A match that had threatened to boil over from the start finally did shortly after Kewell's goal, when a hefty challenge from Bowyer ignited a 22-man brawl. With the adrenaline already pumping from the goal, the Kop was in overdrive, 'If you hate Leeds United, hate Leeds United, hate Leeds United have a go!' When the final whistle blew, Leeds had got the job done, but the highlight of the day was yet to come. In the days before mobile phones we had no idea of the latest scores in the other games, so when the final results were read out over the tannoy system it was pure drama. 'Newcastle three' got an enormously excited cheer, 'Manchester United nil' was treated like a goal, the biggest cheer of the day! It was game on again, and in eight days Leeds would have the chance to pull level on points with their cross-Pennine rivals.

In his programme notes David O'Leary scorned those who had written his team off after the Liverpool defeat, and warned the Leeds fans not to get too downhearted or too upbeat with the result of the Manchester United game; there were still 13 games to play after this one, plenty of time for many twists and turns. O'Leary was right – billing the game as a title decider was preposterous, but it felt imperative for Leeds to get a result and keep momentum going.

Their task was made more difficult with the absence of Stephen McPhail, and with no return date in sight for David Batty it was left to young Matthew Jones and Eirik Bakke to battle it out with Roy Keane, Paul Scholes and Nicky Butt. Leeds were also without their top scorer, Michael Bridges, but these absences were tempered by the return of Lucas Radebe from the African Nations Cup, where he had captained South Africa to a third-place finish (ensuring he missed the maximum number of games for nothing!) When the big screen showed Lucas waiting to lead the Leeds players out of the tunnel, Elland Road burst into song, 'Radebe. Radebe. Radebe, Radebe, Radebe. Radebe, Radebee-ee, Radebe-ee-ee-ee-ee, LUCAS!' The Chief couldn't help but raise a big smile.

There was a surprise absence for the visitors, with David Beckham dropped from the matchday squad after a bust-up with manager Alex Ferguson. Perhaps this was a strategic masterstroke from Ferguson. With the Leeds fans always so keen to abuse their most hated opponent, the absence of Beckham seemed to dampen the atmosphere somewhat; for the fans it was an opportunity lost. The 11.30am kick-off couldn't have helped matters either, and I was frustrated not to be standing in a cauldron of noise that was worthy of such an enormous game.

The match itself was quite low-key too. In the first half Ian Harte was brilliantly denied by Mark Bosnich from three separate free kicks, and early in the second half Andy Cole got the better of Radebe and poked the champions into the lead. It was the visitors' only real chance of the match, and though Leeds never really laid siege to the goal, they were mighty unfortunate not to equalise. Bakke's header cannoned off the bar, Kewell's cross deflected on to the bar, then in the closing stages Bosnich parried a Wilcox drive straight to Alan Smith, but with the goal at his mercy Smith steered the ball against the post, which led to the worst and most significant miss I've ever seen at Elland Road. Smith's shot rebounded off the post into the centre of the penalty box where Bowyer was arriving, all alone, and with Bosnich still in the net from trying to save Smith's effort. Bowyer could have tapped it in, or walked it in, but adrenaline got the better of him and he lashed at the ball as hard as he could on the half-volley, ballooning it into the top of the South Stand. Was luck ever going to start evening out for either of these teams?

Leeds's title dreams were slipping away. Once again they found themselves six points adrift of the luckiest team in the world, a position that no team would fancy overturning. They say a change is as good as a rest, and with no rest period in sight the return of the UEFA Cup was a timely distraction from a domestic blip. Leeds were heading back to the Eternal City, and I was going with them.

AS Roma 0-0 Leeds United
Thursday, 2 March 2000
Stadio Olimpico – 6pm
UEFA Cup Fourth Round, First Leg

It was my first European away trip, so I don't have to describe how excited I was. My dad pulled me out of school for nearly two weeks, a controversial move with my GCSEs around the corner, but my mum was on board as it presented an opportunity for her to visit her 18-year-old son who was living in Florence and had been away from home for nearly eight whole weeks! We went by car and stopped off in Milan to catch up with old family friends, and I was thrilled when they took me on a stadium tour of the San Siro, my favourite stadium in the world (well, second favourite). It was almost surreal being in such an iconic stadium, and the tour itself was even better than Sunderland! For a start there was a trophy room in the San Siro, and a fascinating museum, and we were able to visit the changing rooms and sit in the manager's seat in the press room (a *Championship Manager* addict's dream!)

On Saturday lunchtime we arrived at Gianni's flat in Florence, where he lived with his best mate Nige, a Brazilian called Gee, and a cat called Onion. The flat was in Piazza San Pier Maggiore, a grungy little square that had everything you need: a butcher, an Irish pub, a pizzeria, and *Antico Noi*, which sold the greatest sandwich in the world; *The Tredici* (sausage meat, aubergine, spinach and mozzarella). While my parents settled into their hotel I spent the afternoon in the flat, playing cards and listening to the BBC World Service as Leeds ground out a 0-0 draw at Middlesbrough, while Manchester United scored another late goal to salvage a 2-2 draw at Wimbledon. It was an opportunity missed, but no harm done. The harm was done on the night out. 'We're gonna make you a man tonight,' said Gee. They fell miles short. They kept me out all night but I was in a drunken stupor – clearly the nights of four pints at Trotters had not prepared me sufficiently. In the morning I was in a right state, nursing a stinking hangover by any subsequent standards, and I solemnly declared that I'd never drink again. Words to rival Michael Bridges' delusional post-Sunderland interview.

After a few nights in Florence we headed over to Rome with Gianni. That was always the plan, but now we had the added bonus of another ticket office blunder. When we collected the match tickets we were shocked to find four tickets instead of two, meaning Gianni could come to the game, and my mum too. It would be her first game since 1975, when the Leeds fans rioted after the controversial European Cup Final defeat in Paris. ('Was that when they ripped up all the seats and threw them on the pitch?' was my mum's response when I asked her if she remembered Roma away while writing this book.)

The ticket office's mistake was no blessing for my mum. She had been looking forward to a nice relaxing evening with Gianni, instead she endured the worst night of her life. She was already shaken up by almost getting robbed on the Rome underground, and on entry to the Stadio Olimpico she was subjected to a rigorous search, surrounded by blood-soaked Leeds fans who had been caught up in violence earlier in the day. My dad and Gianni whisked her up to the top row of the away end so she wasn't in the thick of all the boisterous merriment, but behind her stood a line of policemen armed with machine guns and dressed in full armour including helmets. There they stood for the whole match, plus an hour before and an hour after while we were locked in. Furthermore, the stadium's roof was suspended above the stands, and a biting wind was shooting through the gap. Thus, my poor mum spent four hours sitting in her seat (which had no back rest) hunched over with her head in her hands, shivering.

Meanwhile, I was having the time of my life! On entering the ground I bumped into Freddy from the Maverick Whites and ended up standing with his gang for the whole game. Freddy was a lovely lad, a southerner who lived in Guildford yet never missed a game, home or away. Being a few years older than me and my mates he had an almost heroic status to us, so spending the match with him and the Mavericks was the perfect scenario. I did feel guilty for abandoning my dad, but I couldn't have let my mum see what I'm like at football (I turn into a raving lunatic).

The atmosphere in the Leeds end was incredible, and at half-time the 'Champions of Europe' rendition was the greatest ever. I'd never been prouder to be Leeds, in amongst 7,000 bare-chested Yorkshiremen while the Italians gawped and wondered what on earth we were doing, and why on earth we'd waited until half-time to put on such a spectacle. Sadly, this gratifying and amusing half-time tradition was on its last legs. It began as a means of entertainment during the dullest times under George Graham, but under O'Leary the football itself was all the entertainment we needed.

Sandwiching half-time was a brilliant match. Leeds were dressed in their Lazio-inspired away kit, which made the game look like a Rome derby and gave the travelling fans more excuse to wind up the locals by chanting for their bitter rivals. The sky-blue kit acted like a red rag to the bulls of Roma, and they laid siege to the Leeds goal. The first half was the Totti vs Martyn show, and Roma's greatest ever player couldn't beat Leeds's greatest ever goalkeeper, who pulled off three fantastic saves. In the second half Totti's team-mates joined in to help, but neither Montella, Delvecchio, Nakata or Cafu could beat an inspired keeper, on what is generally considered the finest night of his Leeds career (coincidentally, this was the night future Leeds goalkeeping sensation, Illan Meslier, was born). United had their moments too. Harry Kewell was clean through in the first half but finished into the side netting, and in the closing stages his mazy dribble created a shooting chance, which flashed inches wide of the post. There had been no away goal to celebrate, but the 0-0 draw felt like a victory and the Leeds fans saluted their heroes accordingly. It was all to play for at Elland Road.

The return leg was a magical night. Having gone one better than last season's 1-0 defeat in Rome, Leeds went one better in the home leg too, turning a 0-0 draw into a 1-0 win. It was a highly intense game, with Roma a constant threat but never able to breach the Leeds defence, which was helped in no small part by cult hero Alfie Haaland. During that season, Haaland had only ever been deployed as the extra centre-back O'Leary often preferred in the big away games, but with Woodgate and Duberry injured, he was playing alongside Radebe in a back four and played his heart out. Steaming out of defence with the ball had become a trademark of his and always sparked a surge of excitement around the ground, and one such foray set up the only goal of the tie. Haaland charged into the Roma half, through three challenges and all the way to the edge of their box where he was finally stopped in his tracks. The loose ball was picked up by Stephen McPhail, and two passes later Harry Kewell received the ball in space, 25 yards from goal. Seconds after that the Kop was going absolutely mental, as Roma keeper Antonioli could only palm Kewell's blistering strike in off the crossbar.

Leeds held firm through a nerve-wracking last 20 minutes, until injury-time red cards to Zago and Candela all but ended the Italian hopes. At the final whistle David O'Leary ran on to the pitch to hug his babies like a proud father. He had got the better of a world-renowned manager in Fabio Capello; it was the best night of his career to date. It was also the best night of my life, Elland Road was bouncing after the final whistle; I'd never witnessed such scenes before.

Leeds United were in their first European quarter-final for 25 years, and were now the joint favourites to win the UEFA Cup. O'Leary continued to play down their chances of course, but captain Lucas Radebe was pulling no punches, 'The lads feel they can go all the way now. We have a squad packed with confidence and character. We all want to win things, not only for ourselves but also for the fans who have given us such magnificent support.'

Leicester City 2-1 Leeds United

Sunday, 26 March 2000
Filbert Street – 3pm
FA Carling Premiership

Before the tie with Roma, David O'Leary had aired his concerns that continued European commitments could stretch his young squad too far. 'It worries me that in March, if we're still progressing in the UEFA Cup we'll have four Thursday night games in a month, followed by Premiership games on the Sunday. I've seen the effects of that before, and if we lose a few players through injury or suspension we might find it hard.' However, heading into the last weekend of March Leeds were still motoring on nicely. With a comfortable victory over Slavia Prague, O'Leary's babies had booked their place in a European semi-final, and three successive Premiership victories had cut the gap on Manchester United to four points.

Leeds were consistently playing catch-up with their title rivals, but if they were feeling any pressure it was simply driving them on. Manchester United's 1-1 draw at home to Liverpool was capitalised on as Leeds thrashed Coventry 3-0 at Elland Road. The following Saturday Manchester United were stuttering again, but two late goals against Derby opened up a seven-point gap before Leeds made the short trip to Valley Parade on *Super Sunday*. Struggling Bradford were duly dispatched 2-1 in a West Yorkshire derby that would be remembered for a goalkeeping crisis that brought Bantams coach Neville Southall out of retirement, a few years too late and a few stone too heavy. The next Saturday, Manchester United strolled to a comfortable 2-0 win at Leicester, with David Beckham's newly shaved head bizarrely dominating the headlines, but O'Leary's babies again gave a nerveless response on the Sunday, thrashing Wimbledon 4-1.

An inconsequential second leg defeat in Prague ended a five-game winning run for Leeds, and three days later they headed to Filbert Street, once again trailing their cross-Pennine rivals by seven points. The pressure finally told. Leeds's young pretenders were outfought by the galvanised Foxes on an utterly miserable afternoon. Leicester's new signing, Stan Collymore, opened the scoring in the first half with a blistering finish, although the linesman failed to notice he was a yard offside. Leeds rallied, and Harry Kewell hit the post before scoring a brilliant equaliser, darting through the Leicester defence before sliding the ball past Tim Flowers from a tight angle. The Australian had now scored in six successive matches, one away from Peter Lorimer's club record of seven.

At half-time the game was finely poised, but shortly after the break Leeds fell asleep at a set piece, leaving Steve Guppy free at the back post to fire past Martyn and restore Leicester's lead. It was a body-blow that O'Leary's weary team couldn't recover from. An Ian Harte free kick was the best effort they could muster, and the final whistle brought the realisation that the title race was all but over; I gave Leeds no chance of overhauling a seven-point gap in just eight games.

On a day like this O'Leary must have rued the loss of David Batty. Injured in December and not seen again all season, we'll never know what difference his presence would have made to Leeds's title challenge. Losing your best midfielder is enough to derail any team, especially a team with only one other player with any experience of winning a trophy (Jason Wilcox). On the journey home from Filbert Street, it felt like the world had ended, but by the time I wrote my match report I was feeling a little more philosophical, 'Title over, but still clear in second. Only a shocking collapse can stop a Champions League place.'

The title race ended beyond all doubt the following weekend. Chelsea arrived at Elland Road and claimed a scrappy 1-0 victory, while Manchester United smashed in seven goals at Old Trafford. O'Leary conceded the title challenge was over, and Ferguson's men didn't drop another point as they cruised to the finish line. It had been a long and draining season for

Leeds: the number of fixtures, the number of miles travelled, the number of Sunday matches, and the number of criminal charges brought against their players, but it would all pale into insignificance compared with what was to happen next.

Leeds United 2-2 Galatasaray
Thursday, 20 April 2000
Elland Road – 8pm
UEFA Cup Semi-Final, Second Leg

On the morning of 6 April, I woke to the news that two Leeds fans had died following violence in Istanbul on the night before the UEFA Cup semi-final first leg. It was chilling news, and as the details emerged it only became more horrifying. 'Welcome to Hell' was the trademark greeting for English clubs arriving in Turkey to play Galatasaray, but what happened to the Leeds fans was beyond anybody's worst nightmares.

Sticking to the facts, Christopher Loftus and Kevin Speight were brutally murdered in Taksim Square. Neither were hooligans; Christopher was with his brother and friends and Kevin had a young family at home. The attack on the Leeds fans was premeditated; they were drinking in a bar when they were confronted by a group of hooligans who vastly outnumbered them, some armed with machetes and knives. Kevin died at the scene and Christopher died later in hospital, his body identified by his brother along with chairman Peter Ridsdale, who had rushed to the hospital after learning of the attacks.

During the subsequent trial, the defence claimed that the Leeds fans had been rubbing the Turkish flag on their genitals, abusing women, smashing windows and provoking the locals with broken bottles. There was no proof that any of these accusations were true. Nothing untoward was found on the CCTV footage and the West Yorkshire Police, present as 'spotters', submitted evidence to the contrary which was not used in court. The provocation claims were accepted by the judge and led to vastly reduced sentences. The whole process took ten years, during which time the murderers were allowed to live as free men, even serving in the Turkish army, before being brought to justice. By the time they were finally sent to jail, Harry Kewell had already completed two seasons as a Galatasaray player.

While Taksim Square could never be forgotten, it was the aftermath that hardened the animosity many Leeds fans still hold towards Galatasaray (and even Turkey as a whole). The murders were carried out by a group of vicious savages, but Galatasaray and their supporters showed a similar lack of humanity, and the general consensus in Turkey seemed to be that the Leeds fans had got what was coming to them (even if you believe the preposterous provocation accusations, this is still barbaric). Galatasaray denied the murders were connected to their club and refused to postpone the game, refused to hold a minute's silence before kick-off, and refused to wear black armbands. There wasn't an ounce of sympathy afforded to Leeds United officials, players or fans.

Against the wishes of many of the squad, Leeds agreed to play the fixture under advice from the FA's chief executive David Davies, who described it as 'the least-worst option'. On the way to the ground the team coach was pelted with missiles and screamed at, and when the players emerged from the tunnel in the Ali Sami Yen stadium they were guarded by the Turkish army, who held shields high into the air to prevent any missiles hitting the players. Missiles may have been raining down from the stands, but the stands were miles away from the tunnel. It was all done for effect, to terrify the already traumatised players. Leeds's traumatised fans received the same treatment of course, including being subjected to cut-throat gestures from the home fans.

The match itself was a nightmare too. It's fair to say football was irrelevant compared to the deaths of our fans, but what had happened made me even more desperate to win; I couldn't bear the thought of the Turks celebrating. I can't remember the goals, all I remember is being slumped on the sofa feeling desperately upset, the referee blowing his whistle every time a Galatasaray player hit the deck, and Michael Bridges skying a late sitter over an open goal. Leeds fell to a 2-0 defeat, but the travelling contingent can't have cared about anything except getting home to their families.

It was touching to see the national response to the atrocities in Istanbul – British football truly came together to mourn the loss Leeds had suffered. Shirts from clubs from all around the country joined thousands of Leeds shirts and scarves and flowers to form a massive shrine which started at the Billy Bremner statue and snaked around the stadium. The first match after Istanbul was Aston Villa away, where Peter Ridsdale made an emotional visit to the away end to console our supporters. I still remember the Villa fans telling us to 'go win it for them lads now' as we left the ground, which lifted my spirits after a disheartening 1-0 defeat.

In the first game back at Elland Road the Arsenal players all carried bouquets of flowers on to the pitch and handed them to the Leeds players prior to the minute's silence, just as they had done on their first trip to Anfield after the Hillsborough disaster in 1989. While the swell of emotion was comforting for the fans, it was all too much to take for their young team, who fell to a crushing 4-0 defeat. Eight of the players who lined up against Arsenal were 23 or younger, and six of them were academy graduates. Just a couple of weeks earlier they were living out a lifetime's fantasy, playing in the Leeds United first team together, chasing the Premiership title and European glory. Nothing could have prepared them for what they were going through now.

It was all so sad, and when Arsenal scored their third goal, I couldn't take any more. I'm ashamed to report that I was one of many to leave the stadium with ten minutes still remaining, such was my anger at the universe for everything that had happened. Lewis and the remaining fans inside Elland Road sang their hearts out for the lads on the pitch and the lads in heaven, honouring the solemn oath that lives in the hearts of all Leeds fans, 'We're gonna stay with you forever, at least until the world stops going round.'

For the return leg with Galatasaray there was the largest police presence I've ever seen at a football match, this despite there being no away fans. Peter Ridsdale had requested that away fans were banned from travelling to Yorkshire as they could not guarantee their safety, leading Galatasaray to make the disgraceful accusation that Leeds were trying to benefit from the murders of their fans. The Turks insisted the second leg should be played at a neutral venue where their fans could attend safely, but UEFA sided with Leeds and limited the travelling contingent to 70 club officials or guests.

'Welcome to Civilisation' read the banner held up by the Leeds fans as the teams emerged from the tunnel at a highly charged Elland Road. I would have given my right arm to see Leeds triumph, but it was going to be a tall order against a good Galatasaray side with a legendary front two of Gheorghe Hagi and Hakan Sukur. It didn't feel beyond Leeds's capabilities, especially with 40,000 impassioned fans roaring the team on, but after just five minutes Hagi had scored a penalty and now there was a mountain to climb. Leeds needed four goals and Eirik Bakke got the ball rolling straight away by heading in Jason Wilcox's corner. Could this be the greatest European night Elland Road had ever seen? That question was put to bed just before half-time, when Sukur danced around Radebe and fired past Martyn. A minute later the referee flashed his red card at Harry Kewell after Gheorghe Popescu went to ground holding his face, and a minute after that he flashed the same card at Emre Belozoglu for a similar offence; neither player appeared to have done anything wrong.

In the second half Leeds had enough chances to get back into the tie, but by the time Bakke made it 2-2 on the night, from another Wilcox corner, all belief had drained away and the atmosphere had almost turned carnival as the Leeds fans showed their defiance in the face of adversity. There were still 25 minutes left for Leeds to get three goals, but chances came and went and when the final whistle blew, Galatasaray celebrated like the result had been on the line right until the last minute. It was never going to be difficult for Galatasaray players to make it on to my blacklist, and Popescu (for pretending he was hit by Kewell) and Sukur (for pretending to be hit by a missile) were joined by Brazilian World Cup-winning goalkeeper, Taffarel, who sunk to his knees in front of the Kop and pointed to the heavens, the disrespectful swine.

The European dream was over. Instead it would be the Turks that travelled to face Arsenal in Copenhagen, where violence broke out before the game. By the end, Galatasaray had won the UEFA Cup on penalties, the first European trophy ever won by a Turkish club.

Sheffield Wednesday 0-3 Leeds United
Sunday, 30 April 2000
Hillsborough – 4pm
FA Carling Premiership

'Only a shocking collapse can stop a Champions League place.' I'm not sure my words after the title race ended at Filbert Street could be classed as tempting fate, but five weeks later Leeds headed to Hillsborough without a win in eight games, fifth in the league, and five points adrift of a Champions League spot.

'We were the victims of our own success,' concluded O'Leary, whose warnings and concerns had come to fruition. 'The European games took a lot out of us and cost us dearly. If we hadn't had those four games in March, I'm convinced we would already have second place assured and would have pushed Manchester United much harder.'

Still, hopes of salvaging something from a season that had turned so unfathomably sour remained. The draw with Galatasaray had ended a club-record six-game losing streak (has a club ever registered record winning and losing streaks in the same season?), and Liverpool's defeat at Chelsea opened the door for Leeds to re-enter the race for Champions League football. Victory over Sheffield Wednesday would cut the gap to two points with three games to play.

The UEFA Cup exit seemed to have provided some closure on one of the darkest periods the club has ever faced, and things felt somewhat rosy again on a sunny afternoon at Hillsborough. However, walking into the Leppings Lane end always sent shivers down my spine. I found it impossible not to take myself back to 1989 and put myself in the shoes of the Liverpool fans, imagining what they went through on that fateful day, picturing the scenes around me. Once the stand was full of Leeds fans these thoughts disappeared, and as the teams came out the PA system played 'Hi-ho, Silver Lining', with the away end drowning out the home fans, and the speakers, by roaring over the top, 'And it's hi-ho, LEEDS UNITED!'

The feel-good factor grew within 40 seconds of kick-off. While sitting on the floor, Michael Bridges cleverly poked a loose ball through to David Hopkin, who finished calmly to provide Leeds with the perfect start. Bridges had suffered a disappointing second half of the season and his latest goalscoring duck stood at five games, but in the second half the Geordie striker curled in his 20th goal of the season to give Leeds the 2-0 cushion their dominance deserved.

Sheffield Wednesday were on the brink of relegation and desperately needed to win this match, yet their insipid performance was that of a team with their fate already sealed. Even their fans seemed to have accepted the inevitable as the ground wasn't even close to being full, and with relegation now a formality, the Owls were completely demoralised. Meanwhile the swagger returned to Leeds, with Harry Kewell putting the icing on the cake with a sublime goal, a beautifully lofted curler with the outside of his left boot, the ball bouncing into the roof of the net off the underside of the bar.

It was a fitting way to end the match, from which Kewell rushed to the PFA Player of the Year ceremony, having received nominations for both the player and young player of the year awards. Kewell came third in the running for the top prize, but did win the junior title, beating off competition from Bowyer and Bridges. It was the second season running that Leeds had provided half the nominees for the young player award, and they also dominated the PFA team of the year with Martyn, Harte, Kelly and Kewell all voted into the best 11 by their peers. Having been showered with acclaim, it would be desperately sad if these awards were to be the highlight of the season.

West Ham United 0-0 Leeds United

Sunday, 14 May 2000
Upton Park – 4pm
FA Carling Premiership

Having enjoyed an excellent first full season under Gerard Houllier, Liverpool were collapsing at the finish line. They were three games without a win when Southampton arrived at Anfield on the penultimate weekend, and I watched *Super Sunday* in trepidation as the Saints managed to cling on for a 0-0 draw that gave Leeds the chance to take a giant leap towards the Champions League at Elland Road on *Monday Night Football*.

Standing in the way were Everton, and with nothing to play for but pride, the Toffees did their Merseyside rivals proud by giving it everything they had. It was a nervy night at Elland Road and Michael Bridges' opening goal gave Leeds a half-time lead against the run of play. The star of the second half was referee Andy D'Urso, who couldn't keep his cards in his pocket. Early in the second half Everton's Richard Dunne received his marching orders and victory seemed assured, but D'Urso soon evened up the numbers with a red card for Michael Duberry. Shortly after that Nick Barmby evened up the score, capitalising on a rare Nigel Martyn mistake to equalise.

There was still half an hour to go but Leeds couldn't force the winning goal, even after D'Urso completed his hat-trick by sending off Don Hutchison to reduce the visitors to nine men in the closing stages. It was a disappointing way to sign off the season at Elland Road, and although the Leeds players and staff received vociferous support on the traditional end of season lap of honour, I was too downbeat to join in. The point gained at least kept Leeds's chances of claiming the third and final Champions League spot in their own hands, but I had hoped only a draw would be needed in the last game at West Ham. To be guaranteed third, they would now have to win.

I had attended 43 games during the season, 17 of them away from home, but our application for the biggest of the lot was unsuccessful. With the whole season on the line my dad had to think outside the box again to get us into Upton Park and, just as he had for the first away game of the season, he managed to conjure up tickets. This time he wrote a letter to David O'Leary, who was a customer of the family business and had recently had his carpets cleaned for free. In the letter my dad informed O'Leary of our predicament and begged for his help in securing us some tickets for the season's finale. Lo and behold, a couple of days later my dad and I were rolling up at his house with a bottle of Moet in exchange for four tickets in the away end, left on the doorstep by O'Leary's lovely wife, Joy.

So, on a beautiful Sunday morning, Lewis, Paul, my dad and I headed down to London, nervous but expectant. To qualify for the Champions League, Leeds needed to match

Liverpool's result at Bradford City, who needed to win to stay in the Premiership at the expense of Wimbledon. During the first half, news filtered through that was music to our ears. Bradford had taken the lead at Valley Parade, and David Wetherall – who had made over 200 appearances for Leeds United – had scored the goal. The Leeds fans burst into exuberant celebrations as if their team had scored themselves, and chanted for the captain of their local rivals, 'Who put the ball in the Scousers' net? David Wetherall!' The party in the concourse at half-time was my clearest memory of the day, but in the back of my mind it all seemed a bit premature; just one goal in both games would turn the situation on its head.

It was a poor game of football at Upton Park, 'One of the most boring I've been to, but one of the best,' according to my match report. Paolo Di Canio had the best chance, rounding Martyn in the second half but firing into the side netting from a tight angle, while a nervous Leeds team could only muster half-chances. Heading into stoppage time the situation hadn't changed; we were close, but we couldn't afford to concede in case Liverpool equalised at Valley Parade. When the final whistle went Leeds had ground out a 0-0 draw that would be enough to secure Champions League football, as long as Liverpool didn't do a Manchester United and score two injury-time goals. The confirmation finally came through as the players lined up in front of us, Bradford had done it! Their 1-0 win saved them from relegation and ensured Leeds's season hadn't been in vain. It was party time at Upton Park, with players and fans chanting in unison, 'We are Champions League, say we are Champions League!' The party continued all the way back up the M1, as my dad had prepared a celebratory CD in preparation for a happy ending.

It had been a tumultuous roller coaster of a season, but amid the chaos and tragedy David O'Leary had once again met the hopes and expectations he and Peter Ridsdale had laid out at the start of the campaign; Champions League qualification and a good cup run. Although it was an achievement worth celebrating, it was impossible not to regret what might have been: if Hasselbaink had stayed, if he had been replaced, if O'Leary had spent better in the summer (Mills, Duberry and Huckerby had barely contributed), if Batty's season hadn't ended in November, if that night out hadn't happened in January, if Galatasaray hadn't happened. Nevertheless, a title challenge and a European semi-final represented brilliant progress for this young team, and a great learning curve too, and participation in Europe's top competition brought increased income and prestige.

Pundits across the land had always spoken of O'Leary's team winning the Premiership as an inevitability – when, not if – and after five years of Manchester United and Arsenal dominance, Leeds were now primed to challenge seriously for all the top honours.

ACT III

2000/01 – Living the Dream

Pre-Season

Leeds United 2-1 1860 Munich

Leeds United 1-0 AC Milan

Leeds United 6-0 Besiktas

Leeds United 1-1 Barcelona

Bradford City 1-1 Leeds United

Leeds United 4-3 Liverpool

AC Milan 1-1 Leeds United

Leeds United 0-2 Real Madrid

Leicester City 3-1 Leeds United

Newcastle United 2-1 Leeds United

Manchester City 0-4 Leeds United

Leeds United 2-1 Anderlecht

Leeds United 1-1 Manchester United

Sunderland 0-2 Leeds United

Leeds United 3-0 Deportivo La Coruna

Liverpool 1-2 Leeds United

Leeds United 0-0 Valencia

Arsenal 2-1 Leeds United

Valencia 3-0 Leeds United

Leeds United 3-1 Leicester City

Pre-Season

DAVID O'LEARY once again spoke of the need to add quality players in order for his young squad to realise their potential, and nobody at Elland Road could argue with him. In 1999/00, Leeds had played a 55-game season using just 18 outfield players and had run out of steam, albeit in unprecedentedly challenging circumstances. The babies needed help, especially when they were about to embark upon their first Champions League campaign.

Pre-season transfer activity got off to the quickest possible start for United. The day after the final game they announced the signing of French midfielder Olivier Dacourt from RC Lens, for a club record £7.2m. Dacourt had played in England two seasons earlier for Everton, where he was better known for his high number of yellow cards than high level of performance, nevertheless this was a well-received signing and added some continental flair to a very British squad. O'Leary's transfer policy was not altering however, and Leeds continued to be linked with the best of the country's young home-grown talent.

A striker and a left-back were the two clear holes in the squad; Hasselbaink was still to be replaced and the only specialist left-back was Ian Harte. Leeds had been trying to sign an out-and-out centre-forward since O'Leary took the job; Dion Dublin, Pierre van Hooijdonk, Ashley Ward, Emile Heskey and Tore Andre Flo had all failed to materialise, and next to be added to that list was Wimbledon's young target man, Carl Cort. Leeds refused to meet the £7m asking price and, as with Kieron Dyer during the previous summer, Newcastle ended Leeds's interest by stumping up the full fee.

The coveted No.9 shirt instead went to Celtic's Australian powerhouse striker Mark Viduka, a player with an unpredictable temperament and not a lot of pace. He had scored 30 goals in 37 games in Scotland, but that league was weak and even the Celtic fans had split opinions on him, though mainly due to the antics of his trouble-making agent, Bernie Mandic. I was underwhelmed by the signing, and worse still, Viduka would miss the early part of the season as he was insistent upon going to play in his home Olympics in Sydney. Thankfully he would at least be available for the crucial Champions League qualifier.

Another player that Leeds refused to meet the asking price for was Monaco's highly rated left-back, John Arne Riise. Leeds had been tracking the Norwegian for a long time and were close to landing their man until his asking price suddenly jumped from £4m to £6m. Once again, the club would not be bullied into meeting valuations they believed were inflated, and when it became clear the pursuit of Riise was over, Leeds instead swooped for Dominic Matteo, who was struggling to cement his place in Liverpool's first 11. This was not a signing that would cause a boom in season ticket sales but for a fee of around £4m it looked astute business. Matteo was a versatile defender with experience at a big club, had played in Europe and, crucially, was left-footed; finally some cover or competition for Ian Harte.

It had been another exciting summer at Elland Road, yet once again Leeds had strengthened in quality but not quantity. With the departure of experienced squad members Alfie Haaland, David Hopkin, Martin Hiden and Robert Molenaar, Leeds now had an even smaller squad than last season, despite the prospect of battling against Europe's elite, week in week out. Worse still, Leeds were suffering from an injury epidemic, with players dropping like flies throughout pre-season. A new design of boot was rumoured to be the problem, but in the end it cost the physio his job, with O'Leary believing many underlying issues could have been identified and dealt with over the summer, not once the players returned to Thorp Arch.

Despite the threadbare squad, the noises coming out of Elland Road were the same as they had been for two years. Ridsdale maintained that money was available to spend on players, O'Leary maintained that he needed a bigger squad, yet both were adamant that money wouldn't be spent on short-term fixes or over-priced players. O'Leary had identified two more players to complete his squad, but until they were available at the right price Leeds United would bide their time.

Leeds United 2-1 1860 Munich
Wednesday, 9 August 2000
Elland Road – 7.45pm
UEFA Champions League Qualifier, First Leg

Leeds were seeded for the Champions League qualifying draw but managed to pick out the hardest possible tie, 1860 Munich from the German Bundesliga. It was a cruel twist of fate, especially coupled with the host of injuries picked up in pre-season; Kewell, Woodgate, McPhail, Wilcox and Batty were all unavailable for the start of the new season. We were accustomed to the opening day being a sunny afternoon in the Premiership, with a hint of blissful carefreeness in the air; a part of you just feeling happy to be back. This was none of those things. It was Elland Road under the lights, it was the Champions League, and it was critical.

The Leeds fans were in fine voice but their team made a nervy start, struggling to carve open the characteristically well-organised Germans until an uncharacteristic German mistake enabled Alan Smith to break the deadlock. The young striker

– still only 19 – pounced on a weak header back to the keeper and nodded home with ease. Elland Road was rocking and the mood in the stadium improved further when Ian Harte's shameless dive resulted in a straight red card for the 'offending' Munich player. Leeds were firmly in the driving seat, and in the second half would have an opportunity to kill the tie off there and then.

This was not vintage Leeds United in full flow, but they tightened their grip on the tie thanks to another shocking decision from the referee, who awarded a penalty when Smith was fouled a yard outside of the box. The Kop didn't care one jot, nor did Ian Harte, who was fresh from a sensational pre-season in which he had scored eight goals in six games, including a hat-trick of free kicks in a 3-2 victory at Blackburn. No surprise then that Harte made no mistake from 12 yards with no defensive wall in the way.

Two goals and a man up, Leeds were in an almost unassailable position, yet with 15 minutes to go they shot themselves in the foot. Perhaps you could forgive Olivier Dacourt for presuming the referee would fall for anything, but his needless dive resulted in a second yellow card, then four minutes later Eirik Bakke was sent off for the most innocuous of handballs. The complexion of the tie had turned on its head. An away goal would swing it dramatically in the Germans' favour and nine-man Leeds were desperately clinging on. In the 94th minute disaster struck. A deep cross was met by the head of Paul Agostino and the Australian striker found the corner of Nigel Martyn's net, sending the 2,000 Bavarians in the South Stand delirious. I had developed a habit of claiming the referee was the worst I'd ever seen (after nearly every match), but on this occasion the whole country agreed. It was no consolation. I was distraught after the game.

To reach the Champions League group stages, Leeds would have to avoid defeat in Munich without nine first-team players.

I didn't fancy our chances, nor did O'Leary: 'I'm not very confident about going through. I'm not being defeatist, just realistic. I don't know what side I can field.' Reading through the team for the second leg you wondered what all the fuss was about, until you got halfway through. Martyn, Kelly, Harte, Radebe, Woodgate. So far so good. Bowyer, Jones, still making sense, Mills, eh? Duberry, what?! Smith and Viduka. It was a catchphrase that O'Leary must have been sick of wheeling out but, like my 'worst ref ever' jibe, this really was Leeds United 'down to da bare bones'.

Looking back on the O'Leary years brings many, many regrets, but one of the major ones is that I was too young to travel abroad with Leeds; the Roma match was my only European away trip of the era. I was tantalisingly close to being old enough to go, whether my dad could take me or not, and both my dad and my mates talked about going to various games, but it never happened. Business wasn't great at the time and money was tight. Had business been better I'm sure my dad would have taken me to a few games, probably all of them if he could have afforded it!

The most famous nights were all to come, but I bet the 700 Leeds fans that made the trip to Munich treasure it along with the best of them. On a beautiful summer's evening, oiled up with beautiful German lager, the travelling fans did their best to drown out 55,000 Germans in the Olympic Stadium while I sat at home, still too young to even watch in a pub. Although Munich were from one of Europe's top leagues, they weren't a team that Leeds would normally fear, but in the first half Leeds's makeshift team struggled to cope in a makeshift formation. Nigel Martyn was forced into numerous saves as 34-year-old Thomas Hassler pulled the strings and dictated the match for the home team. Hassler may have been past the peak of his powers but you don't play 101 times for Germany without having a touch of class, and in the last minute of the half the old master finally beat Martyn with a stunning free kick, which thankfully smashed off the woodwork to safety.

Leeds capitalised on that let-off straight after the restart. A long Martyn clearance drew three defenders to battle for the ball with Mark Viduka. The Australian showed incredible strength to hold them all off, and even when he eventually fell to the floor, he managed to get a toe to the loose ball and send Alan Smith one-on-one with the keeper. Smith had suffered from 'second season syndrome', having burst on to the scene so spectacularly in 1998/99. He failed to score in the second half of the 1999/2000 campaign but had hit the ground running this time around, and when presented with the chance to score a goal worth £25m to his club, the teenager was coolness personified. Smith slotted the ball home and jumped the advertising boards to celebrate with the Leeds fans, while I jumped around the sofa in jubilation. I'd been waiting for the goal that would knock Leeds out, but Smith had scored the goal that would surely take Leeds through. The rest of the game was still nerve-wracking, as one Munich goal would put the tie back in the balance, but by the final whistle Mills, Duberry and Woodgate had all cleared off the line and Leeds had booked their place in the Champions League proper. O'Leary hailed the victory as the greatest of his career, then took a swipe at the lack of grace shown by his opposite number in the Munich dugout. Care to elaborate, David? 'He was just a sour, sad loser.'

I was now in sixth form, where we had the freedom to attend school or not, and on the Friday morning of the group stage draw I decided to 'not'. We had just subscribed to Sky Digital, which meant access to their revolutionary new 'round the clock' sports news channel. Gone were the days of checking teletext every hour, the '3', '0', and '2' digits on the Sky remote would not be so worn. Sky Sports News were showing the Champions League draw live, so I stayed at home to watch it and what a draw it was! O'Leary's babies were pitted against Italian giants

AC Milan, Spanish giants Barcelona, plus they would have to return to Istanbul to face Besiktas. In terms of glamour, you couldn't wish for more, but I was disappointed, thinking the Champions League campaign was over before it started.

Leeds United 1-0 AC Milan
Wednesday, 19 September 2000
Elland Road – 7.45pm
UEFA Champions League, First Group Stage

Before the Champions League came to Elland Road, Leeds were subjected to the archetypal baptism of fire. In Barcelona's famous Nou Camp stadium there is a little chapel adjacent to the players' tunnel, and Irishmen Gary Kelly and Stephen McPhail shared a pre-match prayer to ask for the Lord's help ahead of the opening game of the group stage. Leeds's task would have been hard enough at the best of times. This was a world-class Barcelona side, with a front three that would send shivers down the spines of any team in history – Rivaldo, Kluivert and Overmars – and with an injury crisis that continued to grow, their prayers were futile. They'd have been better off lighting a candle for their souls. In the 90th minute, when Leeds were already 4-0 down and demoralised, injury was added to insult when captain Lucas Radebe was stretchered off in a neck brace after colliding with his own team-mate, Michael Duberry. A penny for the thoughts of Kelly and McPhail, the Lord certainly works in mysterious ways.

Prior to the first international break of the season everything had been rosy; Leeds had claimed four wins, Alan Smith had bagged five goals and David O'Leary had signed a new six-year contract. However, with such a torrid injury list it was no surprise that a great start had turned sour. Shock home defeats to Manchester City and Ipswich – both newly promoted – sandwiched a disappointing goalless draw at Coventry and the Barcelona humbling, and the Leeds fans were anticipating another extremely difficult night when AC Milan rolled into town.

With Mark Viduka at the Olympics, youngsters Alan Smith and Michael Bridges faced the unenviable task of getting the better of two legends of the game, Paolo Maldini and Alessandro Costacurta. At the other end, right-back Danny Mills joined Michael Duberry in the centre of defence, tasked with keeping quiet the fearsome front two of Andriy Shevchenko and Oliver Bierhoff. Dominic Matteo had been injured since joining the club but was thrust into action ahead of schedule in order to make up the numbers; his first game for Leeds was also his first game as a left-winger. In all Leeds had ten full internationals unavailable, so I arrived at Elland Road with little hope, other than to enjoy an electric atmosphere and the occasion itself.

Perhaps Leeds's chances were boosted by the Yorkshire weather. It was absolutely bucketing down, and O'Leary's team made things even more uncomfortable for the Italians with a high-tempo, up-and-at-'em performance. Leeds were superb and the game ebbed and flowed rapidly, but in the second half Milan took control as the home team's intensity began to wane. The two big chances of the match both fell to the last man Leeds would have wanted, Serie A's leading marksman, Andriy Shevchenko. The first time he raced clean through, Shevchenko was denied by an astonishing tackle by Danny Mills, who appeared out of nowhere to nick the ball off the Ukrainian's toe. The second time he raced through, Shevchenko squared for Oliver Bierhoff to tap into the net, but the German had strayed offside and the goal was ruled out.

With the help of the Leeds fans, the players were able to battle through the second half and looked set to claim an impressive point, until Lee Bowyer picked the ball up in the 89th minute and, with little else on, decided to have a pop at goal. Bowyer's 25-yard drive was well struck, but straight at Brazilian goalkeeper, Dida. 'OOOH' shouted the crowd, as Dida palmed the ball down on to the Elland Road turf, but the ball skidded off the saturated surface and within the blink of an eye it was somehow in the back of the net! Elland Road exploded, the Kop went mental, and Lewis, Paul and I rolled down the gangway in ecstasy. Leeds had stolen a vital and famous victory. Incredible!

If this game had ended 0-0 it would still have been a memorable night, but Bowyer's goal made it unforgettable. I had witnessed one of the greatest moments since the Revie years, but sadly my dad hadn't. His business had branched out into flood restoration, and with major flooding in the south he was too busy to come home for the game. Instead, Paul's mum had chauffeured us to the match and was parked outside the East Stand when Dida did a doo-doo. She reported that the car was literally shaking when the goal went in!

O'Leary's likely lads had ruffled some legendary feathers, their spirit typified by Alan Smith who gave Paolo Maldini a torrid time throughout. 'Before the game I looked into his eyes and there was no apprehension,' said O'Leary about Smith. 'He had the look of someone who was saying, "I want to go out there and show I can play against the likes of Maldini and the rest of them." That's an attitude you are born with.' The manager's words could have applied to every one of his players, and himself.

Leeds United 6-0 Besiktas

Wednesday, 26 September 2000
Elland Road – 7.45pm
UEFA Champions League, First Group Stage

Just a week after the epic victory against AC Milan it was back to Elland Road for another unforgettable Champions League night. The weekend had brought another disappointing Premiership draw, 1-1 away to Derby, and another serious injury which ruled Michael Duberry out for the season. In his first season Duberry had built a rapport with the Leeds fans by leading the anti-Chelsea chants from the sidelines, but this season his football had been doing the talking and his injury was a cruel blow for him and O'Leary. Thankfully, for the visit of Besiktas, Lucas Radebe returned from his neck injury, and the attack was reinforced by the return of Mark Viduka from the Sydney Olympics.

The top-class returnees made all the difference. This was the best performance I had ever seen, from any team, and the biggest victory. Besiktas were no mugs either. They were the league leaders in Turkey and fresh from a stunning 3-0 victory over Barcelona, but Leeds ripped them to shreds. Lee Bowyer opened the scoring, before Mark Viduka and Dom Matteo both scored their first goals for the club. Both should have had braces too, but Matteo was denied by the bar and Viduka missed a one-on-one. Regardless, by half-time Leeds were home and dry, and the only question was how many they would score.

With 89 minutes on the clock the 4-0 scoreline flattered the visitors. Bakke had scored and hit the bar, Smith had hit the post, and countless other chances came and went, but by the final whistle Leeds had the thumping win their performance deserved. Substitute Darren Huckerby scored one himself before skinning the defence and squaring for Bowyer to complete the rout he had started. It was the joint biggest victory in Champions League history. What a night!

Despite missing some of their very best players Leeds had put in an irresistible performance. Smith and Viduka instantly looked a formidable partnership up front, while Lucas Radebe was majestic at bringing an end to any forays into Leeds territory, always one step ahead of the attackers. However, the biggest positive of the night was the performance of Olivier Dacourt. The Frenchman was imperious in midfield, combining elegance and flair with grit and tenacity, sweeping across the park from left to right and controlling the whole game. He was clearly a top-class addition to the team, worth every penny of the club record £7.2m fee that Peter Ridsdale had shamelessly printed on the back of Dacourt's Leeds shirt at his unveiling.

Leeds were top of the group, and next came an emotional return to Istanbul, six months after the murders of Christopher Loftus and Kevin Speight. Just 138 Leeds fans were allowed to travel, all on an official one-day package, and the fans were easily outnumbered not only by police but also the world's media. A two-hour boat trip down the Bosphorus River kept them off the streets pre-match, in what was thankfully an incident-free trip. The match itself would have been incident-free but for a season-ending knee injury sustained by Michael Bridges. Having recently lost Nigel Martyn to a torn thigh and Jason Wilcox to a broken ankle, on top of losing Duberry for the season to a ruptured Achilles, this latest blow was almost beyond belief. In the circumstances, a dull 0-0 draw was a decent result for a team whose average age was just 22, and the point gained meant qualification could be secured in the next game. All Leeds had to do was overcome the mighty Barcelona at Elland Road.

Leeds United 1-1 Barcelona
Wednesday, 24 October 2000
Elland Road – 7.45pm
UEFA Champions League, First Group Stage

Barcelona arrived at Elland Road knowing defeat would send them crashing out of the Champions League. It was a galling prospect for Barca but mouth-watering for Leeds. What a way to avenge the 4-0 humiliation they had suffered just a few weeks earlier. Barcelona were suffering from their own injury problems and travelled without Kluivert, Overmars and Pep Guardiola, although with hindsight it doesn't look such a problem when you are bringing in youngsters like Puyol and Xavi.

Again, my dad was working away and missed the game, so his cousin Gordon accompanied us instead. Gordon had been living in Germany for the past few decades so this was his first trip to Elland Road since the Revie years, and he was treated to an atmosphere like none he could remember. In the fifth minute the noise reached fever pitch as Lee Bowyer's free kick from wide on the left curled over everyone including the goalkeeper and straight into the top corner. The dream start! For the remainder of the match it was wave after wave of Barcelona attacks as they fought for their Champions League lives, but they were met with the firmest defensive wall I had ever seen.

Without the experience of Nigel Martyn behind him, Lucas Radebe alongside him or David Batty in front of him, Jonathan Woodgate had to step up to the plate. And step up he did, playing surely the greatest game of his career. He wasn't the only one. Paul Robinson, the 21-year-old novice standing in for Martyn, embarked upon a sensational duel with one of the all-time greats of the game, Rivaldo, who in the previous 18 months had won La Liga, the Copa America and the Ballon d'Or. The Brazilian's close-range header brought a wonderful reflex save at Robinson's near post, then at the end of the half his deflected free kick skidded off the surface and zoomed towards the unguarded corner of the net in front of us. It was a goal all the way, until Robinson's hand appeared from nowhere to palm the ball to safety. A wonder-save.

In the second half the incessant pressure continued, but Robinson was equal to two more Rivaldo free kicks, then he brilliantly tipped Alfonso's bullet header over the bar. It was so nerve-wracking, worse with Barca now attacking the opposite end of the ground. 'All fists to the pump!' shouted Gordon every time an attack was repelled, but with 15 minutes to go the net finally bulged when Rivaldo's deflected drive squirmed into the corner. The young keeper could do nothing on this occasion, but the linesman could, and he duly raised his flag against Alonso, who hadn't touched the ball but was standing a yard offside and directly in Robinson's eyeline. I was starting to think it was going to be our night.

The game entered injury time with the 1-0 lead still intact, but the fourth official signalled four minutes of added time, to the fury of Elland Road; nobody could understand where the time had come from. Three minutes later and Elland Road was roaring their disapproval again, as the referee wrongly (as he later admitted) penalised Smith as he battled with Carles Puyol on the halfway line. Barca had one last chance. From the resulting free kick Leeds defended desperately but just couldn't clear their lines. Bakke, Mills and Matteo all had chances to, before Bowyer's air-kick enabled Phillip Cocu to swing in a magnificent cross from the left wing, perfectly on to the head of Alonso. Robinson could only stand and watch, along with the other 40,000 people in the stadium, as the ball bounced off the inside of the near post and back into the middle of the box, perfectly into the path of who else but Rivaldo. The Brazilian clinically slammed his half-volley past the despairing dive of Robinson and into the net, saving Barcelona and breaking my heart.

Our dejected heroes trudged off the pitch in disbelief – they had given their all and come so close. David O'Leary struggled to hide his disappointment too, rightly pointing out that if Barcelona had scored earlier nobody could have begrudged them a point, but it was impossible to stomach the equaliser considering how late it had come.

What a night of celebration it could have been. Instead Leeds faced the unenviable task of heading to the San Siro still needing a point.

Eddie's Babies: The culmination of the ten-year plan

Whose side are you on George? Contrasting emotions in the directors' box at White Hart Lane

The Battle of the Prospective Managers

The first failed attempt at kicking Ferguson's butt

The look of love

A proud father hugs his babies

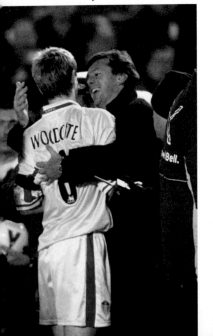

Kewell wins the tie vs AS Roma

The tragic trip to Istanbul

Trauma on the faces before the UEFA Cup semi-final second leg

*We Are
Champions
League*

Give us a break ref

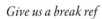

*Me, Lewis and Paul, celebrating
outside the East Stand*

Rivaldo breaks 40,000 Yorkshire hearts

Arguably the greatest defender of all time leads his team out to face Paolo Maldini's AC Milan

Nightmare on Filbert Street

Bowyer writes the perfect script vs Anderlecht

The goalkeeper trying to sneak a peak at Ian Harte's thunderbolt

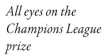

All eyes on the Champions League prize

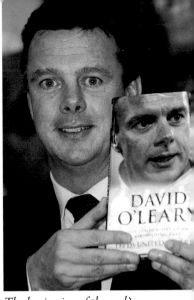

The Damned United, robbed by a referee again

The beginning of the end?

The Other Man

*The Titanic
hits the
iceberg in
Cardiff*

*A fond and
unexpected
farewell*

Bradford City 1-1 Leeds United

Sunday, 29 October 2000
Valley Parade – 4pm
FA Carling Premiership

While Leeds were tearing it up in the Champions League, their domestic form had suffered significantly, and heading into the West Yorkshire derby they were languishing in the bottom half of the table, with any hopes of a title push already over. The spine of last year's team was all missing through injury – Martyn, Radebe, Batty, Kewell and Bridges – and, coupled with the physical and mental exertions of the Champions League campaign, O'Leary only expected one thing from his depleted squad: 'to show courage'.

Prior to the West Yorkshire derby Leeds suffered a 3-0 defeat at Old Trafford, which was made memorable not by the players on the pitch but the players in the stand. They surely formed the greatest team of unavailable players in Premiership history; Martyn, Mills, Radebe, Duberry, Harte, Bakke, Batty, Dacourt, Wilcox, Kewell and Bridges. Despite the injuries, and the league table, I was massively excited for the Bradford match. I had been to Valley Parade before and loved the away end; a tiny two-tiered stand, with the upper tier stacked directly on top of the lower, and so close to the pitch that in the upper tier you were right on top of the action. The game I had attended had only been a friendly though, and I couldn't wait to experience a proper local derby awayday in the Premiership, having been unable to get a ticket for the previous season's 2-1 victory.

The sky was black (despite it being a 4pm kick-off) and the rain torrential, and fans in the new stand that Bradford were constructing all wore plastic rain covers, making it look like a racist fancy dress party; a stand full of the Ku Klux Klan. It all set the scene for a classic battle and Leeds got off to a fast start. Bowyer's speculative shot was tipped on to the bar and

Danny Hay and Dom Matteo both had headers cleared off the line, but after 20 minutes it was the home side who took the lead. Stan Collymore had recently joined the Bantams, and after helping Leicester to end Leeds's title hopes last season, he now scored a stunning overhead kick on his debut to send the home fans delirious. It had the opposite effect on the Leeds fans when Collymore began to goad them. Being in the upper tier we couldn't really see the reaction of the fans below us, only the swarm of police struggling to keep them from ripping the striker's head off. Collymore continued to wind the Leeds fans up throughout the first half, bizarrely with monkey gestures, as if trying to incite racist abuse.

The antics of Collymore, the exhilaration of the home fans, the weather and the scoreline, set up a frantic second half. Bradford goalkeeper Matt Clarke was enjoying a brilliant season. The form of his life had taken him to the brink of the England squad and he did his international prospects no harm at all by keeping Leeds at bay with some brilliant saves. 'Matt the Cat' had lady luck on his side too. When Viduka rounded him, his lobbed finish from a tight angle dropped agonisingly wide, then Clarke escaped with only a booking after obstructing Viduka from an open goal, but with ten minutes remaining it was third time lucky for Viduka, who planted Matteo's cross firmly into the bottom corner. The Leeds fans were jubilant, and the relief of denying Bradford a famous victory, together with the courage O'Leary's players had shown, overshadowed another two dropped points.

On leaving the ground we were confronted by hundreds of angry Bradford fans. I'd never witnessed such a scene. Only a line of police separated them from the Leeds fans, but my dad's strategy was to stay close to the police, surmising that the nearer to them we were, the safer we would be. However, when 'missiles' started flying towards us it was time to bolt, and we rushed back to the car as quickly as we could.

Just two days later Leeds were back in action in the League Cup at Tranmere Rovers. The third-round ties had been postponed due to the 9/11 terrorist attack, and with the draw already made, Leeds were set for a fourth-round trip to Filbert Street for the third year running, if they could escape Prenton Park unscathed; a graveyard for Premiership teams in recent years. Injuries prevented O'Leary from freshening up his side, so only two changes were made from the team that had played the blood and thunder West Yorkshire derby in energy-sapping conditions. At half-time Leeds held a 2-0 lead, but in the second half they hit the wall and Tranmere fought back to force extra time. The worst possible outcome for O'Leary's exhausted players became a reality when Tranmere scored the winning goal just seconds before the final whistle. Yet another gut-wrenching League Cup exit.

Leeds United 4-3 Liverpool
Saturday, 4 November 2000
Elland Road – 11.30am
FA Carling Premiership

With my dad working away again, my mates and I had to make our way to Elland Road ourselves. We were a group of five now; Paul had become a season ticket holder the previous season, and now another school friend, Rick, had joined us in the Kop, having previously been in the East Stand, courtesy of his boss. I was almost 17 and old enough to go alone, but we had my older brother in tow anyway, who would be in with the Liverpool fans of course. It was my first time on the 'Elland Road Special', the bus that runs fans from the city centre to the ground, and it was a raucous experience despite the ridiculously early kick-off. The fans were packed in like sardines and chanted all the way to the ground, while banging on the windows so hard I'm surprised they didn't pop out. The atmosphere turned sour when the bus was caught in a traffic jam on the M62, just a few hundred metres from the ground. With no sign of the traffic moving, and kick-off fast approaching, the passengers became extremely agitated, imploring the driver to open the doors and let them walk the rest of the way. The driver would not relent, begging for patience because opening the doors on the motorway would apparently cost him his job. It was quite distressing to see how upset he became when patience expired and the passengers forced the doors open themselves, but it was also a relief to know we would make it to the game.

Morning kick-offs were a real bind, I despised them. They would often bring an underwhelming atmosphere which could take the edge off even the biggest occasions. By the end of this game even a 9am kick-off couldn't have taken the edge off it, but at the start O'Leary's boys played like they'd just got out of bed. Liverpool were looking to pull level on points with Manchester United and Arsenal at the top, if only for a few hours, and took advantage of Leeds's sluggish start by cruising into a 2-0 lead within 20 minutes. Even worse for the hosts, Jonathan Woodgate had hobbled off injured. Would this injury curse ever cease? Woodgate's replacement was Danny Hay, and with Jacob Burns in midfield, Leeds had three Australasians in their team, another on the bench, and Harry Kewell in the stands. When Paul Robinson saved a one-on-one it seemed like a damage limitation job, but midway through the half Leeds were sparked into life. Alan Smith's persistence in chasing down defenders resulted in an opening for Viduka, who expertly chipped over the advancing goalkeeper. Suddenly Leeds found their rhythm and almost equalised when Ian Harte's free kick deflected against the upright, then Dacourt was denied by a brilliant Sander Westerveld save.

The half-time break came at the perfect time for Liverpool, but within two minutes of the restart they conceded the equaliser anyway. Gary Kelly sprinted down the right wing, skinning Patrik Berger and delivering a perfect cross, plumb on the head of Mark Viduka, who powered a bullet header into the top corner. What a goal, what a striker! It was the Australian's third consecutive Elland Road brace since returning from the Sydney Olympics. The burly striker was certainly making up for lost time. A chance to complete the turnaround fell to Alan Smith, but with no goalkeeper to beat, he complacently passed the ball towards goal from 20 yards, allowing Carragher to recover and clear off the line. Rather than ruing the miss, the home fans sensed blood and Elland Road was rocking, until Vladimir Smicer silenced the crowd by restoring Liverpool's lead. Now it was time to rue the miss, Leeds had it all to do again.

Ten minutes after Smicer's goal Leeds were back on level terms. Dacourt expertly threaded a ball through to Viduka who bore down on goal, shaped to shoot, but instead turned on a sixpence to leave Berger on the deck before drilling low past Westerveld to complete a wonderful hat-trick, 3-3! 'HE'S THE BEST PLAYER IN THE WORLD!' I screamed, as I grabbed, pushed, pulled, and squeezed Lewis, Paul and Rick. I'd never seen a performance like it. Just as the wild celebrations were settling down, with the atmosphere now at boiling point, Leeds were on the attack again. Dacourt took a high ball on his chest and spun his man beautifully, but this time his through-ball to Viduka was blocked. The ball rebounded back to Dacourt who fired at goal. Again it was blocked, this time by the expert first touch of Mark Viduka, which set the ball perfectly in his path. 'Here he is again, it's Vidukaaaaaa... IT'S FOUR!' Martin Tyler's words still send shivers down my spine, his voice perfectly capturing the disbelief in the stadium. It was another ice-cool finish, sending the Kop into meltdown!

Leeds hung on for the final ten minutes to complete an incredible victory, one that would enter the history books as one of Elland Road's greatest days. O'Leary ran on to the pitch at full-time, arms outstretched, straight to his goal-machine striker. They laughed and joked, before Viduka headed over to take the plaudits from the Kop with the match ball in hand. 'MARK VIDUKA!' Clap clap, clap clap clap! 'MARK VIDUKA!' It's not often you chant a player's name at the top of your lungs but Viduka had earned every decibel. As he walked off towards the tunnel he turned to the Sky cameraman, waved down the lens and said, 'Hi mum!' She must have been the proudest lady on the planet.

AC Milan 1-1 Leeds United
Wednesday, 8 November 2000
San Siro – 7.45pm
UEFA Champions League, First Group Stage

My fondness for the San Siro stadium stems from Italia '90, the World Cup in which my love of football really exploded. I was six years old and obsessed with Diego Maradona (my dad hadn't informed me about the 'Hand of God' goal in the previous World Cup), and I remember being bewitched by the San Siro as my beloved Argentina fell to a shock 1-0 defeat in the tournament's opening match. The four swirling pillars in each corner of the ground, the way the roof hung above the stadium, the moat around the pitch, the sheer size of the place; what an arena for a football match. The stadium tour of the San Siro en route to Roma away was thrilling, but being there for a game would have been a completely different experience, especially with 6,000 Leeds fans packed into the lower tier of the Curva Sud. We talked about going, and 20 years later it remains a great regret that we didn't. I should have moved heaven and earth to get there but the campaign boiled down to a few half-hearted conversations with my dad and a few pie in the sky conversations with Lewis, Joe, Paul and Rick.

Normally in football it's difficult to raise your game again after an epic victory, but heading to the San Siro to play AC Milan in the Champions League, with qualification up for grabs, meant there was no chance of a post-Liverpool hangover for Leeds. Lucas Radebe returned from his latest injury so once again O'Leary had enough players to cobble a team together, but not enough for the bench. Only six of a possible seven substitutes were selected; Danny Milosevic, Danny Hay, Jacob Burns, Gareth Evans, Alan Maybury and Matthew Jones, all of whom were in their early twenties and in five years' time would be playing for New Zealand Knights, Perth Glory, Wisla Krakow, Blackpool, Hearts and nobody (Jones retired through injury, bless him).

Milan were already qualified and just needed a point to secure top spot in the group, and when a draw suits both sides you often see them playing out a lifeless contest. Immediately it was clear that wouldn't be the case as Milan made a fast start, with Brazilian wing-back Serginho causing all sorts of problems for Gary Kelly. On his 300th appearance for Leeds, Kelly endured a tough night in the absence of any of the luck his Irish heritage should have afforded him. After 26 minutes the referee gave a terribly soft penalty against him when Serginho's shot struck his hand, but Shevchenko's spot kick struck the post. It was a surprise let-off and Leeds took full advantage on the stroke of half-time, when Bowyer's near-post corner was met by Dom Matteo, whose twisting header beat Dida at his near post. Delight was etched on the faces of the Leeds players, their fans in the San Siro and their fans in my lounge. It was a great time to score, not least because it allowed us to savour the goal for 15 uninterrupted minutes during the safety of half-time. In fact, the goal has been savoured ever since, with the Leeds fans still singing about it to this day.

After the break Milan upped the intensity and Robinson was called into action to deny Serginho and Shevchenko, before tipping Oliver Bierhoff's header over the bar, but with 20 minutes to go Milan finally got the equaliser they craved. Serginho surged past Gary Kelly, with the help of a divot that bobbled the ball over Kelly's leg as he slid into the tackle, and the Brazilian wing-back lashed the ball past Robinson and into the far corner, Carlos Alberto style.

With Barcelona 5-0 up against Besiktas, Leeds knew that another Milan goal would eliminate them, so while both teams continued to search for the winner, neither was willing to take too many risks. It remained nerve-wracking right until the final whistle, but when it finally blew Milan were the happy group winners, with Leeds the delirious runners-up. O'Leary's babies had knocked out the mighty Barcelona, and the players celebrated with the fans long into the night, re-emerging after their showers to dance and sing with the locked-in travelling army. Alan Green, commentating for 5Live, called it the most powerful bond between players and fans he had seen in his long career. Leeds were marching on together, into the last 16.

Leeds United 0-2 Real Madrid

Wednesday, 22 November 2000
Elland Road – 7.45pm
UEFA Champions League, Second Group Stage

Once again I skived off school to watch the Champions League draw. In those days the Champions League format included two group phases, so the last 16 was split into four more groups, with the top two in each qualifying for the quarter-finals. Having had the hardest possible draws in the qualifier and the first group phase, incredibly Leeds received the hardest possible draw again: European champions Real Madrid, Serie A champions Lazio, and Belgian champions Anderlecht. I was again disappointed despite the glamour, though this time I had the belly for the fight. Leeds had got through the first group; they could get through this one too.

First up was a first-ever clash with Real Madrid, a poignant tie. One of the first things Don Revie had done when becoming manager of Leeds was to change their colours, dressing them like Real Madrid in order to emulate their achievements on the pitch. Pretty heady heights for a club that had never won anything or even established themselves in the top flight – Real Madrid had won the European Cup five times in a row! In 2000/01, Real Madrid were gunning for two in a row, and new president Florentino Perez had just launched the age of the 'Galacticos', promising to sign the world's greatest player every summer. Their team was already littered with legends; Iker Casillas, Roberto Carlos, Fernando Hierro, Claude Makelele, Raul, and the current holder of the Ballon d'Or, Luis Figo. Their manager wasn't bad either, Vicente del Bosque, a man who would end his career as one of the all-time greats, winning all the top trophies at domestic, European and international level. Tests didn't come any sterner than this.

It was a shame Leeds couldn't face this challenge with their full team available. O'Leary wasn't just cobbling together line-ups, but creating formations he could cobble them together in. For this game he fielded a back three, with a midfield trio of Lee Bowyer, Jacob Burns and Dom Matteo. It was far from ideal, but Leeds made a decent fist of it in a first half of few chances. A goalmouth scramble almost resulted in an early goal for Woodgate, but his effort hit the post, after which Real Madrid took control. They hit the post themselves but Leeds defended resolutely and the scores remained level at half-time.

Having spent 55 minutes keeping Real's flowing, attacking football at bay, O'Leary would have been frustrated that Leeds came undone at a corner. Fernando Hierro headed home unmarked and in the blink of an eye the game was gone when Raul finished off a brilliant sweeping move to make it 2-0. Leeds never looked like getting back into the game. It had been a masterclass by Real Madrid, the best team I'd ever seen. It was hard to feel too downbeat.

Two weeks later O'Leary's team headed back to Rome for the third successive season, this time to face Sven-Goran Eriksson's star-studded Lazio team. After previously losing 1-0, then drawing 0-0 in the Stadio Olimpico, Leeds continued their progress by claiming a stunning 1-0 victory. New heights were reached in Rome, 'One of the best performances by a British side in Europe in the last 20 years,' according to Glenn Hoddle, on punditry. They faced a team with Angelo Peruzzi in goal, Alessandro Nesta in defence, a midfield trio of Diego Simeone, Juan Veron and Pavel Nedved, and a front two of Hernan Crespo and Marcelo Salas, but United dominated the match.

As impossible as it seems nowadays, the game wasn't televised. I had to listen on the radio, and the commentators on 5Live couldn't believe the standard of football Leeds were playing. But as time ticked by, and chances slipped away, my delight at the performance turned into agitation that we weren't going to get the result we deserved. Then, in the 80th minute, the returning Harry Kewell slipped the ball to Smith, who passed to Viduka on the edge of the box, looking for the give-and-go. Viduka held off Nesta until the time was just right and casually flicked a back-heel through to Smith, who passed the ball calmly into the far corner. It was a goal worthy of winning any game, and afterwards the Leeds players and staff held another sing-song with the travelling fans. O'Leary's likely lads were back in the chase for the quarter-finals.

Leicester City 3-1 Leeds United

Saturday, 2 December 2000
Filbert Street – 3pm
FA Carling Premiership

With the European campaign on the back burner until February it was time to concentrate on the league, where Leeds's patchy form had left them stranded in mid-table. O'Leary was struggling to transfer the inspired European form into the domestic campaign, and after a 0-1 defeat at home to West Ham the alarm bells were ringing. For the first time, and not the last, Peter Ridsdale decided to push the boat out.

Before a much-needed 1-0 victory at Elland Road against Arsenal, courtesy of Olivier Dacourt's deflected free kick, Leeds paraded a new signing. They had broken the British transfer record by spending £18m on Rio Ferdinand, making him the world's most expensive defender. Leeds had been courting the cultured centre-back for some time, with O'Leary earmarking him as the ideal long-term replacement for Lucas Radebe, and with the guarantee of a further six Champions League games adding extra revenue, coupled with Woodgate's impending trial and Radebe's ongoing knee troubles, Ridsdale came up with an offer West Ham couldn't refuse.

The transfer signalled a change of tack by the club. Player valuations had previously been in the hands of the manager, and although the club had delivered his number one target, it was rumoured that O'Leary was aghast at the fee. Rio joked that his parents thought he was worth double, but £18m was certainly an eye-watering amount for a centre-back who was more potential than the finished article, and his manager was quick to distance himself from the money spent: 'My job is to nominate the players I think will make this squad better, then the board decide if we can afford them and try to buy them. I don't put a gun to their head and I don't interfere with the financial side of the club. I prefer to leave that to the financial experts.'

Those experts had now sanctioned £65m in transfer fees in the two years O'Leary had been in charge, an extraordinary investment which would amplify the pressure for immediate results. Age, experience, spending power and squad size had regularly been touted as reasons not to expect Leeds to challenge for major honours, but now there was no hiding place; the board would expect results. The fans already expected results. They had booed the players after the early-season home defeat to Ipswich, an incident that hit O'Leary so hard that he described it as the lowest point of his first two years at Elland Road, 'It saddened and disappointed me. We are now certainly aware that there is a tiny, fickle group who quickly forget the progress we've made.' It was the first chink in his relationship with the Elland Road faithful, and he would regularly lambast 'the boo boys' in the months ahead.

I really didn't know what to make of the Ferdinand transfer. It was exciting to land such a highly rated talent, and mind-blowing that Leeds had broken the British transfer record, but I was sceptical about his ability, and we already had Woodgate and Radebe, the two best centre-backs in the league in my book. You couldn't leave out the world's most expensive defender, so I wondered how Ferdinand would fit in.

O'Leary threw Rio straight into the team for the trip to Filbert Street, switching the formation to incorporate all three centre-backs. The result was spectacular. On paper Leeds were fielding surely the greatest back three in British football history, but in practice it was a disaster. Within half an hour Leicester had breached the impregnable defence three times and Jonathan Woodgate had been hauled off. And when Lucas Radebe was sent off in the second half Leeds were in disarray.

The Leicester fans were loving it – their team only cost half a million more than Leeds's last remaining centre-back yet they were 3-0 up and coasting. There was no worse venue for this calamity to take place. I'd now been to Filbert Street four times, each one a horrendous experience, and now I was watching grown men in replica shirts goading us by holding up three fingers (one for each goal) and licking them. What a strange bunch! Yet with ten men Leeds started to come back into the game. Viduka pulled a goal back with 15 minutes remaining, Dacourt was denied a second goal by the post, and it wasn't until Kewell missed a sitter in the 88th minute that all hope was lost.

It was one step forward, two steps back for Leeds in the Premiership. One good game had been followed by two bad

ones nearly all season, and after beating Arsenal and losing
to Leicester the pattern continued with a catastrophic trip to
Southampton the following week. I went on the coach with Paul,
and the highlight was a stunning 45-yard volley from Harry
Kewell which flew into the top-corner, drawing gasps from the
Leeds end, such was the quality of the strike. Unfortunately,
this came during the half-time interval when Kewell was just
having a kick-around with the other substitutes. The lowlight
was James Beattie scoring the only goal of the game, or was it
him celebrating by dancing around like an imbecile right in
front of us? Or was it when the bus broke down on the long
journey home? Regardless, this was the first time I'd been so
annoyed by a result that my match report contained a mistake,
zero effort, and didn't even fill the page.

Newcastle United 2-1 Leeds United
Tuesday, 26 December 2000
St James' Park – 3pm
FA Carling Premiership
After the defeat at Southampton, Leeds bounced back with
a 2-0 victory over Sunderland at Elland Road, a result which
David O'Leary referred to as an early Christmas present. It
wasn't his only one; in fact he had been spoilt rotten before the
busy festive period even got underway.

The injury crisis had finally eased up, and with only
Duberry, Bridges and McPhail on the sidelines, O'Leary finally
faced selection headaches that he could only have dreamt of
since taking the Elland Road hotseat. His substitutes' bench
against Sunderland cost the club £18m (Martyn, Mills, Batty,
Huckerby and Wilcox), whereas two months earlier the bench
at Bradford had cost £350k (Milosevic, Jones, Evans, Burns and
Hackworth). There was more positive news when Lucas Radebe
received the coveted FIFA Fair Play award for his role fighting
racism in football and his charity work with children in his

native South Africa. It was wonderful to see our beloved captain receive global recognition for the calibre of man he is, and the words of FIFA's Dr Antonio Matarrese provided a fitting tribute: 'Lucas Radebe is not only a fantastic and fair player on the field, but also a great personality off the pitch, with a big heart for the children in this world. He is a real ambassador of fair play for our youth and all footballers.'

But a fair play award and clean bill of health could never compete with the excitement of signing a shiny new striker. O'Leary must have been as thrilled as me when Leeds beat off competition from Chelsea for the signature of Robbie Keane, on loan from Inter Milan. To make way for Keane, Darren Huckerby was sold to Manchester City after a disappointing 16 months at Elland Road. He had made only 14 starts and never showed the quality David O'Leary was so sure he possessed. Keane was a really exciting upgrade; a whippet of a forward, as inventive as he was rapid, and a natural finisher too. At just 20 years of age his big money move to Italy had come too early in his career, or perhaps it was simply a bridge too far competing for a starting place with Christian Vieiri, Alvaro Recoba, Hakan Sukur and 'El Fenomeno' himself, Ronaldo.

The task of breaking into the Leeds team wouldn't be easy though. The Viduka/Smith partnership was proving too hot for some of the world's best defences to handle, but with Kewell being eased back into the team after injury and Bridges out for the season, this signing made sense to all parties. Leeds would have the option to make the move permanent at the end of the season for £12m (they could have signed him for half that instead of signing Huckerby), although to afford such a fee they would need to string together a long sequence of wins to get back into the Champions League, or win the bloody thing.

O'Leary learned from the Leicester debacle and refrained from shoe-horning his new signing into the team, but Leeds still lost their next game, 2-1 at home to Aston Villa. The manager was keen to remind everyone that all teams suffer difficult periods, but it was difficult for the supporters to keep a level head with the Whites languishing in 12th position, 18 points behind leaders Manchester United after 18 games.

For the second season in three, Boxing Day brought a trip to St James' Park, and in the two years between the fixtures the stadium had been transformed; it felt like a different ground. From being tightly packed in the corner of the ground with barely any segregation to separate us from the Geordies, we were now up in the gods, in a vast new upper tier that swept around half the stadium, so far from the pitch it was hard to tell who the players were. The stairs up to the away end seemed never-ending, and the atmosphere, apart from being thinner, was nothing like it had been prior to the redevelopment. The poor acoustics made it sound like there were 20,000 less fans, rather than 20,000 more in St James' Park.

That said, after ten minutes furious noise was bellowing around the stadium as referee Andy D'Urso moved a Leeds free kick ten yards forward due to dissent from the Newcastle players. It was a new rule that only lasted two seasons, and Olivier Dacourt took full advantage by placing the advanced free kick into the corner of the net at the Gallowgate end. The Geordies were as incensed as we were delighted. It was the perfect start for Leeds, and with Bobby Robson suffering an injury crisis of his own, the Whites looked set for their first away win since the first away game of the season. Newcastle didn't even have Alan Shearer up front; teenager Shola Ameobi was leading the line on his own, a full debut up against England's finest young defenders, Woodgate and Ferdinand. Even so, the following 80 minutes were like a bad dream.

To a man Leeds were awful, with the exception of Olivier Dacourt in midfield, who continued to shine amongst the shrinking performances around him. It took Newcastle until the 40th minute to equalise, Acuna heading home unmarked from inside the six-yard box, and Leeds conceded again before half-time, Nolberto Solano celebrating his 100th appearance for Newcastle by scoring a stunning free kick. 'Where's your famous atmosphere?' the Leeds fans had asked just five minutes earlier; here it was. The second half brought a slight improvement from Leeds, and Bowyer was extremely unfortunate not to equalise when his shot hit the inside of one post and somehow spun wide of the other, although if Leeds had claimed a point it would have been a travesty.

After the game a bitterly disappointed O'Leary bemoaned the 'disgraceful defending' for the equaliser, and labelled the performance the worst since he'd arrived at the club. To compound his misery, Harry Kewell's Achilles injury had resurfaced and it would be another six weeks until O'Leary could call upon his star player again. Leeds United ended the year 14th in the Premiership.

Manchester City 0-4 Leeds United
Saturday 13 January 2001
Maine Road – 3pm
FA Carling Premiership

David O'Leary must have been delighted to see the back of the year 2000. His team had lost more games than they had won, having collected more points than any other team in the calendar year 1999. Bizarrely, Leeds were still voted 'team of the year' in *Match* magazine, perhaps an indication of the progress the club had continued to make despite the poor domestic results. They had continued to build a top-class squad of hungry young players, and continued to raise their international profile, just as O'Leary had planned when taking the job.

On New Year's Day Elland Road welcomed 19th-placed Middlesbrough, who were just six points behind O'Leary's team. The Teessiders had brought in Terry Venables to 'help, not replace' struggling manager Bryan Robson, and Leeds, despite a much-improved performance, needed a late penalty just to earn a point, with Robbie Keane assuming responsibility on his full debut. Keane converted the spot kick emphatically, then stood motionless on the penalty spot for a second, drinking in the cheers from the Kop, before darting off to the corner flag to perform his trademark cartwheel-into-pistols celebration. It was two more dropped points for a team still targeting European qualification, though the mischievous may have suggested the point gained maintained breathing space from the drop zone.

Next up was another match that could legitimately be billed as a relegation six-pointer, away to Manchester City, who had taken Boro's 19th position and were also only six points behind Leeds. It was almost a year to the day since the clubs had met in the FA Cup at Maine Road, but it felt half a world away. So much had happened in the meantime, and the circumstances couldn't have been more different. The previous year, in bright winter sun, the two teams were in excellent form, top of their leagues and set for glorious seasons. This time, the match was played on a gloomy afternoon, between two teams who couldn't buy a win (as much as Leeds were trying to).

The result may have been similar to the earlier 5-2 thrashing, but United's performance was a long way short of that sparkling display. Nothing was coming off for Viduka and Smith, and stand-in full-backs Matteo and Mills failed to match the threat of Kelly's pace down the right and Harte's wand of a left foot. It wasn't all bad, though – Ferdinand and Radebe were rock-solid in defence, Dacourt controlled the midfield and Eirik Bakke popped up to give the visitors a 1-0 half-time lead.

Due to Nigel Martyn's return to fitness and the team's results, rather than his own performances, Paul Robinson's place in goal was coming under scrutiny, but the youngster justified his selection by keeping City at bay in the second half. He made one great save from Danny Tiatto and one brave stop at the feet of Paulo Wanchope. These were nerve-wracking times, but anxiety turned to fury when the Man City fans progressed from the standard chants about the impending court case, to goading us about the murders of our fans in Istanbul. There was an explosion of rage in the Leeds end when the chants went up, uncontrollable anger, and supporters began to clamber over the segregation to attack the home fans. The stewards halted their progress, but the best retribution would be served on the pitch, and who else but Lee Bowyer duly popped up on the edge of the box to smash a loose ball into the net. What timing! The emotions were so raw that the joy was amplified by the anger, and vice-versa. I was pleased my dad wasn't there so I didn't have to watch my potty mouth as I screamed obscenities at the City fans, before we turned our attention to my favourite player, 'BOWYER FOR ENGLAND!'

With 89 minutes on the clock, the game was done, but Leeds weren't. Bowyer split the depleted City defence for substitute Robbie Keane to race through and apply an exquisite finish past Nicky Weaver, and there was still time for Keane to bundle home a fourth goal from an injury-time corner. I was bouncing off the walls after the game; it had been an exhilarating end to an excruciating match.

Any hopes that this result was the start of a surge up the table were dashed the following Saturday. Robbie Keane continued his excellent start by opening the scoring inside two minutes, but Leeds fell to another home defeat, 3-1 against Newcastle. The following weekend O'Leary recalled Nigel Martyn to the team after eight games sitting patiently on the bench, but he couldn't prevent an FA Cup exit at the hands of Liverpool at Elland Road. Leeds rediscovered their best form but the Reds scored two goals in the last two minutes, their only shots on target in a 'smash and grab' 2-0 victory. Once again United's conquerors went all the way to the final, by beating relegation-bound Manchester City, Tranmere Rovers of Division One and, in the semi-final, Wycombe Wanderers of Division Two. If Leeds had managed to take one of many glorious openings created against Liverpool, or if Andy D'Urso had awarded a late penalty when McAllister fouled Bowyer in the box, David O'Leary would surely have been leading his team out for his dream FA Cup Final against Arsenal. Oh, what could have been!

No matter what O'Leary tried he just couldn't spark any consistency from his squad, and now it was time for the trial of four of his players to commence. Who would have thought such a morbid event would kick-start Leeds's season? Legal wrangling delayed the start of the trial proper, but that didn't spare the accused players from having to spend every weekday at Hull Crown Court, putting their availability for midweek fixtures in jeopardy. Before even considering that the players were unable to train, court proceedings would only finish at 4.30pm, leaving a maximum of two hours to get to the match. Home games would be fine, European away games would be impossible, and domestic away games would each be a challenge of varying difficulty.

The first challenge required a helicopter to fly Lee Bowyer from east coast to west, and he took his place in the starting 11 for the trip to Everton, with Leeds heading into the game on the back of their first successive victories since August. Robbie Keane's spectacular bicycle kick had secured a narrow 1-0 win over Coventry, and, having been named Premiership player of the month for January, Keane kicked February off by bagging again in a vital victory at Ipswich, who surprisingly occupied one of the European spots O'Leary was now optimistic of claiming. The Premiership table was so tight that United suddenly had the European places in their sights, and two second-half equalisers at Goodison Park shunted Leeds into the top six. Then at the weekend they moved up to fifth, despite a disappointing goalless draw with Jim Smith's Derby County. Ipswich, Leicester and Chelsea all had games in hand, but Leeds had dragged themselves back into the hunt for European qualification, and now Champions League football was back on the agenda in more ways than one.

Leeds United 2-1 Anderlecht
Tuesday, 13 February 2001
Elland Road – 7.45pm
UEFA Champions League, Second Group Stage

The jury were summoned to Hull Crown Court on Monday morning, as the prosecution began presenting their case against Woodgate, Bowyer, Hackworth, Duberry, and two of Woodgate's childhood friends; finally we would hear what had happened that night. The undisputable facts were that there had been some argy-bargy in the Majestyk nightclub between a group of Woodgate's friends and some students, and when they were all kicked out it all kicked off. The students fled but Sarfraz Najeib stumbled over in a side-street called Mill Hill, where he was set upon in a stomach-churning attack. He was left unconscious in a pool of blood with a broken nose, broken cheekbone and a broken leg. He was lucky to escape with his life.

First to present their case was the prosecution, who suggested Woodgate and Bowyer had been trailing behind Woodgate's friends, Neale Caveney and Paul Clifford, but were central to the attack. On arrival at the scene Woodgate allegedly took a standing jump, slamming both feet into the victim's body, while Bowyer was accused of inflicting the bite mark on his cheek, 'locking his jaws and shaking his head like a dog'. The morning after that day in court – the morning of the Anderlecht game – the story was front-page news. 'Bowyer the Savage' read the headlines, but 24 hours later the Bowyer headlines would be back in their usual place, on the back pages.

Walking down to Elland Road I clearly remember a statement my dad made about Bowyer, 'I won't chant his name ever again, unless he's proved innocent.' It was a sentiment that few other fans shared. Bowyer went from the dock straight into the pressure-cooker of a huge Champions League night, and received a rapturous welcome from the Elland Road crowd.

Anderlecht were always going to be difficult opposition; they had overcome Manchester United earlier in the competition and boasted a red-hot strike force: the towering Jan Koller and lightning-quick Tomasz Radzinski. But they were never going to have it easy against Rio Ferdinand, who was making his Champions League debut. Rio had settled in quickly at Elland Road, brushing off any pressure his price-tag may have brought, and in this game he delivered a colossal performance which limited the Belgians to long-range efforts in an evenly matched first half. At the other end, Viduka and Ian Harte were denied by excellent saves and at half-time the game, and the group, was in the balance.

The second half was a tense affair. With the return match in Brussels only a week away, Leeds couldn't afford a bad result, and Elland Road was silenced when a terrific move resulted in a goal at the South Stand end. Leeds's Champions League hopes were hanging by a thread. On came Harry Kewell, almost returning from injury with a bang as he immediately drew a fine save from the keeper. With Kewell on the wing Leeds were a totally different proposition and with 15 minutes remaining Ian Harte lashed in a 30-yard free kick to equalise. Leeds grew in confidence as the visitors tired, although Jan Koller could have immediately reinstated their advantage but hooked over the bar with Martyn stranded.

The Kop were doing all they could to suck the ball into the net, and in the 86th minute they succeeded. A visiting defender trod on the ball which fell at the feet of Alan Smith. He spotted Bowyer on the move and his slide-rule pass split the defence perfectly; Bowyer was in. The Kop took an intake of breath as a loose touch forced him wide, but Bowyer rifled low towards goal, under the goalkeeper, and the net in front of us bulged! It was a moment that will stay with me forever; it simply couldn't have been scripted better. The chaotic celebrations resulted in me travelling from the very back row of the Kop down to the very front of the upper section, screaming at the top of my voice, pointing as ferociously as I could, 'LEE BOWYER! LEE BOWYER! LEE BOWYER!' I glanced to my left to see my dad doing the same! All morals out of the window, because the defendant had kicked the football into the goal.

The following week Leeds headed to Anderlecht on the verge of qualification for the quarter-finals. One win was all they needed and they had three chances to get it. After the game at Elland Road, Anderlecht's manager claimed Leeds were 'not a good side' and vowed that things would be very different in Belgium. His confidence was understandable, as Anderlecht had won all 20 of their home games that season, but his disparaging words inspired O'Leary's team into arguably their greatest performance yet, demolishing their opponents with a virtuoso first-half display.

Alan Smith opened the scoring – his first goal since the winner at Lazio – then Viduka doubled the lead with a wonderful header, hanging high above the defender to meet Matteo's deep cross, and using all the power of his neck muscles to arc a looping header perfectly into the far corner. The third goal was a classic, a beautiful interchange of one-touch passes and flicks, before David Batty split the defence and Smith scooped his finish nonchalantly over the advancing keeper. 3-0 to Super Leeds, what a team!

In the second half Anderlecht did all they could to save the match and when Jan Koller pulled a goal back, I felt very uncomfortable, but the visitors quickly re-asserted their authority. An Ian Harte penalty made the game safe and Leeds were through to the Champions League quarter-finals, as easy as that!

'Good teams deal with the bread-and-butter stuff when they've had a great result in Europe,' said a bullish and perhaps slightly cheeky David O'Leary, after his team followed up their tremendous victory with a 2-1 away win over George Graham's Tottenham. It was the first defeat George had suffered at White Hart Lane that season but it also proved to be his final home game. He was sacked the following week, with his team on a run of two wins in 14 league games. He has not worked in football since.

The struggles of the first half of the season seemed to be firmly behind Leeds. They were still missing the long-term absentees – Kelly, Woodgate, Duberry, McPhail and Bridges – but the spate of injuries had eased and O'Leary now had a settled team. Batty and Dacourt were as dominant in midfield as Ferdinand and Radebe were in defence. Kewell and Harte was a partnership down the left that was envied across Europe, and Bowyer was excelling down the right, backed up by the ever-improving Danny Mills. Robbie Keane was cup-tied for the European fixtures but was forming his own deadly partnership with Viduka in the Premiership, a rotation with Smith that was working a treat. O'Leary's likely lads were flying again, and had given themselves a great chance of remaining at the top table of European football the following season.

Leeds United 1-1 Manchester United
Saturday, 3 March 2001
Elland Road – 11.30am
FA Carling Premiership

As the trial progressed things started to look up for the Leeds players. There seemed to be little evidence that Bowyer was at the scene of the attack, and dental records proved that it wasn't Bowyer who bit the face of Sarfraz Najeib, which in turn discredited the witness who had also identified Woodgate as the two-footed stamper. Woodgate was further aided by witness statements that all agreed he was acting as peacemaker in the nightclub, while the only evidence that Tony Hackworth was at the scene came from the testimony of the paramedics, who reported that Hackworth had shown great concern for the victim. Hackworth was therefore acquitted mid-trial, and the young striker walked away with damages paid, free to continue his life and football career.

Talking of football, it was time for the big one: David O'Leary's sixth attempt at 'kicking Alex Ferguson's butt'. Ferguson had only had his butt kicked twice all season, and a 6-1 demolition of Arsenal in the previous match all but secured his team's third Premiership title in a row. Nevertheless, O'Leary believed the gap was closing, his view supported by how well Leeds were coping with battling on two fronts. 'We are going into the last part of the season and I think we are getting stronger. Last season we ran out of steam because of too many games, but over the last few weeks we have become more powerful.'

Frustratingly it was another morning kick-off, but there was still a hostile atmosphere inside Elland Road. One of the great customs of the time (which was sadly lost when we started hating our players through the club's demise) occurred as the players entered the pitch and prepared themselves for kick-off. Each one received their own special welcome, their names chanted until the player in question clapped back to the Kop. It nearly always went in the same order too (only the tail-enders would be mixed around):

'England's No.1 … England's, England's No.1'

'Radebe, Radebe, Radebe Radebe Radebe. Radebe, Radebe-ee, Radebe-eeeeeee, LUCAS!'

'Bowyer for England! (clap clap, clap clap, clap)'

'Oh Harry Kewell, Harry Harry Harry Kewell, Harry Harry Harry Kewell. Harry Harry Harry Kewell'

'Mark Viduka (clap clap, clap clap, clap)'

'Smith, Smith, Alan, Alan Smith. Gets the ball and scores a goal, Alan, Alan Smith.'

'Batty, Batty, Batty, Batty'

'Ian Harte, Harte, Harte. Ian Harte, Harte, Harte'

'Rio, Rio, Rio, Rio'

'Oli, Oli Oli Oli, Oli, Oli'

'Danny Mills is fucking brilliant (clap, clap, clap, clap, clap, clap clap, clap clap)'

The visitors won the toss and turned Leeds around, but attacking the Kop led to a blistering first-half performance by the Whites. Batty and Dacourt were at the heart of everything, and with Radebe and Ferdinand behind them, the champions-elect couldn't lay a glove on Nigel Martyn's goal. After 45 minutes of probing, Leeds's big opening finally arrived, thanks to the stupidity of the opposition goalkeeper, Fabien Barthez. As the Manchester United defence pushed out having cleared a Bowyer corner, suddenly there was a roar from the Kop. Barthez had kicked out at Ian Harte and, amazingly, it had been spotted by the ref who pointed to the penalty spot. What a gift! More amazingly, the French keeper escaped with a yellow card, and the lucky swine then saved Harte's penalty. Bloody typical! What a bitter way to end a brilliant half.

Leeds continued to dominate but received a sucker punch when Manchester United's first shot of the game slipped out of Nigel Martyn's hands and Luke Chadwick pounced to score against the run of play. Leeds continued undeterred, and the pressure finally told in the 84th minute. A rampaging Danny Mills powered down the right wing, his cross was flicked on at the near post by Bowyer and met at the far post by Mark Viduka, who equalised with a superb diving header. Elland Road went berserk but my reaction was delayed – I wanted to be sure there was no flag before committing myself to the wild celebrations.

With the game heading into injury time, seemingly destined for a draw, the Leeds fans were desperate to at least claim a moral victory for their team's fantastic performance and a new chant bellowed around Elland Road, 'What's it like, what's it like, what's it like to be outclassed?' Moments later Leeds were on the attack again; Bowyer received the ball in the box and his low cross was diverted into his own net by Wes Brown. Elland Road exploded! There was no delayed reaction this time, I celebrated like a man possessed! Leeds had done it; O'Leary's babies had finally beaten the scum! But after five seconds of euphoria came the devastating realisation that this time the flag was up, and the goal wouldn't count. But how could that be when it was an own goal? Well, it turns out that the linesman was flagging against Mark Viduka, who had peeled off the back of Wes Brown, waiting for a tap-in, but was clearly not offside. It was a scandalous decision which not only cost O'Leary and the fans the victory they craved the most, but also cost Leeds two vital points in the race for Champions League qualification. Those two points would prove far more vital than anybody outside the Elland Road boardroom could possibly have imagined.

Despite the disappointment it had been another fantastic performance by Leeds; more proof, if it were needed, that they could mix it with the very best. Every year O'Leary was getting closer to kicking Alex Ferguson's butt, and although it seemed inevitable that one day it would happen, it was unlikely his team would ever outplay their rivals as emphatically as they did on this bright spring day.

Sunderland 0-2 Leeds United
Saturday, 31 March 2001
Stadium of Light – 3pm
FA Carling Premiership

March had been another dramatic month at Leeds United, even though there had only been one Premiership match between the Manchester United game at the start of the month and the trip to Sunderland at the end of it; a vital 2-1 victory over fellow

European hopefuls, Charlton, although every game seemed to be against European hopefuls, with only five points separating tenth and third. March also brought a trip to the Bernabeu, where Leeds put on a great show against Real Madrid. They took the lead through Alan Smith, before falling behind to a Raul goal that was punched into the net, and a Figo cross that bounced at a 90-degree angle off a divot, past the bewildered Nigel Martyn. Leeds equalised in the second half through Viduka, but Real nicked a 3-2 victory that sealed their place as group winners.

The main drama of the month was in the courtroom. It reflected badly on all of the accused when dental records proved Woodgate's friend, Paul Clifford, inflicted the bite mark on the victim's cheek, then Michael Duberry sensationally changed his story whilst in the witness box. Having previously denied any knowledge of the incident, Duberry now told the court he had picked Woodgate and his friends up in Leeds (not including Bowyer) and driven them back to his house, where Woodgate revealed they had been in a fight with some Asians. Duberry did stand by his claim that Woodgate and his friends had only disposed of clothing because somebody had been sick on them, rather than to deceive forensics.

Clothing and shoes played a central role in the trial, and none of the shoes that the defendants claimed to be wearing that night matched the prints on the victim. The prosecution wasn't buying it. They believed the CCTV footage proved that Bowyer's shoes had a buckle, whereas the ones he'd presented as evidence did not. Bowyer insisted it was his skin they were seeing on the footage, not a buckle, as he wasn't wearing socks. When he was asked to change into the trousers he was wearing (to see if they were short enough to reveal the skin on his foot) the court had to be emptied as Bowyer sheepishly revealed he wasn't wearing any underwear. It was a light-hearted moment in an otherwise turgid case. Before sending the jury out to consider their verdicts, the judge asked them to consider the fact that a group of people did attack Sarfraz Najeib, and if it wasn't this group then who was it, where did they come from, and where did they go?

Again, it was a relief to get back to football. I drove up to Sunderland on a bitterly cold spring afternoon, with my dad in the passenger seat as my driving instructor. In fact, it was so cold that my dad resorted to buying a Sunderland bobble-hat in order to keep warm (he turned it inside out to hide the badge). This was another huge six-pointer with Leeds and Sunderland next to each other in the table, and the home side raced out of the blocks, spurred on by a red-hot atmosphere at the Stadium of Light, where Peter Reid's side had only lost once all season. Julio Arca came close with a volley and David Batty hacked a header off the line, but once Leeds had survived the early onslaught they began to settle into the game. Bowyer should have opened the scoring but dragged a one-on-one wide, then Smith did open the scoring, less than a minute after a tangle between Rio Ferdinand and Kevin Phillips which should have seen the Leeds man sent off. It was a rare but deserved stroke of luck and the Sunderland fans were seething.

The referee appeased the home fans in the second half by reducing Leeds to ten men. Now it was the Leeds fans who were seething, convinced that the referee was incorrectly levelling out his earlier mistake, though the truth of the matter was revealed on *Match of the Day*. Alan Smith had needlessly kicked out at the defender, an act of petulance that added to his growing reputation as a hot-head. Having spent the second half soaking up the Sunderland pressure with relative comfort, the last 20 minutes would now be backs to the wall and all hands to the pump. Leeds defended like lions but were thankful for Nigel Martyn's acrobatics, and a sitter missed by Arca who thrashed the ball over the bar after Martyn dropped a high cross at his feet. Martyn had earned his slice of fortune.

The closing stages were played in a toxic atmosphere after the Sunderland fans added themselves to an undistinguished list, becoming the third club (the first outside of Manchester) to taunt Leeds about their murdered fans. As at Maine Road, this amplified the celebrations when, in the final minute, Robbie Keane broke clear and fed Mark Viduka, who expertly prodded the ball into the corner of the net with the outside of his foot. The victory was sealed and, knowing three points would lift Leeds into the third Champions League spot, we went ballistic! At the final whistle the players were as elated as the fans: what an astonishing turnaround it had been since languishing near the relegation zone just three months earlier. Anything seemed possible now, an improvement on last season's third place finish wasn't even out of the question, nor was winning the Champions League.

Leeds United 3-0 Deportivo La Coruna
Wednesday 4 April, 2001
Elland Road – 7.45pm
UEFA Champions League Quarter-Final, First Leg

Leeds welcomed Deportivo to Elland Road with the utmost respect, with David O'Leary suggesting victory over the reigning Spanish champions would be an incredible achievement for his young side. The respect was not mutual. Deportivo's manager, Javier Irureta, made no attempt to hide his satisfaction at drawing the team he considered the weakest left in the competition.

While Deportivo were clearly a top side, their first ever La Liga title had been claimed with an extraordinarily low points tally of just 69, the same number Leeds had collected in the last season's Premiership campaign. In fact, the teams had identical league records in 1999/00; 21 wins, six draws and 11 defeats. Despite O'Leary's words, he must have known this was a beatable team, and on one of the most glorious nights Elland Road has ever seen, his likely lads delivered their greatest performance.

Viduka and Smith led the line with aggression, strength and skill, while at the other end Rio Ferdinand, captain for the night in place of the injured Lucas Radebe, was powerful and elegant in equal measure. Danny Mills was a freight train up and down the right, Ian Harte a constant threat from the left, and Lee Bowyer was everywhere, doing everything. But it was in the middle of the park where Leeds won this game, with Olivier Dacourt putting in yet another sparkling display alongside the simplistic brilliance of David Batty. Dacourt had initially been signed to cover for the absence of Batty, but together they were awesome, even greater than the sum of their parts.

Leeds attacked the Kop in the first half and terrorised the visitors from the off; by half-time they had only scored once but could have had five. Bowyer and Batty were denied by the keeper, Smith flashed a header inches wide, and Kewell's mazy dribble and shot flashed inches over. The goal came from the left boot of Ian Harte, a 20-yard free kick which was synonymous with Leeds's performance, an unstoppable thunderbolt. It flashed in off the bar before the keeper could flinch and at half-time the Spaniards must have sat in the Elland Road changing room dazed and bewildered, not knowing what had hit them.

Once back out on the pitch the punishment resumed. The second half was only minutes old when Ian Harte's cross was headed home by Smith to give Leeds some breathing space. Shortly after came another goal, Harte the architect again, his corner swinging beyond the reach of the goalkeeper but not Rio Ferdinand, who buried his header into the roof of the net. Elland Road was bouncing, the rafters ringing. Leeds had a foot in the Champions League semi-finals! However, everybody knew that one goal for Deportivo would change the whole complexion of the tie, so when they finally got their act together for the last five minutes it was nail-biting stuff. Leeds fully deserved a 3-0 victory – anything less would have been a huge disappointment – and they duly clung on after surviving a couple of goalmouth scrambles and a sitter missed by Dutch striker Roy Makaay, who shot straight at Martyn from six yards.

What a sensational performance and result; I was bouncing off the walls. It was the best game I had ever witnessed, and afterwards came my first ever post-match piss-up. We were still only 17, but it was the Easter holidays and someone at our school had arranged a party at Rok bar in Leeds. My last memory was stepping outside to leave my brother a voicemail about how incredible Leeds were. I rambled on for five minutes until Gianni's voicemail cut out, and probably much longer thereafter. Then I'm told I fell asleep, using the club's main speaker as a pillow, probably dreaming of Lucas Radebe holding the European Cup aloft.

Leeds arrived in northern Spain two weeks later, knowing that there was still work to be done. Deportivo were fearsome at the Riazor. They had lost only once in their last 31 home games and genuinely fancied their chances of turning the tie around. Their faith wasn't blind; earlier in the competition they had overturned a 4-1 deficit at home to AC Milan to win 5-4, and in their last European home game they'd only needed the last 35 minutes to turn a 3-0 deficit into a 4-3 victory against Paris Saint-Germain. I headed to my nanna's to watch with my dad and Lewis, and my brother Gianni came along too. Strangely, my nanna was the only person we knew who had the channel that was showing the game.

It was a horrific experience, the polar opposite of the first leg. Deportivo tore through Leeds from the first minute to the last. Harry Kewell gave away a penalty after only nine minutes, but somehow this was the only goal Leeds conceded in a first-half mauling. Leeds could even have gone in level, with the tie all but won, but on the stroke of half-time Alan Smith missed a golden chance to grab the vital away goal. Smith had done the hard work but having rounded the keeper he could only fire into the side netting.

In the second half the crossbar came to Leeds's rescue twice as Nigel Martyn's goal was peppered with shots, but in the 74th minute the home side finally doubled their lead to set up a harrowing end to the game. One mad scramble left me so petrified that I suffered a temporary loss of vision, black flashes appearing in my eyes which must have been panic-induced. It's never happened to me before or since, but the net didn't bulge and Leeds United were in the Champions League semi-finals!

Nobody could have predicted the meteoric rise the club had experienced under David O'Leary's management; what an extraordinary job our beloved manager had done. O'Leary was already regarded as the best young coach in Britain, possibly for a generation, but now he was becoming recognised as one of the best young coaches in the world. In his first two seasons in management, he had overcome the champions of Serbia, Russia, Belgium, Italy and Spain, and got the better of legendary managers Alberto Zaccheroni, Sven-Goran Eriksson and Fabio Capello. O'Leary would be quick to share any accolades with the players and his chairman, and rightly so. Everybody at the club was on the cusp of greatness.

Liverpool 1-2 Leeds United
Friday, 13 April 2001
Anfield – 12pm
FA Carling Premiership

The week following the Deportivo home leg was quite a week at Leeds United, even by Leeds United standards. On the Friday after the greatest night of his managerial career, David O'Leary was brought crashing back down to earth when he attended the funeral of his former Arsenal team-mate, David Rocastle. 'Rocky' had played for Leeds for a short period too, and although he made little impact on the pitch you could tell from afar what a lovely person he was. The outpouring of emotion when Rocastle succumbed to cancer said everything about him, and his death hit O'Leary as hard as anyone in the game.

On Saturday it was back to the football, and Leeds claimed a routine 2-0 Premiership victory over Southampton at Elland Road. It's never good when football provides an escape from the stresses of off-field matters but that had been the case in the spring of both 2000 and 2001 for Leeds. At least the trial of Woodgate, Bowyer and Duberry was reaching its climax, or so we all thought.

On Monday, Paul and I skived off school and jumped on a train to Hull. This was expected to be the day the verdicts would be reached, and we turned up at Hull Crown Court not quite believing we would be allowed to just waltz in. That's what we'd been told and that turned out to be the case. Once through the security scanners we headed up some stairs and spent the day hanging around the concourse outside the courtrooms, waiting to be summoned in for the verdicts, if they ever came. There was media, there was Bowyer's entourage, and there was Woodgate's entourage, and the two footballers never mixed, everyone was just keeping their noses clean, and waiting. There were two other young lads there too, clearly fans like us but, taking a lead from the players, we all just kept ourselves to ourselves. The atmosphere was tense, although Bowyer seemed relaxed and in good spirits, certainly compared to Woodgate, who looked like he had the weight of the world on his shoulders. Gaunt and tired, it was no wonder he hadn't played for the first team since the trial began.

After lunchtime Bowyer must have realised we were fans and wandered over to where Paul and I were loitering, purposefully opening the door for a brief conversation of which I can only remember my opener, 'What was it like scoring against Anderlecht and having your name sung by thousands of Leeds fans?' I must have been trembling with apprehension, but Bowyer was pleasant and receptive and it meant the world to us, we were buzzing! We didn't just take the memories from court that day, we also took Bowyer's empty can of 7-Up which he had left on a table. We treasured that can, it lived in Paul's bedroom for years, until one day we eventually realised it was lost.

In the afternoon a commotion started; had the jury reached a verdict? Everyone swarmed into the court, but we were not permitted, and when they came out it was confusion all around. We tried to understand through the chitter-chatter of the journalists what was going on; something clearly wasn't right, and there was talk that the trial had collapsed. Did that mean they were off the hook? I had no idea. As Bowyer headed out of the courtroom we hurriedly followed behind, down the stairs and out of the main entrance into a media circus. We were right on Bowyer's shoulder and could be seen on the six o'clock news!

It was only when we got home that we found out what had happened. The *Sunday Mirror* had printed an interview with the victim's father, which spoke of an alleged racist element to the attack, something the judge had emphatically dismissed right at the beginning of the trial. The interview was in contempt of court and some of the jurors had read the article, forcing the judge to abandon proceedings there and then. It would mean a retrial, a horrendous outcome for all involved: the defendants, the victim and his family, the taxpayer and Leeds United. A cloud would hang over everyone for another nine months.

On Good Friday, Leeds headed to Anfield for the biggest match of their Premiership season. With six games remaining, the race for Champions League qualification could not have been much tighter. Liverpool were the main threat, three points behind but with two games in hand, though Ipswich Town were the current occupants of the all-important third spot, tied with Leeds on 53 points. Sunderland and Chelsea were still in the running too, trailing Leeds by four and five points respectively, and Chelsea had a game in hand.

With Liverpool, Chelsea and Arsenal to play in the next four games, and two legs of a Champions League semi-final mixed in between, even a UEFA Cup spot was far from guaranteed for Leeds. There was at least the safety net of the Intertoto Cup, which offered a back-door route towards qualification into the UEFA Cup for the team finishing seventh, although it may have been the threat of an Intertoto campaign that was spurring Leeds on. For the players it would feel more like a punishment than a consolation, robbing them of their summer holidays as the competition commenced in June, a little over three weeks after the Champions League Final.

Gianni and I were both learner drivers and took turns in driving over to Liverpool. It was a calm journey with all arguments already exhausted and any distracting conversations banned by our instructor. Gianni was adamant that Liverpool would wipe the floor with Leeds, insisting Houllier's was a much better side regardless of O'Leary's European exploits. Up front perhaps Liverpool edged it: they had the choice of Owen, Fowler and Heskey, a pretty fearsome trio of strikers. Keane, Smith and Viduka were also a top-quality trio, but Michael Owen was a phenomenon and tipped this particular argument in Liverpool's favour. Gianni would accept Nigel Martyn was a better goalkeeper than Sander Westerveld, but that's where the harmony ended. That said, a sign of weakness emerged when Gianni predicted that if Leeds won the toss and Liverpool attacked the Kop and failed to take a lead into half-time, Leeds would win.

It was the only thing he got right. Leeds won the toss, turned Liverpool around, and put on a virtuoso performance which, considering the circumstances, possibly even eclipsed the Deportivo match. Olivier Dacourt again was my man of the match, as he had been against Deportivo (from ten match reports since December, Ferdinand or Dacourt had won my man of the match in nine), but it could have been anybody. To a man Leeds were impeccable. Rio Ferdinand headed home an Ian Harte corner after just five minutes, then midway through the half Lee Bowyer made it 2-0. The goals and celebrations happened right in front of us, we were bouncing off the walls, 'He's here, he's there, he wears no underwear, Lee Bowyer, Lee Bowyer!' Liverpool couldn't get the ball. Their fans were stunned into silence, only springing to life when trying to pressurise the referee into helping their hapless team.

In the second half Liverpool came out fighting and ten minutes after the restart pulled a goal back through Steven Gerrard. However, Gerrard was then sent off following a foul on David Batty, leading the Anfield crowd to give Batty dogs' abuse for the rest of the game. The fact Batty tried to talk the referee into giving Gerrard a reprieve had gone unnoticed. The red card came just at the right time for Leeds, taking the sting out of Liverpool's revival, but they weren't able to restore their two-goal cushion. Viduka hit the post, then missed a one-on-one, before finally hitting the net in injury time, only to see the goal ruled out for offside. It mattered not, Leeds had their priceless win and I'd never been prouder of them. They had shoved Gianni's insults down his throat.

Now trailing Leeds by six points, Liverpool headed to Goodison Park on Easter Monday and played out a rip-roaring Merseyside derby. With injury time almost up and the score level at 2-2, Liverpool won a free kick not even halfway inside the Everton half. While Everton sorted their defensive line on the edge of the box, Gary McAllister marched the ball forward a full ten yards without anybody noticing, or probably caring, as he was still 40 yards from goal. The former Leeds captain had been an inspired signing by Houllier – he was now in his mid-30s but added experience and expertise to a young side. McAllister used both of these virtues to unleash a low drive at goal, catching out goalkeeper Paul Gerrard, who had started to advance to collect a cross. The keeper scrambled across his goal, but the ball was nestled in his net and the Liverpool fans, players and manager celebrated in disbelief. Despite all the glories that Liverpool have enjoyed since, this moment remains the biggest high Gianni has experienced in football.

McAllister's goal was a body blow to Leeds, but O'Leary's side shrugged it off and responded with a solid 2-0 victory at West Ham the following week. It was Rio Ferdinand's first return to Upton Park since leaving the Hammers, and he received a warm reception despite continuing his hot scoring streak. His third goal in five games sealed Leeds's eighth win in the last nine Premiership away games. Qualification for the Champions League was now a three-horse race and Ipswich led the way, but if Leeds and Liverpool won their games in hand, all three teams would be level on points. It really could not have been any tighter.

Chelsea still retained a mathematical chance of stealing third spot and visited Elland Road on the last Saturday of April. It was Jimmy Floyd Hasselbaink's first return to his old stomping ground, having signed for Chelsea after a year in Spain. His season at Atletico Madrid had been a roaring success on a personal note – he had been La Liga's top scorer, and received a standing ovation from the Real Madrid fans for his performance at the Bernabeu – but otherwise it was a horrific failure as Atletico were relegated and lost the Copa Del Rey Final. With Hasselbaink and Gianfranco Zola up front for Chelsea, and Marcel Desailly and John Terry at the back, this was never going to be an easy game, and safe in the knowledge that Leeds could afford no slip-ups, O'Leary fielded his strongest 11, despite hosting Valencia in just three days' time.

Leeds toiled without success, then with the game still goalless in the 88th minute, Robbie Keane popped up with a priceless poacher's goal. Two minutes later Mark Viduka chased a ball over the top, shrugged off Desailly like a fly on his shoulder, then thundered the bouncing ball first time into the top corner of the South Stand net. It was a stunning goal to seal a stunning win, which guaranteed Leeds a place in the next season's UEFA Cup, while keeping their Champions League hopes alive. Now it was back to fighting for the current season's Champions League.

Leeds United 0-0 Valencia

Wednesday, 2 May 2001
Elland Road – 7.45pm
UEFA Champions League Semi-Final, First Leg

'Nine months ago, I wasn't too sure how we would do against 1860 Munich in the qualifying round of this great competition,' wrote O'Leary in his programme notes, 'but tonight we face last year's runners-up, Valencia, for the right to appear in the final of the biggest club competition in the world. And on my birthday too!'

The Champions League Final was only three weeks away and we had already applied for our tickets before the semi-final kicked off. As exciting as that was, I couldn't help feeling uneasy at the tempting of fate. The date is ingrained in my head, Wednesday, 23 May, as is the venue, the San Siro in Milan, the stadium that had been the holy grail to me since my first memory of watching a football match. Leeds's opponents in the final would likely be the mighty defending champions, the team Don Revie had changed Leeds's kit to emulate 40 years earlier, Real Madrid. Beating them in the final would be a poetic realisation of Don's quest to make Leeds United the top club in Europe. If not Madrid, it would be an even more fitting opponent: Bayern Munich, the club who cheated Revie's team from winning the 1975 European Cup Final, according to anyone connected to Leeds and anyone who watched the game, and even some of the Bayern players too (well, they just put it down to a bad day at the office for the referee).

So, in 2001 the scene was perfectly set and I fully expected O'Leary's team to reach the final. Valencia were clearly a very good team, but I doubted whether they were worthy of reaching successive finals. They were only fifth in La Liga, battling for the last Champions League spot but well adrift of champions-elect Real Madrid, having finished third the previous season – identical to Leeds's Premiership exploits over the last two years. However, Valencia were a team with the experience to match their undoubted ability. In goal was Santiago Canizares, Spain's number one and a former Champions League winner with Real Madrid. Mauricio Pellegrino and Roberto Ayala were a solid pair of Argentina internationals at the back, protected by Ruben Baraja, a Spanish international who was good enough to keep France's World Cup-winning captain, Didier Deschamps, on the bench at Elland Road. Up front they weren't prolific – Juan Sanchez was their top scorer with only 12 goals, alongside young Norwegian target-man, John Carew – but the supporting act were top notch. Their talisman was their captain, Gaizka Mendieta, a Spanish playmaker at the peak of his powers, one of the top players in Europe. Either side of Mendieta were Argentinian internationals, Kily Gonzalez and the latest 'new Maradona', Pablo Aimar, who had signed in January for a club record €24m (which converted to only £13m in those days!).

There was a hint of trepidation both on the pitch and in the stands for the first leg at Elland Road. This was not the swashbuckling performance the players had delivered against Deportivo, nor was the atmosphere as buoyant. In the quarter-finals Leeds were enjoying the ride and had nothing to lose, but now that a Champions League Final was on the line they had everything to lose. That said, O'Leary's young side certainly didn't freeze on the occasion – they played their part in a riveting encounter.

The first half was one of half-chances. Ian Harte's early free kick was tipped over by the keeper and his resulting corner was inches away from being converted at the back post by Mark Viduka. Bowyer couldn't keep a volley down, Batty's long-range drive was straight at the keeper, while Kewell and Smith saw speculative efforts comfortably saved. Valencia's manager, Hector Cuper, was a renowned tactician, and his game plan was working well. His team were happy to protect their goal and look to punish Leeds on the counter, and the best chances of the half all came Valencia's way. Mendieta's looping header struck the face of the crossbar and Sanchez should have done better when denied by Martyn, who also saved smartly from a John Carew overhead kick.

The second half followed the same pattern – Leeds probing, Valencia countering – however, this time it was the visitors who were restricted to half-chances, while Leeds could have, should have, and maybe did score the opening goal. Smith was the man who could have, but on the night his finishing deserted him. He snatched at two very decent chances, one a header, one a volley. Viduka was the man who should have. With Canizares out of his goal Smith's looping cross just needed to be nodded in from three yards. Viduka had two defenders to contend with, but they had no chance of beating the big Australian to the ball. Yet Viduka mis-timed his jump and everyone missed the ball entirely, which bounced instead to Lee Bowyer at the back post, who strained to reach it but could only head against the bar. Dom Matteo was the man that maybe did score. His close-range header was miraculously clawed from on or behind the line by Canizares; without technology we will never know.

Valencia had their moments too, and every time Mendieta drove them forward it reduced Elland Road to a chorus of anxious boos. With the very last attack of the match the visitors were also denied by a goal-line clearance, from a mishit volley that bounced over Martyn and towards the top corner. Thankfully, Rio Ferdinand was on hand to head it clear, with no question marks over whether it had crossed the line.

Thus, when the final whistle blew there was an element of relief to accompany the regret, but overall Leeds were quite content with the final score. O'Leary had spoken of the importance of not conceding an away goal and the 0-0 draw meant his likely lads would reach the final if they avoided defeat in Valencia, or face a penalty shoot-out at worst.

Arsenal 2-1 Leeds United
Saturday, 5 May 2001
Highbury – 3pm
FA Carling Premiership

In between the Valencia games came a pivotal trip to Highbury. Leeds had given themselves a fantastic chance of Champions League qualification and with just three matches remaining they were level on 62 points with Ipswich and Liverpool, with Liverpool in the driving seat due to their superior goal difference. Arsenal themselves were only four points ahead of the chasing pack, so this was a real six-pointer; victory would turn a three-horse race into four. In different circumstances this would have been the biggest game of the season. However, with the second leg in Valencia just three days away David O'Leary made no secret of his priorities: 'I could do without the trip to Arsenal. Having already made certain of European football next season, my priority now is to get into the final, and Arsenal is not the ideal match in between the two legs of the semi-final.'

It was only Lewis and me in attendance for this one, and we headed down to London on the supporters' coach. Being almost last to board we weren't sitting together, I sat next to an OAP and Lewis was just across the aisle from us. We started chatting to the older gentleman but a nice conversation turned into one-way traffic as 'The Incredible Talking Man' just wouldn't stop chattering on. Four hours later, with the finishing line in sight and our tremendous patience wearing thin, the bus driver drove over a boulder and got stuck. Thankfully we were close enough to our destination to be allowed to walk the remaining distance, so we duly bolted to the pub that was reserved for away fans, where they were more than happy to serve 17-year-olds. By the time we were making our way into the Clock End we were absolutely paggered. It was our first time being drunk at a football game, and with Valencia on the horizon and the booze dulling our senses, the match felt like an end-of-season dead rubber when it was really anything but. Lewis and I basically spent the whole game taunting an Arsenal fan, aka 'Spice Boy' across the segregation.

Leeds weren't the only team with split priorities. Arsenal were looking forward to an FA Cup Final against Liverpool the following week and my best memories of the game were the two sets of fans goading each other: 'What you doing Tuesday night?' asked the away fans. 'What you doing Saturday?' replied the home fans. But while Arsene Wenger's team concentrated on the job in hand, O'Leary's pre-match words resonated with his players. Leeds seemed as distracted as Lewis and me.

During an ill-tempered clash at Elland Road back in November, David O'Leary had incensed Robert Pires by sarcastically blowing him a kiss after he pretended to be hurt one too many times. A war of words ensued but today Pires finally got his revenge. The Frenchman ran the show, he was untouchable as Arsenal cruised into a 2-0 lead. Ian Harte struck a superb free kick to drag the visitors back into the game, then he hit the post, but Leeds were unable to equalise, succumbing to a defeat that guaranteed Arsenal's Champions League spot and left United's own qualification hopes on the brink. If O'Leary's side were going to be dining at Europe's top table again, they would probably have to do so as holders.

Valencia 3-0 Leeds United

Tuesday, 8 May 2001

Mestalla Stadium – 7.45pm

UEFA Champions League Semi-Final, Second Leg

Leeds arrived in Spain full of confidence, but their confidence was soon rocked by the controversial, if not scandalous, suspension of Lee Bowyer. Bowyer was the heartbeat of the team. His energy was vital to their high intensity game, as were his goals; 15 this season, six of them in the Champions League to put him in the frame to win the competition's golden boot. In the first leg he had landed on a Valencia defender in a tangle. If the referee had booked Bowyer UEFA wouldn't have been able to review the incident but legendary Italian referee, Pierluigi Collina, instead made the players shake hands, so review it they did, and at 5pm on the eve of the game UEFA announced an immediate three-match ban. Bowyer wasn't just out of the semi-final, he was out of the final too.

It was an outrageous decision. Bowyer's momentum clearly meant he had nowhere else to go, there was no extra force applied, and his reflex reaction was apologetic as soon as his feet landed. At best it was a marginal call that should have fallen well below what could be considered violent enough to make such a significant ruling, so close to such a big game. In an act of solidarity the Leeds players took to the pitch at the Mestalla with shaven heads, everyone except Ian Harte because of his impending wedding.

The Mestalla stadium was a genuine fortress. Valencia hadn't lost a European home game for ten years, winning 15 of 17 Champions League ties. Yet having managed to avoid conceding the precious away goal, Leeds began the game in a position of strength; if they scored first Valencia would need two. That position of strength didn't last long; within 15 minutes Valencia were in the lead, and for the second time this season the ball had been punched into Nigel Martyn's net without the officials noticing. The Leeds players were livid. A sea of yellow shirts surrounded the referee but the protests were in vain.

Having spent the first part of the match under incessant pressure, the next half-hour reverted to the pattern of the first leg; Leeds pushed and pushed but could only carve out half-chances. Beneath my fury at the injustice of the opening goal, I remained confident at half-time. Valencia knew one goal could knock them out and I suspected they would be caught in 'stick or twist' mode: that they would get more nervous as time ticked by, while Leeds threw everything at them.

It never transpired. The second half was a nightmare. Within two minutes Sanchez had doubled the lead, his speculative shot beating an out-of-position Martyn, who had lost his bearings and couldn't reach the bobbling ball which nestled in the corner. Five minutes later it was game over. Mendieta celebrated his 300th appearance for Valencia by booking their place in the final, scoring a replica of Sanchez's goal, just with a better execution to beat a well-placed Martyn into the same corner. In the end nobody could quarrel with the result. Sanchez was denied a hat-trick by the post and the only mark Leeds left on Valencia was a frustrated injury-time lunge from Alan Smith that earned him a straight red card. The European adventure was over.

By the time the final whistle blew I'd already had 30 minutes to process the result. There were no tears, I just felt empty, almost numb. The thought of watching Leeds United in the European Cup Final, at the San Siro, had always seemed too good to be true, so it was easy to accept that it wasn't happening. But once it all sank in, the aftermath was littered with questions and regrets, as always with Leeds. Would it have been different if Bowyer hadn't been suspended? Or if the linesman had spotted the handball? Or if Radebe hadn't been injured? Or if the linesman had awarded Matteo's first-leg 'goal'? These were external factors that conspired against O'Leary's team, but inexperience had told too. The occasion had got the better of them in the vital moments, certainly in the first leg, when on another occasion they might have scored a hatful.

Leeds had lost to a team that were not superior, even if Valencia did win La Liga the following season (with Deportivo as runners-up), but I found solace in the clear belief that O'Leary's likely lads would be back. This was just the beginning: they had reached the semi-finals at the first attempt, with a young and naïve team that was plagued by injuries throughout the campaign. There was so much more to come. McPhail and Bridges would return from injury and grow in stature, Kewell would blossom into one of the world's greatest playmakers, and Woodgate would be free from injury and criminal charges to form a partnership with Rio Ferdinand that would take Leeds and England through the next decade. I was still gutted, but faith is an underrated healer, even better than time.

In the final, Valencia faced Bayern Munich and lost on penalties. It should have been Leeds in that final. They should have been given the chance to avenge 1975 and finally become official European champions. O'Leary's babies had come tantalisingly close to the holiest grail. Oh, what could have been!

Leeds United 3-1 Leicester City

Saturday, 19 May 2001
Elland Road – 3pm
FA Carling Premiership

While Leeds were losing in Valencia, Liverpool faced Chelsea at Anfield knowing a win would settle the race for Europe there and then. Perhaps with half an eye on the weekend's FA Cup Final, Liverpool stuttered to a 2-2 draw, Jimmy Floyd Hasselbaink's brace keeping the dream alive for his old team, and for Ipswich too (though it wasn't enough to get him off my blacklist). At the weekend Liverpool completed the domestic cup double, with Michael Owen's late double-salvo stealing the FA Cup from Arsenal, and the next day Leeds hosted already-relegated Bradford City. By half-time O'Leary's team were 5-1 up and Bradford captain Stuart McCall exchanged blows with his team-mate, Andy Myers, as they headed down the tunnel. The final score was 6-1, a handy goal difference boost which further dented Ipswich's hopes heading into the final game of the season; they now needed both Leeds and Liverpool to slip up if they were to complete the fairy-tale two-year journey from Division One to the Champions League.

Whereas the previous season it had been Leeds who had held the one-point advantage on the last day, this time it was Liverpool, but my confidence was still high. Gerard Houllier's men had completed an unprecedented cup treble in midweek, adding the UEFA Cup to the FA and League Cups already in the trophy cabinet by beating Alaves 5-4 in Dortmund, thanks to a 'golden goal' scored three minutes from the end of extra time. My brother had been at all three finals and it was impossible not to be jealous of what he had experienced, when all I'd experienced was 'what ifs'. Nevertheless, I was sure this epic victory, on top of their dramatic FA Cup win, would have drained Liverpool's resources, and Charlton away was a tricky last fixture.

Leeds's last match was against their bogey team, Leicester City, at Elland Road. Mind you, the Foxes no longer provided the tricky proposition they once did – their successful cycle of the late 90s was over. The previous summer Martin O'Neill had finally left them, heading north of the border to help Celtic end Rangers' decade of dominance in Scotland. His replacement was another young, up-and-coming manager, Peter Taylor, and he made a great start. Leicester were third at Christmas, but they dropped like a stone when O'Neill took midfield maestro, Neil Lennon, to Celtic. By the time they arrived at Elland Road they were 13th, having just ended a run of eight straight defeats.

It was a typically sunny afternoon for the last day of the season, and after almost half an hour of probing Leeds took the lead – and third place in the live table – through a goal from Alan Smith. They were in the ascendancy for only five minutes as Ferdinand's own goal levelled the scores, so at half-time everything remained in the balance. Liverpool were still locked at 0-0 at The Valley, while outsiders Ipswich trailed 1-0 at Derby.

Roared on by a passionate and hopeful Elland Road crowd, Leeds tore into Leicester, knowing a goal would take them back into third. They had been denied three times by the woodwork when they finally took the lead in the 77th minute through Ian Harte's 20-yard free kick – his 11th goal of a terrific season – but by then all hope was lost; Liverpool were 3-0 up and cruising. Any dreams of a miraculous Charlton comeback ended when Robbie Fowler capped off Liverpool's incredible season with an overhead kick to seal a 4-0 win and Champions League football to accompany their three trophies. Alan Smith brought the curtain down on Leeds's season, sealing a futile victory in the 90th minute, amid a defiant Elland Road atmosphere. The fans were determined to salute the heroes who had come so close to immortality.

For the first time in management David O'Leary had failed to fulfil his season's objective (qualifying again for the Champions League), yet nobody could describe season 2000/01 as a failure. Leeds had built a squad that was now proven as capable of challenging the elite at home and abroad simultaneously. Nobody had collected more points than O'Leary's team in the second half of the Premiership season, and both chairman and manager praised the performance of the team in finishing fourth, and claimed to be content with UEFA Cup football. Ridsdale reassured supporters that missing out on the Champions League would not affect Leeds's transfer plans, while O'Leary believed it would present an opportunity to go 'full-tilt' for the Premiership title in 2001/02. The time was now for O'Leary's likely lads.

2001/02 – The Fall

Pre-Season

Arsenal 1-2 Leeds United

Leicester City 0-6 Leeds United

Liverpool 1-1 Leeds United

Manchester United 1-1 Leeds United

Sunderland 2-0 Leeds United

Fulham 0-0 Leeds United

Leeds United 3-4 Newcastle United

Leeds United 3-0 West Ham United

Cardiff City 2-1 Leeds United

Chelsea 2-0 Leeds United

Leeds United 0-1 PSV Eindhoven

Everton 0-0 Leeds United

Leeds United 3-4 Manchester United

Leeds United 1-0 Middlesbrough

Pre-Season

IT WAS a quiet summer at Leeds United, but by keeping the same squad together it was perhaps their most ambitious yet. While the club could have been forgiven for balancing the books, having lost their Champions League status, there were no key departures from Elland Road, despite the cream of Europe sniffing around the likes of Harry Kewell, Mark Viduka, Olivier Dacourt and Paul Robinson. On the contrary, a further £12m was spent to convert Robbie Keane's loan into a permanent deal, taking the club's transfer outlay in the previous 12 months to almost £50m.

A lack of further incomings was not for the want of trying either. Links to Frank Lampard had long been rife but Leeds refused to pay eight figures for the young West Ham midfielder, and the fans were not too disappointed when Chelsea completed an £11m deal. Another long-term target, John Arne Riise, headed to Liverpool for just £4m, the same fee Leeds had failed to land the left-back for a year earlier. They may not have added any new players, and McPhail, Bridges and Radebe would miss the whole season due to injury, but Leeds still had one of the strongest squads in the country and David O'Leary was no longer talking long-term: 'My top target is a Champions League place, and there is no reason why, with the luck all teams need, we can't pick up some silverware along the way.' O'Leary was even happy to field questions about winning the Premiership title: 'While I don't see us as favourites, it is a possibility this season.'

O'Leary had the squad of 20 quality players he had spoken about when he took the job (23 if you include the long-term absentees), but his lust for better-quality players remained, 'We have keen competition for every position, but we want to make the squad even bigger and better. I will try and buy the players we can afford if we can get them. Unfortunately, the ones I wanted in the summer we couldn't get.' That message was backed up by his chairman: 'Let me reassure you we have always backed David's judgement in the transfer market, and we are ready to continue to do so as and when the players who would add further value to the squad become available.'

Peter Ridsdale's ambitions seemed to have no ceiling, and during that summer he revealed plans to build a new 'world class stadium for a world class team'. Ridsdale insisted the club would only leave Elland Road if the move was backed by the fans, then revealed that a club survey had found 90 per cent of fans to be in favour of a move. There was suspicion amongst the fanbase as almost nobody wanted to leave Elland Road, but Ridsdale was adamant that moving stadiums was necessary to continue the growth of the club. The intention was to move into a new home for the start of the 2004/05 season, and the project would be funded by selling the naming rights. The site selected was a patch of land next to the A1 which was renowned for its toxic odour but the whole thing smelt toxic. I was so opposed to the idea that I proclaimed I'd rather Leeds were relegated than leave Elland Road.

In pre-season Leeds once again trounced their opposition. They scored 16 goals without reply on a three-game tour of Sweden, then thrashed Dublin City 6-1 and Preston 5-0, before signing off with a 6-1 thrashing of Sparta Rotterdam. It wasn't so easy when the real work of the Premiership started, but a

2-0 victory at home to Southampton was still the perfect start, sealed at the death by a classy goal from Alan Smith, who turned Dean Richards with a back-heel flick before finishing clinically. Next up was a midweek trip to Highbury, where O'Leary's team had always been soundly beaten. It provided an early opportunity to lay down a marker, a chance for Leeds to really show their Premiership title credentials.

Arsenal 1-2 Leeds United
Tuesday, 21 August 2001
Highbury – 7.45pm
FA Barclaycard Premiership

By now my dad had totally stepped back from away games whereas I had gone the opposite way, buying my first away season ticket to guarantee my place at every match. Lewis and Paul followed suit, but, while we were embarking on our last year of sixth form, Joe was a year older than us and embarking on his first year at university. Thus, his place in the travelling contingent went to our Burnley-supporting friend, Sam, who bought an away season ticket just for the craic.

Being old enough to have an away season ticket and travel the country unattended was a double-edged sword – I was also old enough to need a weekend job to pay for the privilege. My dad would no longer supplement his nearly full-grown child, and I had lost my job as garage manager as the family business had outgrown such a humble abode. So, I got my first 'proper' job, earning £4 per hour at the pub over the road from our house. I was employed as a waiter and absolutely hated it, worse still, I was expected to work Sundays which would mean missing the odd game. The only upside was the comedy value of working for the female version of Basil Fawlty, who would regularly lament customers for making her job more difficult. I did enjoy it more after breaking my wrist playing football; it forced them to deploy me behind the bar as I couldn't carry plates of food.

I was a rubbish waiter and an even worse barman, but at least I could chat football all night with our best customer, Sid, who would joke that it should be 'three for two' when I pulled pints, due to the enormous head on his Guinness (or ask if it came with a spoon).

This was my fourth visit to Highbury, a ground which was unfairly nicknamed 'The Library' by opposing fans. Perhaps Leeds brought the best out of the home fans, but it had always been a great atmosphere when I'd been there, and tonight had all the ingredients to expect nothing less. It was Arsenal's first home game of the season, an early-season blockbuster that was live on Sky, which was still a rare enough occurrence to stoke the atmosphere. It was also Sol Campbell's home debut after his highly controversial free transfer to Arsenal from their arch-rivals Spurs, and despite having no stake in the deal, the Leeds fans booed Campbell throughout for his treachery.

In terms of rivalries between supporters, Arsenal were insignificant compared to Leeds's other title rivals. Manchester United and Chelsea topped the list – they were both bitter enemies – while the rivalries with Liverpool and Newcastle were heated, but more about northern pride than hatred. On the pitch it was a different story entirely: the players of Leeds and Arsenal had built up a unique rivalry since O'Leary had taken the helm at Elland Road. Perhaps the fact O'Leary was a Gunners legend played a part, the night Leeds beat Arsenal to cost them the title must have played a part, and the matches were always feisty battles, packed with incidents, flare-ups and flashed cards. This match was no different.

With Dom Matteo continuing his successful partnership alongside newly appointed club captain Rio Ferdinand, and Bakke preferred to Batty after an impressive pre-season, O'Leary's bench was unquestionably the strongest in the club's history: Robinson, Woodgate, Kelly, Batty and Keane. But having a strong bench counted for nothing as Leeds struggled to get to grips with the Gunners, who flew out of the blocks, roared on by the loudest 'library' in Europe. After only 20 minutes Leeds had already picked up four bookings, but they took the lead against the run of play when referee Jeff Winter allowed Ian Harte to take a quick free kick. Harte curled the ball inside the far post while David Seaman was standing by the near post lining up his wall, leaving the England keeper totally helpless and the home fans furious. Arsenal's fury was channelled in the right direction, leading to an instant equaliser when Sylvain Wiltord headed home in front of the North Bank. The home fans were ecstatic; a goal always tastes better when marinated in retribution.

It was a relief to get to half-time level, and a thrill to take the lead just after the break. Harry Kewell had struggled to return to his scintillating best since overcoming his injury troubles, but he showed signs that a full pre-season was all he needed when his trademark body-swerve bamboozled his marker and set up a chance for Mark Viduka, who side-stepped Tony Adams and fired an unstoppable low drive past Seaman. The Leeds fans in the Clock End went crazy, but my delight was tempered by the knowledge that the rest of the game would now be excruciating.

On came Dennis Bergkamp, fresh from a brace in an opening-day 4-0 thrashing of Middlesbrough, but even the Dutch master could do nothing to inspire an equaliser, Leeds were defending so resolutely. After 20 minutes of fruitless pressure, Jeff Winter decided to give the home side a leg up and flashed his red card at Bowyer for an innocuous challenge. Bowyer saw red alright, unleashing a barrage of swear words at the referee that were so clear and so abusive that they'd need to blur out Bowyer's face on any future re-runs. The Leeds fans, meanwhile, decided to tone down the swearing for once, and chanted at the ref, 'You don't know what you're doing!' Breaking from the norm somehow felt more impactful.

Now Leeds were really up against it. The ten men spent ten minutes repelling wave after wave of Arsenal attacks, but with O'Leary on the verge of his biggest Premiership scalp, Jeff Winter took more drastic action, sending off Danny Mills for trying to win a throw-in off Ashley Cole, who was laid on the floor feigning injury. It was an outrageous decision and the Leeds end went ballistic; in our heads there was no doubt Winter was trying to influence the game in Arsenal's favour. Now down to nine it took a heroic effort, but fuelled by the injustice, Leeds's warriors in electric blue held on for the last five minutes and injury time to claim a landmark victory. Energy, flair, organisation and Yorkshire grit – O'Leary's likely lads had it all. They would take some stopping this year.

Leicester City 0-6 Leeds United

Tuesday, 9 October 2001
Filbert Street – 7.45pm
League Cup, Third Round

Two disappointing 0-0 draws followed the Arsenal victory, but those results looked a lot better after a 2-0 win at Charlton was followed by a 3-0 win at home over Derby. Leeds were already top of the league before a *Super Sunday* clash with Ipswich offered the chance to establish a three-point lead heading into the first international break. United fell behind in the first half, conceding for only the second time in the season, but roared back after the interval. Harry Kewell provided a truly world-class assist for Robbie Keane to equalise with 20 minutes remaining, before Mark Venus completed the comeback with an own goal in the closing stages. Curiously, Keane and Venus had been Leeds's goalscorers in the previous season's 2-1 victory at Portman Road. Everything was going swimmingly for O'Leary: if not quite better than he could have expected, then certainly as well as he could have hoped.

Next up was the obligatory League Cup tie at Leicester, although this year it came around sooner than normal. The previous two ties had been heartbreakers, and my three trips in the league had been no more enjoyable, but tonight O'Leary's side were hot favourites to break my Filbert Street jinx. Leicester City were managerless and bottom of the Premiership, and with O'Neill, Heskey, Lennon and Guppy all gone, Matt Elliott's legs gone, and expensive flops such as Ade Akinbiyi and Trevor Benjamin replacing them, this was a club hurtling towards relegation.

A day out at Wembley was no longer up for grabs but the cups still meant something, so Leeds were at full strength and broke the jinx in some style. Within 15 minutes Robbie Keane had helped himself to a brace, both poacher's goals from Eirik Bakke knock-downs. By half-time it was 3-0, as Keane returned the favour with a stylish back-heel that sent Bakke through on goal to rifle past Ian Walker. Leeds were all but through. The vibrant first-half performance was replaced by a second-half swagger, and by the 65th minute the visitors led 6-0. Keane helped himself to a hat-trick with another poacher's goal after Bakke caused more havoc in the box, then Viduka curled a magnificent left-footed strike into the top corner, so good that it drew a round of applause from the appreciative home fans. Harry Kewell completed the rout, drilling home after Dacourt's searching cross-field ball undid the defence.

We were absolutely loving it and milking it for all it was worth, against fans who had mocked us time and time again down the years. However, with nothing to entertain them on the pitch the Leicester fans found a different form of entertainment: me! I suppose I was asking for it. I had positioned myself as close to them as I could and didn't hold back as goal after goal flew in, but the last 20 minutes really put a dampener on the 6-0 win. 'Rent boy, rent boy, give us a song!' chanted the home fans, and every time I had a go back, I was threatened with ejection by the stewards, to chants of, 'He's gonna cry in a minute!' Bloody Filbert Street!

Having been the media darling for much of his young managerial career, the pressure to win things seemed to be having an adverse effect on David O'Leary's cheery disposition. The 'young and naïve' catchphrase was long gone, as was the affection he used to show his babies; they were all grown up now. He would eventually develop a reputation for complaining that led sections of the media to nickname him 'O'Dreary', and his comments after this stunning win may have been the first step on that journey: 'They are still immature and can do daft things on the pitch, like charging around when six goals up.' Dreary me.

Liverpool 1-1 Leeds United
Saturday, 13 October 2001
Anfield – 12pm
FA Barclaycard Premiership

We were tantalisingly close to our 18th birthdays, but when it came to drinking, in those days if you were persistent enough you were old enough. So, driven by my new brother-in-law Josh, Lewis, Paul and I headed over to Liverpool on the Friday night ahead of a Saturday lunchtime kick-off for a night on the town with Gianni and his uni mates. Being surrounded by students, we blended in sufficiently to not require our fake IDs, nor was there any swapping of jumpers and shoes to bamboozle any doubting door-staff. We had a great night, and by the end Lewis was being paraded on our shoulders like he'd just scored the winner in the World Cup Final. 'Hey, Lewis Ramsey, ooh, ahh, I wanna knooow how you pulled that girl!'

In the morning we were rough as old boots, but, with our bodies well accustomed to alcohol abuse by now, we headed over to Anfield in good spirits, hoping for a repeat of spring's impeccable display. We got what we wished for in the first half; Leeds were superb, in total control of proceedings and in the lead at half-time thanks to a goal from Harry Kewell.

Unbeknown to the fans in the ground, dramatic scenes were developing in the Liverpool changing room. Gerard Houllier was rushed to hospital after suffering from a heart attack that would have killed him had it not happened in the eye of the storm of the matchday traffic. O'Leary was great friends with Houllier, and with his father having recently suffered similar heart trouble this must have been a very chilling experience. Houllier's assistant, Phil Thompson, took charge of the team in his absence, an absence which lasted five months and probably ended too soon.

Being blessed with a larger than usual scent detector, Thompson's increased presence on the touchline inspired a new song from the terraces, with the Leeds fans changing the lyrics of 'We've got Dom Matteo, you've got our stereos', to 'We've got Dom Matteo, you've got Pinocchio'. The chant soon developed into, 'Sit down Pinocchio, sit down Pinocchio', and eventually, and perhaps predictably, 'Fuck off Pinocchio, fuck off Pinocchio'. Thompson had the last laugh though, inspiring Liverpool to a much-improved second-half display and an equaliser through Danny Murphy. At the final whistle it felt like two points dropped. I was disappointed that Leeds seemed to take their foot off the gas after such a dominant first half; nevertheless, this was another positive result away to a title rival.

On the way home we had a surprise encounter as we stopped at the services on the M62. As we walked through the car park, out of the bushes popped Rio Ferdinand and Jonathan Woodgate. They looked more startled than us and ignorantly barged past us like we were paparazzi, before speeding off in their 4x4. Never meet your heroes, unless it's Lee Bowyer.

The following week brought another clash with a title rival, a clash of the Premiership's two remaining unbeaten teams. Chelsea twice cleared efforts off their own goal line, and in the final minute Nigel Martyn pushed Emmanuel Petit's free kick on to the bar, but once again both teams were content with a draw, which was enough to take Leeds back to the top of the Premiership.

Manchester United 1-1 Leeds United
Saturday, 27 October 2001
Old Trafford – 12pm
FA Barclaycard Premiership

If David O'Leary was going to kick Alex Ferguson's butt, he was going to have to get a move on. Ferguson had announced his intention to retire at the end of the season, so if the two old foes weren't paired together in a cup competition, this would be O'Leary's penultimate chance. Speculation about Ferguson's successor seemed to be centred around O'Leary, and everyone at Elland Road was praying it wouldn't be a case of, 'if you can't beat them, join them'. O'Leary had been getting closer and closer to beating them since that 3-2 defeat in his first trip to Old Trafford three years ago, and only a controversial flag had denied him on his latest attempt. Today his team would go closer still.

Having won three Premiership titles in a row, Ferguson was looking to finish his career in record-breaking style; no English team had been champions four years running. However, Ferguson's last team had its frailties and came into this game off the back of a shock home defeat to Bolton which left them fifth in the league. Defensive stalwart Jaap Stam had been sold to Lazio in the summer and his replacement, Laurent Blanc, was struggling to adapt to the pace and physicality of the English game. He may have been a World Cup-winning centre-back, but Blanc's best years were clearly behind him. Ferguson also broke Leeds's British transfer record in the summer by spending £28m on Juan Sebastian Veron, but the Argentine playmaker was struggling to settle too. Perhaps their main problem was the trial of a new formation. Ferguson ditched the tried and trusted 4-4-2, which had dominated English football since I was

187

born, and instead played Veron alongside Keane and Scholes in midfield, with Ruud van Nistelrooy deployed as a lone striker. It just wasn't gelling.

There were no such problems at Elland Road. Having passed the test at Highbury with flying colours, and come away from Anfield disappointed with only a draw, Leeds arrived at Old Trafford full of confidence. The first half was as tight as a good battle between two top teams should be. Viduka missed a one-on-one with Barthez and Beckham prodded against Nigel Martyn's post, and at half-time the game was locked at 0-0.

It wouldn't be a fair reflection on the previous play to say the game burst into life on 55 minutes, but the heat of the battle was raised a notch when Robbie Keane reacted to a foul from David Beckham with a double-handed shove to his face. Seeing Beckham decked so spectacularly by a Leeds player was a dream come true and the away end celebrated it like a goal, but seconds later came the realisation that Leeds were about to be reduced to ten men. Over came the referee, first dealing with the initial foul and booking Beckham, then, to our astonishment he flashed the same card at Keane. Never have I been more shocked and delighted to see a booking; what a let-off! Within two minutes Keane capitalised on his escape by floating a beautiful free kick into the top corner and sending the Leeds end into raptures, but the referee disallowed the goal, claiming he hadn't blown the whistle. I broke into a fit of rage, adamant he only disallowed it due to the amount of earache he would get from Ferguson having not red-carded Keane.

Soon enough it was all forgotten. With 77 minutes on the clock, Ian Harte sent an innocuous-looking ball into the box which caught Mikael Silvestre on his heels. Viduka got in front of the defender, and with Fabien Barthez glued to his line, the big Aussie was able to let the ball bounce across his body before firing a close-range volley through the keeper's legs and into the net in front of us. Cue ecstasy in the Leeds end. After all those near misses down the years, Leeds had finally taken a pivotal chance at Old Trafford and were primed for the result I'd waited my whole life for. Cue the Manchester United onslaught.

Leeds were pegged back continuously but Rio Ferdinand was oustanding, ably assisted by Dom Matteo. Each minute seemed like five, but every time an attack was repelled the Leeds fans belted out 'Marching on Together' in full belief that their 20-year wait for a victory at Old Trafford was about to end. It wasn't. In the 89th minute Ryan Giggs swung a cross to the back post which landed plumb on the head of super-sub, Ole Gunnar Solskjaer, who headed perfectly into the far corner. Old Trafford erupted, then roared their team on, sensing another famous late turnaround. It offered some consolation that they didn't get it, especially when they came so close. Leeds had the heroics of Nigel Martyn to thank for preventing a painful defeat; first he saved from a Dom Matteo deflection, then he miraculously denied van Nistelrooy what looked a certain goal.

Ferguson praised the quality and excitement of the game in his post-match interview, but David O'Leary was seething. He felt his players had let him down by taking their foot off the gas once they had the lead, allowing Manchester United back into the game. It was becoming the story of the season – a big game had ended in a respectable and positive result, but not a win.

The following week's 2-1 victory over Spurs made the consecutive draws against Liverpool, Chelsea and Manchester United look like the results of champions and ensured Leeds would again spend the international break leading the Premiership. Expectation was rising and O'Leary wasn't shying away from it. 'I demand a lot from the players and the question they have to answer is have they got the desire and discipline to see it through? It's entirely in their hands. They have the ability; they just have to have the hunger.' O'Leary ended with a pearl of wisdom that, with hindsight, was chilling, 'We've built something good here and the only way it can go wrong is if it self-destructs from within.'

Sunderland 2-0 Leeds United
Sunday, 18 November 2001
Stadium of Light – 4pm
FA Barclaycard Premiership

Leeds had the chance to open up a three-point lead at the top when they returned to action on *Super Sunday*, against a Sunderland side in terrible form. With only one win in their last nine games, the Mackems found themselves in 16th place, and their home form against Leeds was even worse – no wins in 21 years. It made a mockery of the cliché, 'it's never an easy place to go', but that still felt true, especially when facing the predatory strike partnership of Niall Quinn and Kevin Phillips.

Of added concern for O'Leary was the absence of key players for this game – Mark Viduka, Harry Kewell and Lee Bowyer – although Leeds had plenty of quality in reserve, especially as the squad had recently been bolstered by the addition of combative midfielder Seth Johnson from Derby County. A 22-year-old with an England cap already to his name, Johnson had the potential to blossom into a top first-team player, and his versatility would immediately add depth to the squad. Being left-footed, he would cover for the long-term absence of Stephen McPhail and provide cover at left-back, a job that was vacant again with Dom Matteo established at centre-back in the long-term absence of Lucas Radebe. On paper Johnson was a perfect fit, yet this transfer would become a symbol of the excesses that caused the fall of Leeds United.

There were two problems with the Seth Johnson transfer. Firstly, he was far too expensive. Johnson's contract negotiations entered folklore and led to Peter Ridsdale obtaining the nickname 'Father Christmas', both inside and outside the club. The story goes that he was on £5k per week at Derby and hoping for £15k per week at Leeds. He and his agent were left dumbfounded with Ridsdale's opening offer of £30k per week, and eventually negotiated it up to £37k. Leeds also overpaid on the transfer fee. At £7m it wasn't silly money, but Chelsea had just paid £7.5m for Emmanuel Petit, a combative, left-footed midfielder from Barcelona who had won nearly every honour at club and international level. And Arsenal had just paid £8m for Giovanni van Bronckhorst, a combative, left-footed midfielder who would go on to play 100 times for Barcelona and 100 times for the Netherlands.

Which brings us to the other problem: Johnson simply wasn't that good and his first start at Sunderland was a sign of things to come. Granted, he was given the thankless task of filling in for Harry Kewell, but nothing went well for Johnson, or any of his team-mates, and Leeds crashed to their first defeat of the season. It could have been a different story but Leeds missed their first-half chances, and a two-goal salvo at the beginning of the second half was too heavy a blow for the Whites to recover from. On 48 minutes Jason McAteer's stinging drive was parried straight to Julio Arca who fired home the rebound, and on 56 minutes Sunderland scored a trademark goal; a high ball to Quinn, a chest down to Phillips and the ball was in the back of the net.

It still could have been a different story had Robbie Keane been awarded a penalty rather than being incorrectly booked for diving. There was still over 20 minutes to go at that point and Leeds could have fought back, but Sunderland deserved their victory, Leeds's first Premiership defeat for ten months.

Leeds failed to bounce back in their next game. Alan Smith scored and was sent off within the first half hour in a 1-1 draw at home to Aston Villa. It was now one win in six for O'Leary's men, and those draws against their title rivals were no longer looking so great. They were still in second place, only two points behind Liverpool, but draws would need to be turned into wins in order to maintain the title challenge.

Fulham 0-0 Leeds United

Sunday, 2 December 2001

Craven Cottage – 4pm

FA Barclaycard Premiership

Another disappointing result followed the draw with Villa, a 2-0 League Cup defeat at home to Chelsea in which Michael Duberry was used as an emergency striker for the last 15 minutes. It was a strange move from O'Leary. Perhaps there was an alternative motive: to justify the club's decision to pull off their highest-profile signing since paying £53,000 to bring John Charles home from Juventus in 1962.

Robbie Fowler was often called the most natural goalscorer of his generation by pundits and coaches across the land, but in Liverpool he was simply called 'God'. At 26 he was theoretically yet to reach his prime, despite having already notched up 120 goals in 236 games for Liverpool, and won the FA Cup, two League Cups, the UEFA Cup and the UEFA Super Cup along the way. During the previous season Fowler had scored 17 goals in 48 appearances, but many of those appearances were from the bench as manager Gerard Houllier preferred the physical presence of Emile Heskey alongside the 2001 Ballon d'Or winner, Michael Owen. Fowler felt under-appreciated and his relationship with Houllier broke down, so in swooped Leeds with an £11m bid and 'God' was on his way to Yorkshire.

I had just turned 18 and Fowler was the best present I could possibly have wished for. I woke up every day counting my lucky stars, Leeds had signed Robbie Fowler! It was so strange seeing him in the white shirt, with a Leeds badge on his chest and talking as a Leeds player, but so exciting too. I was sure this was the last piece in the jigsaw; how could we possibly fail now? Every time Fowler got the ball in the box it would be a goal! Gianni, meanwhile, was heartbroken. His love and respect for Houllier quelled his anger somewhat, but he was still disappointed there weren't any protests at Liverpool's next game. The fact Fowler had signed for Leeds just compounded his misery; seeing how happy my dad and I were kept the pain closer to home.

I did wonder how Leeds could afford to buy all these players. A big chunk of last season's Champions League earnings had already been spent on Rio Ferdinand, and this season we weren't in the competition but had still spent another £30m on transfers, while significantly increasing the wage bill. Nonetheless, I assumed it was all good, the club must know what they were doing. And even if they didn't, Leeds were going to win the league so all would be fine, regardless! At the very least they would be back in the Champions League next season, especially as the top four now qualified rather than just the top three; Ridsdale was probably just spending next season's money.

As it happened, Leeds United plc's annual general meeting took place on the Friday after Fowler signed, with many people questioning the ability of the club to afford such transfers. Peter Ridsdale's response was as emphatic as when the fans were accusing the club of not spending enough, 'I can assure everyone – shareholders and supporters alike – that your board are managing the club for sustained success, and that the club's long-term financial position is healthy.'

Fowler's debut was broadcast live on *Super Sunday*, at Craven Cottage where he had scored on his Liverpool debut as an 18-year-old in 1993. My excitement was magnified as it would also be my debut standing on a terrace, but the terrace turned out to be a mammoth anti-climax – a poxy little paddock down the side of the pitch, with nowhere near enough room to swarm about like the crowds did on *Match of the 70s*. Fowler's debut was equally disappointing.

The highlight of the day was the team news. O'Leary couldn't resist the temptation and threw Fowler straight into the team alongside Mark Viduka, with Alan Smith shifted to the right wing and Harry Kewell down the left. With such attacking talent Fulham must have been quaking in their boots, yet, similar to our superstar three-pronged defence capitulating at Leicester, our superstar four-pronged attack failed to click and Leeds barely created a chance. The closest either side came to scoring was in the opening minutes, when Seth Johnson lost possession in a dangerous area and needed Gary Kelly to bail him out with a terrific goal-line clearance. Fowler did have a late sniff at goal but couldn't connect cleanly with a close-range volley and the ball was smothered by Edwin van der Sar. Thus, the game fizzled out into a drab 0-0 draw.

Leeds's title charge was officially faltering. They had registered only one win in their last seven outings and now trailed leaders Liverpool by four points, having played a game more. The following week there was a much-needed win at Blackburn, 2-1 thanks to a second-half brace from Harry Kewell, then came Leicester at Elland Road. This was the first game I was forced to miss due to my weekend job, and waiting tables was almost impossible with the distraction of the Leeds game on the kitchen radio. 'Sometimes he leaves his brain at home,' commented my boss to my parents when singing my praises one day, but my brain wasn't at home, it was at Elland Road. Inside ten minutes Leeds were ahead through Harry Kewell, but despite a brilliant performance my anxiety was rising with each missed chance. Mark Viduka eventually doubled the lead on the hour, and for the next 20 minutes I could concentrate on my job, until Leicester pulled a goal back out of nothing. For the last ten minutes I was torn between hiding in the kitchen or hiding from the kitchen. I chose the latter as the least painful and most responsible solution, and I could hardly believe it when the chef told me an 89th-minute equaliser had salvaged a 2-2 draw for the Premiership's basement boys. An absolute sickener.

Three days later United conceded two late goals at Elland Road again, though this time they had built a three-goal lead and so returned to winning ways. Robbie Fowler had waited all month for a goal and then two had come at once, fittingly against Everton, a club with whom he had a hate-hate relationship. Fowler was off the mark and Leeds seemed to be hitting their stride again heading into the hectic Christmas period.

Leeds United 3-4 Newcastle United
Saturday, 22 December 2001
Elland Road – 3pm
FA Barclaycard Premiership

What a mouth-watering pre-Christmas clash this was. The top of the Premiership could barely be tighter, and Bobby Robson's visitors were leading the way thanks to a stunning midweek victory at Highbury which lifted them above Liverpool on goals scored. Leeds were just one point behind, Arsenal three points behind, and a chasing pack of Chelsea, Manchester United, Spurs and Villa were six points behind. But even more mouth-watering than the football was the prospect of welcoming Lee Bowyer back on to the Elland Road pitch.

Since mid-October the retrial of Bowyer and Woodgate had been taking place, and while the start of the first trial sparked a dramatic upturn in results, you could say the start of the retrial had the opposite effect. Leeds had just drawn at Anfield after the 6-0 thrashing of Leicester, but three wins in nine games since, plus a League Cup exit, had punctured their season.

The retrial was a drain on everybody (even Bowyer), this time lacking the drama and intrigue of the initial proceedings; we'd heard it all before. The only difference was that Michael Duberry went from defendant to star witness for the prosecution, but only in the case against Woodgate – Duberry had no knowledge of Bowyer being at the scene. After another eight weeks in Hull Crown Court, Bowyer was found not guilty on all charges, while Woodgate was cleared of GBH but found guilty of affray (as was his friend Neale Caveney). Woodgate was spared the jail sentence his career could ill afford, and would instead serve 100 hours' community service. Woodgate's other friend, Paul Clifford, was the only person convicted of GBH, thanks to his dental records matching the bite marks on Sarfraz Najeib's face. He got six years in jail.

Leeds United slapped unprecedented fines on both players, four weeks' wages for Bowyer (for breaking club protocol by being drunk in the city centre late at night), and eight weeks' wages for the convicted Woodgate. Woodgate accepted his punishment, but the exonerated Bowyer was livid, and when he refused to cough up Ridsdale slapped him on the transfer list. It was an extraordinary turn of events and yet another off-field distraction, prolonging the effects of the trial despite the case finally being closed.

Bowyer wasn't just transfer-listed, he was dropped too, and watched the 3-2 victory over Everton from the stands. Bowyer received the full support of his team-mates, who rounded in front of him to celebrate Fowler's second goal in his honour. It was a statement of solidarity from the team, which in turn confirmed a rift in the club. The players were not happy with their chairman for fining Bowyer, nor their manager for dropping him. Looking back, it's hard not to view this incident as the first crack in the O'Leary era.

Within hours of the Everton match all had been resolved, on the surface at least. By the time Newcastle arrived at Elland Road just three days later, Bowyer had paid the fine, been removed from the transfer list and was reinstated into the starting line-up. The atmosphere at Elland Road was rocking, and when the players took to the pitch all the fans were chanting in unison, 'BOWYER FOR ENGLAND!' The chant had been born in protest at the FA's decision to ban both him and Woodgate from international selection, but with Bowyer's name cleared the chant was now sung in celebration that the two-year campaign was set to triumph.

In such partisan surroundings you could have forgiven Newcastle for crumbling, but the league leaders were determined to prove their title credentials and took the sting out of the atmosphere before taking a 38th-minute lead through Craig Bellamy. It proved to be just the catalyst Leeds needed. Less than a minute later Viduka cleverly played in Bowyer, who had burst beyond the Newcastle defence. Bowyer jinked inside the desperate covering defender, almost left the ball behind, but managed to sort out his twinkle toes just in time to nudge his finish under Shay Given and into the net. The commentator on *Match of the Day* summed it up very nicely, 'That's his way of putting two fingers up to the world. That's Lee Bowyer, doing what he does best.' Nobody inside Elland Road was going crazier than me, although Bowyer came a close second. It was a shame the goal wasn't in front of the Kop but Bowyer didn't mind. He unleashed all his pent-up aggression in a tirade towards the away fans in the South Stand, who, to Bowyer, represented every rival supporter who had abused him in every game for the best part of two years.

Attacking the Kop in the second half, Leeds had the bit between their teeth. Mark Viduka scored a wonderful goal, turning Andy O'Brien before curling the ball beautifully into the far corner, then Ian Harte drilled in a third from the edge of the box. Leeds were 3-1 up and heading back to the top of the league. The current leaders had other ideas, though. Robbie Elliott headed them back into the game within three minutes of Harte's strike, and in the 70th minute the referee awarded a hotly disputed penalty for handball against Eirik Bakke. Whether playing for Southampton, Blackburn or Newcastle, Alan Shearer's record against Leeds was immense. He rarely failed to score at least one, and he was never going to miss from the spot: 3-3.

As the game headed into injury time David O'Leary must have been preparing his answers to why his team were drawing so many games, but Newcastle weren't finished. In the last minute the visitors won a scrap for the ball in midfield and Kieron Dyer broke forward before playing a lovely ball inside Ian Harte for Nolberto Solano to chase. Harte's lack of pace was badly exposed as Solano left him for dead and sent a low finish beyond Nigel Martyn into the far corner. The Toon Army went berserk, Bobby Robson's team were Christmas number one and dreaming of the title themselves. This was a sucker-punch that knocked the stuffing out of me; Christmas was ruined.

Leeds United 3-0 West Ham United
Tuesday, 1 January 2002
Elland Road – 8pm
FA Barclaycard Premiership

I may have sulked throughout Christmas, but I was more bothered about the handball decision that swung the game away from Leeds rather than any deficiency in the team. I still believed O'Leary's team were the best in the land, but with Chelsea and Manchester United heading into Christmas on the back of 5-1 and 6-1 wins respectively, the top of the table had become very congested; six points separated the top six.

On Boxing Day Leeds headed to the Reebok Stadium to face Bolton, and so too did my dad – a rare away game for him – and so too did Jonathan Woodgate. With the trial behind him Woodgate was given his first start in the Premiership for 11 months, alongside Rio Ferdinand. It would be a dream partnership if Woodgate could recapture his best form. The visitors made an ideal start, thanks to the realisation of the dreams I'd had when Robbie Fowler signed; each time Leeds found Fowler, Fowler found the net. His first goal came after a minute, when he plucked Batty's hopeful high ball out of the air and slammed it inside the far post. 'SUPER, SUPER ROB, SUPER ROBBIE FOWLER!' His second came after 15 minutes, when he plucked Viduka's clever high ball out of the air and gently caressed it past the advancing keeper. 'SUPER, SUPER ROB, SUPER ROBBIE FOWLER!' With Leeds rock-solid in defence there was going to be no way back for Sam Allardyce's struggling team. The only question was whether Fowler could complete his hat-trick. In the closing stages he fluffed the chance to do so from the spot, to the delight of the defeated Bolton fans who bizarrely taunted the match-winner with chants of 'What a waste of money!' With the last laugh already in the bag, Fowler proceeded to claim his hat-trick anyway. Alan Smith sent him clean through and he rounded the goalkeeper, jinked inside the covering defender, and scored into the empty net to the acclaim of the triumphant Leeds fans, 'WHAT A WASTE OF MONEY! WHAT A WASTE OF MONEY!'

Next up in the busy Christmas schedule was the long trip to Southampton's new St Mary's stadium. Injuries had been a constant feature of his tenure, and they were still hampering O'Leary. His midfield over the festive period was a real mishmash – Kelly, Bowyer, Batty and Smith – and on the south coast Leeds lacked balance and cohesion. However, with Ferdinand and Woodgate in defence there was no joy for Southampton's dangerous-looking strike partnership of James Beattie and Marians Pahars. Due to a bout of 'the runs' I was at home listening on the radio, and with 90 minutes almost up and the game heading for a bore draw, I felt relieved to have dodged the ten-hour round trip. Suddenly, Radio Leeds commentator Ian Dennis's voice grew in excitement as Mark Viduka's clever flick split the defence, then exploded with joy when Lee Bowyer calmly finished to snatch all three points for Leeds, his 50th goal for the club. I went absolutely crazy, but in the back of my mind I was gutted to have missed what would have been an unforgettable moment. I had put in the hard yards, going to nearly every game, only to miss this last-minute winner by my hero – it almost felt cruel, despite it being so kind. An addict had missed a major hit.

The Christmas period ended with a New Year's Day clash with in-form West Ham, under the lights at Elland Road and live on Sky. 'You might not necessarily choose Lee Bowyer as your son-in-law, but as a football manager you'd rather have him in your team than facing you,' said the commentator ahead of kick-off, a charming fellow. Leeds were fourth going into the game but had the chance to move to the top of the league with a victory, and grabbed their opportunity with both hands.

A light film of snow covered the Elland Road pitch, and a rip-roaring start caught the visitors cold. In three minutes flat Leeds had torn the Hammers open and Mark Viduka was on hand to apply the finishing touch. Three minutes later Danny Mills steamed forward to dispossess the hesitant Trevor Sinclair, skin the startled Nigel Winterburn, and put a perfect cross on the head of Viduka to double the lead. The Kop was buoyant, taking great pleasure in the failure of their 'southern softy' opponents to handle the Yorkshire conditions, taunting them with an obscene chant which greeted any team based in and around the M25. I often wondered what Bowyer must make of it considering his London roots, but I'm sure he had developed a thick skin by now.

Glenn Roeder's side weathered the metaphorical storm and would have been happy to get back to the changing rooms with no further damage, especially as Leeds would be attacking the much less vociferous South Stand in the second half. Any hopes of an unlikely comeback were dashed just five minutes after the restart. The points were sealed in some style by Robbie Fowler, who, from only 18 yards, nonchalantly dinked a bobbling loose ball perfectly over the 6ft 5in frame of goalkeeper David James and down into the bottom of the net. The trajectory couldn't have been drawn better, a divine finish from the artist formerly known as 'God'.

A 3-0 victory was the perfect start to 2002 for Leeds. It was their 38th Premiership game since New Year's Day 2001 and in that time they had lost only four games and collected 80 points, the same total as Manchester United had won the previous season's title with, and more than any other team had collected in the calendar year (a feat they also achieved in 1999 with 78 points, the same total Arsenal had won the 1998 title with). More significantly, O'Leary's likely lads were top of the league, and the realisation of all their potential seemed to be only months away.

Cardiff City 2-1 Leeds United
Sunday, 6 January 2002
Ninian Park – 3pm
FA Cup, Third Round

There's no doubt the FA Cup lost its appeal in the 21st century, with a shift in focus towards other more lucrative prizes. For me though, the demolition of the Twin Towers was the most significant blow to the competition. The prospect of getting to the final has been diminished by the characterless arena that replaced a historic old stadium, and holding the semi-finals at the same venue further devalued the final and soured the prospect of getting to the semis. Robbing the fans of the enchanting neutral venue stage was bad enough, but this decision also presented a dilemma for thousands of supporters who couldn't afford the vast sums it costs to visit Wembley twice in a month (especially northerners, who have to pay for excessive rail transport and possibly accommodation too).

In 2002, the FA Cup may have lost its most glamorous attraction, but it was still a major trophy and winning it would constitute a fantastic season for Leeds United, whatever happened in the title race. While Wembley was under reconstruction the temporary home of the cup final was Cardiff's Millennium Stadium, and the road to Cardiff started in Cardiff for Leeds. It was the tie of the round, a real David vs Goliath contest, pitting the now expensively assembled Leeds squad against a third-tier club led by the man who had steered Wimbledon to the greatest FA Cup story of all time, Sam Hammam.

The eccentric Lebanese chairman led Wimbledon's 'Crazy Gang' from non-league to the top flight in just nine years, then won the FA Cup against the all-conquering Liverpool side of the 1980s. His attempt to replicate the achievement in South Wales was well underway. Cardiff had been promoted from the fourth tier the previous season, and had assembled a team containing a blend of seasoned campaigners like Graham Kavanagh and Spencer Prior, alongside bright young prospects like Danny Gabbidon and Robert Earnshaw. Despite a run of four winless games, they were flirting with the play-off spots, and hopeful of successive promotions.

There was extra spice to this tie off the pitch too. The hooligan problems of the 80s had been all but eradicated from football grounds but hooligan gangs still existed; they just conducted their business away from the CCTV-ridden stadiums. Football hooliganism really enthralled me at the time. I loved reading about the exploits of the various 'firms', so I was all too aware that Cardiff's 'Soul Crew' had a fearsome reputation while Leeds's 'Service Crew' was notorious as well. This added to the excitement as Lewis, Joe, Sam and I headed down by coach to Ninian Park, an old-school ground where, after my shambolic debut on the terracing at Fulham, I would finally be able to experience what football was like 'back in the day'. Little did I know I'd get far more than I bargained for.

Just over 22,000 fans packed into the ground on a Sunday afternoon as the sun started to set, and the atmosphere was electric from the word go. The 2,500 Leeds fans had a third of the terrace behind the goal, right beside Cardiff's most boisterous fans, but although we did our best to make ourselves heard, the Cardiff fans were just too loud. It was the first time

I'd experienced Leeds's away following being out-sung, and to such an extent that we just had to give up trying in the end, it was futile.

As always, O'Leary fielded his strongest team, but within minutes you could see Leeds were rattled by the atmosphere. They had played at the Nou Camp, Bernabeu, Riazor, Mestalla, San Siro, and the Olympic stadiums in Rome and Munich, but they were nothing compared to Ninian Park, which must have taken the players back to their awful experience in Istanbul. Not only was the stadium and atmosphere akin to the 80s, so too was the football. Cardiff players were flying into tackles as if it was a game of fouling football and the referee, the notoriously flappable Andy D'Urso (the man who failed to book any Manchester United players under intense intimidation two years earlier) let every challenge go unpunished. Within ten minutes Rio Ferdinand hobbled off after one such ugly foul, which meant Michael Duberry partnered Jonathan Woodgate in defence. The two former best mates hadn't spoken since Duberry informed Woodgate he would be testifying against him, but now they were thrown into the trenches together. This wasn't looking good.

However, two minutes after Ferdinand hobbled off, Mark Viduka fired United into the lead with an unstoppable drive from the edge of the box. My mates and I made the most of celebrating on the terracing, flinging ourselves around as wildly as we could; one less item for the bucket list. But the goal did little to dampen Cardiff's spirits and 20 minutes later they were level when Graham Kavanagh's stunning free kick flew past Nigel Martyn. Then, two minutes before the interval, disaster struck when Andy D'Urso finally reached for his pocket and controversially sent off Alan Smith for an apparent elbow. This really wasn't looking good.

In the second half it was backs to the wall for the Premiership leaders as they strived to get out of this madhouse with a replay.

Cardiff knew this was their big chance, their only chance; if they were going to knock Leeds out, they had to do it now. With 15 minutes remaining, their chairman Sam Hammam decided he was no help to the team while sat in the directors' box and headed pitch-side, walking down the touchline and past the shocked Leeds fans to take his place behind Nigel Martyn's goal, in front of Cardiff's baying fans. It gave those fans an injection of adrenaline (not that they needed it), which transmitted to their team, and with three minutes to go, a header from a corner was blocked on the line by Batty, only for the rebound to be smashed into the net to send Ninian Park ballistic. Everybody around us was going crazy, the rafters were ringing and all the celebrations were directed at the Leeds end. It was horrible. When the final whistle blew the Cardiff fans burst on to the pitch. Some celebrated with their team, others confronted the Leeds players and for the rest it was an excuse to attack the Leeds fans. Only 80s-style fencing separated the two sets of supporters, and the police were nowhere to be seen. This definitely was not looking good.

The lack of preparation for a potential pitch invasion was ludicrous considering the obvious warning signs; the Cardiff fans had been throwing 'missiles' on to the pitch throughout the match. A bottle had missed Ian Harte by inches in the opening stages, Andy D'Urso needed treatment when he was struck by a coin in the closing stages and one of his linesmen had also been struck. Objects were raining into the Leeds end: coins, lighters and even advertising hoardings. The Leeds fans weren't taking it lightly either, flinging back whatever they could find. Finally, the police stormed the pitch with batons and dogs to force the home fans back, but that wasn't the end of it. On leaving the ground we were confronted by the very people that were supposed to be protecting us. The police turned on the Leeds fans but I managed to escape back to the coach, where my clearest memory of the day took place. As we waited to board, a policeman with a vicious and angry dog came bounding towards us. The gruesome twosome were shouting and barking in unison as I cowered against the coach. 'COME ON THEN LEEDS!' he screamed, a hooligan in uniform. Thankfully I made it on to the coach injury-free, which was not the case for many bloodied Leeds fans.

The nightmare still wasn't over though. On the coach back we listened to 5Live as Aston Villa faced Manchester United in the evening game and raced into a two-goal lead: a crumb of comfort to soften the blow of Leeds's exit. The consolation was short-lived. After a stop at the services, we re-boarded to find that Ferguson's team had scored two late goals to level at 2-2, and then we listened in disbelief as they scored the winning goal too. When would we get a moment like that? For Manchester United and Liverpool it seemed to be epic glory on tap, for Leeds it was nothing but torture and heartache.

In the aftermath the behaviour of the Cardiff fans, Sam Hammam, and the policing came under intense scrutiny. The FA took decisive action, slapping a tiny £20k fine on the Welsh club for their pitch invasion, and instructing them to put half-page warning notices against bad behaviour in their matchday programmes and erect warning signs inside and outside the ground. That'll learn 'em! Unfathomably, the charges for missile throwing were dismissed (a missile had literally hit the head of the referee, live on television!) and there was no action taken against Sam Hammam's pitch-side antics either. There were sterner repercussions for some of the Cardiff hooligans. Only four arrests were made on the day but CCTV footage led to many more, most notably Dai Thomas, a former Cardiff player. He was the man who threw the advertising hoarding into the Leeds end, which was caught on film and led to a 60-day jail sentence and a six-year ban from football grounds.

While Cardiff City escaped practically scot-free, Leeds had lost their captain to injury, Alan Smith to suspension, and their place in the FA Cup. The club appealed Smith's red card – backed up by a statement from the victim of his 'violent conduct' – but the appeal was dismissed, and Smith's four-match ban was eventually extended to five.

Once over my dismay, I became philosophical about the Cardiff affair. It had been one hell of an experience, and an FA Cup exit at least meant there was one less distraction for O'Leary's team in their pursuit of the Premiership title. There was plenty to look forward to as well; the next four games were all huge six-pointers against fellow title-chasers. Four wins would make Leeds hot favourites to become champions of England for the first time in ten years.

Chelsea 2-0 Leeds United

Wednesday, 30 January 2002
Stamford Bridge – 8pm
FA Barclaycard Premiership

In December David O'Leary had released a book that gave readers the inside story of Leeds's 2000/01 season. The book centred around the team's wonderful run to the Champions League semi-finals, but a big chunk of it was dedicated to the trial of Lee Bowyer and Jonathan Woodgate (which hadn't even concluded when the book was released). Having spent two years trying to convince the world that Leeds United were not on trial, just two of their players, Peter Ridsdale was furious with the title of the book, *Leeds United on Trial*.

At the time I thought nothing of the fact our manager had released a book. I read it and I loved it, and never considered the negative effect it could have on team spirit. The book was extremely candid, packed with information that most professionals would expect to be kept in-house. O'Leary revealed details of training ground incidents, dressing room dressing downs, the foibles and frailties of his players, and his thoughts on the highly sensitive court case, which were thinly veiled at best. The overall message was that the manager loved his players, but almost all of them received some form of criticism along the way, and as O'Leary wrote himself, 'players these days do seem to take constructive criticism personally'.

O'Leary's book added further weight to a growing consensus that the club's success had gone to his head, and Peter Ridsdale faced similar allegations, having just released a video entitled *My Leeds United*. Had the leaders of the club lost their focus? Looking back, it seems preposterous that O'Leary was allowed to write the book at all, never mind release it in the middle of a vital season!

After a week spent licking their wounds from Cardiff, Leeds returned to Premiership action with a trip to Newcastle, a club who were challenging Aston Villa and Leicester for the title of 'Leeds United's Bogey Team'. Leeds started the day on top of the table, two points clear of Manchester United, Arsenal and Newcastle, but they were leapfrogged by the Geordies who triumphed 3-1 at St James' Park, just three weeks after they'd won 4-3 at Elland Road. For the second season running the Toon Army had completed the double over Leeds, and this was a chastening defeat. Bobby Robson had spent a fraction of what O'Leary had, but with Kieron Dyer, Craig Bellamy, Nolberto Solano and Laurent Robert rampaging through midfield, Alan Shearer leading the line and Gary Speed pulling the strings, his team looked a cut above. Despite taking the lead within a minute of kick-off, Leeds were battered from the second minute to the last. Their plight wasn't helped by an own goal from Duberry (deputising for the injured Ferdinand) and an idiotic red card for Danny Mills (for blatantly kicking out at Craig Bellamy), but these incidents were reflective of the battering Leeds had taken, rather than the reason they lost. Perhaps it was wrong to refer to Newcastle as a bogey team: they simply looked a better team.

The Whites were just a point behind the Premiership leaders, but David O'Leary's programme notes before the next match revealed the stark reality of life at Leeds United. 'We went to Newcastle in first place in the league, but psychologically, with all that's happened over the last couple of months, it felt a bit as though we were down at the bottom and hadn't had a win in 20 games.'

Regardless of what was happening behind the scenes, Elland Road was rocking for the next instalment of the Leeds–Arsenal rivalry. Confidence on the terraces was high, with Ferdinand back to partner Woodgate in defence, and rose another notch when Robbie Fowler planted a lovely header into the South Stand net in the opening minutes. Fowler had now scored seven goals in ten games since signing for Leeds, but with him paired with Viduka up front, Leeds lacked some pace, and had lost much of their intensity. Never had that been more apparent than on this occasion. The Arsenal defence, so used to being tormented at Elland Road, were barely troubled for the remainder of the game. There was no vibrancy or harrying to deal with as United failed to press home their advantage, and it was no surprise when Robert Pires struck a brilliant equaliser right on half-time. The second half was a lifeless affair, with both teams hindered by blustery conditions and unwilling to risk losing a point. David O'Leary's post-match words summarised an underwhelming occasion, 'I didn't think either team deserved to win.'

While their rivals toiled in the FA Cup there was a weekend off for Leeds, who returned to action with a midweek trip to Chelsea. Champions Manchester United were now back on top of the Premiership after a great run of form since Alex Ferguson had reversed his decision to retire, although a defeat at Anfield reminded everyone that they were still a team in transition, and their rivals had a great chance to dethrone them. Leeds had slipped down to fifth but had the chance to pull level at the top with a victory at Stamford Bridge.

Paul and I bunked off school for the afternoon and Fan, my brother's friend who was a few years older than us, drove us down to London. Well, that was the plan, until disaster struck halfway down the M1. Throughout my childhood, literally every match, home and away, my dad would play a trick on me and pretend to have forgotten the tickets when parking up at the ground. I adopted this half-hearted wind-up and would always play the same trick on my mates. They never fell for it, but when I started panicking as we passed Leicester, they suspected something wasn't right; why was I playing the trick so early in the journey? I really had forgotten the tickets. They realised it was no joke when I called the ticket office to explain our plight, but there was nothing the club could do to help us. Fan turned the car around and we headed back to Yorkshire while debating what action to take, and in the end we had to abort the mission. At best we would have made it down for the second half but, having already driven for two hours, Fan really couldn't face driving back to Harrogate to then go again, and neither could we. The game was live on Sky anyway, so with our tails between our legs we all went home and watched it on telly.

By the end of the game Paul and Fan were thankful for my act of lameness. We weren't the only ones who didn't turn up at Stamford Bridge: none of the Leeds players did either, and not having to drive home afterwards was a comforting consolation for a terrible performance. United conceded after just two minutes, were 2-0 down after half an hour and didn't muster their first effort on goal until the 65th minute. To rub salt into the wounds, Jonathan Woodgate pulled his hamstring on the stroke of half-time and would be unavailable for six weeks. Almost as alarming was seeing David O'Leary sporting two black eyes following plastic surgery on his nose. In isolation this would not have been a newsworthy procedure but instead, perhaps unfairly, it was taken as further evidence that the manager was losing sight of the job in hand.

Four days later Liverpool arrived at Elland Road and romped to a humiliating 4-0 victory. Leeds's title bid was in tatters and there were no positives to be taken – nobody could have imagined a worse start to 2002. In back-to-back games against four of their title rivals, Leeds had taken one point from a possible 12 and were now down to sixth in the table, nine points behind the leaders and out of the FA Cup. They had been in a similar position at the same stage last season, but this was more concerning; Leeds were totally bereft of confidence, energy or togetherness, on and off the pitch.

All was not lost but there was no time to waste in getting back to form, and the following week Leeds looked set for a confidence-boosting 2-1 win at Middlesbrough until Dean Windass fired home a late equaliser to extinguish any flickering hopes of winning the Premiership. I couldn't believe how abruptly things had turned. After the FA Cup defeat at Cardiff, I had found solace in a lack of distraction from the league, but now I craved a distraction and was grateful for the resumption of the UEFA Cup campaign. A good run in Europe could kick-start Leeds's Premiership season, and momentum could be built with fixtures coming thick and fast. On the flip side, elimination would confirm another trophyless season for David O'Leary.

Leeds United 0-1 PSV Eindhoven
Thursday, 28 February 2002
Elland Road – 7.45pm
UEFA Cup Fourth Round, Second Leg

When league form deserted Leeds in the first half of the previous season, the bad performances and results were at least sprinkled with good ones, mostly in European competition. In the first half of this season, it had been the other way around. Amid a solid league campaign, O'Leary's team had managed to navigate themselves through the opening rounds of the UEFA Cup, but it was far from plain sailing. Perhaps we shouldn't have been surprised. Before the campaign began, O'Leary was pouring scorn on the UEFA Cup, claiming it needed a facelift to give teams an incentive to win it. Hardly the motivation the players needed when they were preparing to face European minnows, having become accustomed to mixing with Europe's elite.

Leeds kicked off their UEFA Cup campaign in Madeira, losing 1-0 to Maritimo as they had done in George Graham's final match in charge. They recovered well in the second leg, winning 3-0 to set up a tricky second-round clash with French side Troyes. Despite racing into a 4-1 lead just 46 minutes into the first leg at Elland Road, Leeds were on the verge of elimination in France, before Robbie Keane's 77th-minute goal earned a nail-biting 6-5 aggregate victory. In the third round Leeds struggled again, trailing nearly all night against Grasshoppers, before late goals from Ian Harte and Alan Smith meant Leeds left Switzerland with a 2-1 lead and a foot in the next round. The second leg was no walk in the park, but with a nervy 2-2 draw the Whites progressed to the last 16, where they would face formidable opposition in Dutch champions PSV Eindhoven.

United's previous trip to Eindhoven ended in a comprehensive 8-3 aggregate defeat in the mid-90s, and while there was no Ronaldo in the PSV line-up this time around, the opposition still boasted an abundance of quality players who were constantly linked with moves to the Premiership: Marc van Bommel, Mateja Kezman, Dennis Rommedahl, Kevin Hofland, Wilfred Bouma and the wonderfully named Jan Vennegoor of Hesselink. Leeds would need to rekindle something near their top form in order to progress; if they did they were lined up to face Rangers in the quarter-finals, in a re-run of the 1992 'Battle of Britain'.

For the first leg, in the atmospheric Philips Stadion, O'Leary reverted to his trusty Champions League eleven, a refreshing move that was enabled thanks to an easing in the injury list, and the fact Robbie Fowler was cup-tied. It brought a much-improved performance. In the opening stages Mark Viduka was denied twice in a minute by goal-line clearances, while at the other end Matteo cleared one off the line for Leeds, with the help of his arm, unbeknown to the officials. After a breathless first half, the second half was much more cautious, with both teams seemingly happy with a clean sheet, content to decide the tie from a standing start at Elland Road the following week.

In the driving Yorkshire rain Leeds were made to attack the Kop in the first half, and just like in the first leg they made a great start and should have taken the lead. Mark Viduka was denied from close range by the goalkeeper, then set up Harry Kewell whose lovely effort clipped the post. Moments later the two Australians combined again, this time forging a golden chance when Viduka's cut-back found Kewell alone in the box and faced with an open goal. Astonishingly, Kewell flashed the ball over the bar. Viduka was proving a real handful and teed up the final chance of the half for Eirik Bakke, but the Norwegian's blistering long-range drive was brilliantly tipped over the bar. It was tough not to be disappointed to be heading into half-time without an advantage (especially with Leeds attacking the opposite end in the second half), but it had been great to see O'Leary's team playing like their old selves again.

With the tie finely poised, the second half was once again a cagey affair, and exactly as I'd hoped would happen in the previous season's Champions League semi-final in Valencia, the visitors took control as the hosts became more and more wary of a killer away goal. Jan Vennegoor of Hesselink saw two great chances go begging but, in the 90th minute with extra time beckoning, it was third time lucky for the big Dutchman, who dived to head home the winning goal from practically on the goal line after Theo Lucius had struck the bar. Leeds were out. There would be no Battle of Britain, and no trophy. Yet another hammer blow in a season that had unravelled at breakneck speed.

Everton 0-0 Leeds United

Sunday, 3 March 2002

Goodison Park – 3pm

FA Barclaycard Premiership

From leading the Premiership on New Year's Day, Leeds had now gone two full months without winning a match. I had never known such a catastrophic collapse, perhaps it had never happened before? A 13-point gap to leaders Manchester United was insignificant compared to the nine-point gap to the Champions League spots; in fact, things had got so bad that talk had turned to the Intertoto Cup, with David O'Leary publicly airing his annoyance that Peter Ridsdale had applied for the competition in case his struggling team failed to finish in the top six. He had no right to be upset. There now seemed to be no limit to how bad the season could become.

With ten games remaining, Manchester United, Arsenal, Liverpool and Newcastle were in a riveting four-horse race for the title and it hurt so much that Leeds were nowhere to be seen. All hope and enthusiasm had seeped out of me, and I was so disconsolate that on the Saturday night before Everton away I sold my match ticket to Joe for £5. I was drunk at the time, but it speaks volumes that a fiver was the most I could get for the ticket, having spent 20 minutes touting it around while waiting for a taxi outside Creation in Leeds city centre. In the cold light of day there were no regrets, except from Joe, who didn't even bother going himself.

Leeds were 11 points behind fourth-placed Newcastle by the time they kicked off at Goodison, and another drab 0-0 draw cut the gap to ten. Typical of the season, Leeds also lost their two centre-backs: Ferdinand to a back injury sustained on the morning of the match, Matteo to a red card handed out by that man Andy D'Urso, Leeds's sixth red card of the season. United were now ten games without a win, and while I sat at home in silent protest, more bothered about my hangover than missing the match, the travelling fans at Goodison made their concerns loud and clear at the final whistle. Their fury wasn't directed at the players though, nor the manager or board; it was directed at the head coach, Brian Kidd.

Kidd had been running the Thorp Arch academy until the day after the 4-1 victory at Anderlecht which booked Leeds's place in the Champions League quarter-finals. He was promoted so that O'Leary could 'step back from training and concentrate on higher levels of management', and while many fans were uncomfortable with the decision, they accepted it, with the club beyond criticism due to results on the pitch. Now that the results had turned, the anger was released. Kidd was a legend at bitter rivals Manchester United and was hated by association, but apart from this, the appointment undermined club legend and assistant manager Eddie Gray, the man who nurtured the Thorp Arch graduates. The fans also felt the style of football had changed since Kidd joined the coaching team, and surmised that the players were happier working with Eddie Gray and probably weren't too happy to see their old mentor silently demoted. O'Leary was quick to point out that Gray's role hadn't changed, but there could be no denying that Brian Kidd was now O'Leary's right-hand man, and Kidd was always lodged between the manager and his assistant in the dugout.

After the final whistle at Goodison Park, Peter Ridsdale marched across the pitch to remonstrate with the Leeds fans, while O'Leary denounced them in his post-match interviews: 'I am disgusted with the fans. Have you heard so much lunacy as fans wanting to get the number two out? Brian is a soft target.' The following day the players called a press conference – represented by Rio Ferdinand, Alan Smith and Nigel Martyn – to confirm their backing for Kidd, defend his commitment to Leeds, and to threaten the fans. 'If someone like Brian Kidd could be driven out of this club,' warned captain Ferdinand, 'it would make us think, "is this where we want our futures to lie?"'

Monday's public backing was a short-lived reprieve for Kidd. On Tuesday the 'soft target' took another hit when David O'Leary announced he would be returning to the training pitch. Although he maintained that Kidd was a top coach and criticism of him was unfair, O'Leary believed he was too lenient with the players, who were allowed to get away with 'a bit too much' when he wasn't at training himself.

The situation had become toxic, the whole club was disjointed. Players, staff and fans were all taking swipes at each other and we were at the stage where O'Leary couldn't come out of this looking good. If results picked up, he would face questions on why he had taken a step back from training in the first place. If results didn't pick up, it would look like he had lost the dressing room. He could even lose his job.

Leeds United 3-4 Manchester United
Saturday, 30 March 2002
Elland Road – 12pm
FA Barclaycard Premiership

As it happened, O'Leary's return to the training pitch did succeed in waking Leeds from their slumber. Three days after the Everton game the ten-match winless run came to an end with a 2-0 victory over Ipswich, then another home win followed, 3-1 over Blackburn. Next up was my sixth and final trip to Filbert Street, which was due for demolition in the summer. Leicester would be moving into their new Walkers Stadium as a First Division club with their relegation now a formality, and Leeds waved them goodbye with a routine 2-0 victory. There was no racism, no penalty misses, no mocking the dead, no red cards and no personal abuse for me; the demons were laid to rest. I left Filbert Street feeling on top of the world again: Leeds had now won three on the bounce, Fowler had netted in all three games, and Alan Smith had finished the game wearing the captain's armband, something I'd always wanted to see (Smith would always be my choice of captain on *Championship Manager*).

Suddenly, the race for the Champions League was back on. Heading into the Easter weekend, Leeds were just two points behind Newcastle, who had failed to keep pace in the title race and were now stuttering. However, a stonking 6-2 thrashing of Everton on Good Friday piled the pressure back on Leeds, whose run-in commenced the following day with Manchester United's visit to Elland Road. I dreamt of a victory that would confirm that Leeds had turned the corner (while denting Ferguson's title push), but the reality was another worst nightmare.

After only eight minutes Woodgate and Mills got in each other's way when faced with a harmless long ball, a calamity that set the tone and set the visitors on their way. Within seconds Paul Scholes was left completely free in the middle of the box to thump Silvestre's cut-back past Nigel Martyn. Leeds rallied, and equalised when Bowyer's excellent burst through midfield culminated in an even better pass to split the defence, which was finished off exquisitely by Mark Viduka. That was as good as it got for Leeds. The players ran around like headless chickens and were torn to shreds by a team too good to be ruffled by such a chaotic performance. Seth Johnson was lost in midfield, as was Smith, leaving Batty and Bowyer with too much to compensate for. Ferguson's men regained the lead when Solskjaer pounced on a rebound quicker than the defenders, and with the away fans still singing his name, Solskjaer added another.

The debacle became humiliating early in the second half. David Beckham was a wide midfielder whose weakness was a lack of pace, but minutes after the restart he ran almost the full length of the pitch down the right wing while Ian Harte chased in vain behind him. Beckham squared for Ryan Giggs, who tapped in the fourth. It was painfully easy. Moments later, with our enemies cheering their team's every pass, Ronny

Johnsen headed against the bar when he really should have made it 5-1.

At this point I was praying for the final whistle, but when it came it was the away fans who were relieved to hear it. On the hour mark, Ian Harte whipped a beautiful 30-yard free kick into the top corner, and when Lee Bowyer diverted Fowler's fluffed shot into the net it was game on at 4-3. With the last kick of the game another Ian Harte free kick beat Barthez all ends up, but fizzed agonisingly wide of the post. Leeds had restored some pride, and the last 30 minutes suggested there remained some fight in O'Leary's team, but the first hour of the match had exposed the truth – this was a team in crisis. Worse still, a club in crisis.

On Easter Monday, two days after the Manchester United defeat, Leeds travelled to White Hart Lane and lost 2-1, putting an end to any lingering hopes of Champions League qualification and leaving the Whites in sixth spot. They bounced back from their disastrous Easter weekend with a solid 2-0 victory over Sunderland, but within 48 hours O'Leary was faced with yet more off-field ignominy, as Jonathan Woodgate was ruled out for the rest of the season after breaking his jaw while out drinking in Middlesbrough. Keen to avoid any further controversy, the club swept the incident under the carpet and accepted Woodgate's version of events – 'it was just horseplay between mates' – but it was another blatant example of the lack of discipline, respect and professionalism within the club, from a player who was already on a 'final warning'. O'Leary refused to answer questions on the matter, then gave away his feelings in his next programme notes, before contradicting himself within the same sentence: 'I was totally disgusted by what happened, but I have dealt with it internally and that's the way things should be done.'

As the season reached its conclusion, O'Leary's programme notes reflected a desperate and deluded manager. It was as sad to read as it was maddening. What had happened to the breath of fresh air who had reignited the club? Defending his team's position in the table, O'Leary pointed to the 'tremendous resources and spending power' of Newcastle and Chelsea which had enabled them to join Manchester United, Arsenal and Liverpool at the top of English football, yet Leeds had a greater net spend over the past three seasons than Newcastle and Chelsea combined! In fact, no Premiership club had spent more on transfers (total or net outlay) than Leeds United over the course of O'Leary's three full seasons in the job. Regardless, O'Leary continued to portray his team as plucky young upstarts who were doing tremendously well just to be rubbing shoulders with the 'big boys'. 'I think we are firmly established in the top six these days, and have a young and improving squad.' The sentiment was all wrong.

A strand of dignity was saved as Leeds secured UEFA Cup qualification with a relatively strong end to the season. The Whites won four of their last five games, but the performances weren't impressive and they only scored five goals in the process. Prior to the final game of the season, they also suffered a degrading 4-1 defeat at home to Celtic in Gary Kelly's testimonial, a result which may have been immaterial, but was not insignificant. O'Leary had fielded a strong side and taken a battering; it was the polar opposite of the swashbuckling victory at Celtic Park three years earlier. There was no spark left in his team, all the joy had been sucked out of them.

Leeds United 1-0 Middlesbrough

Saturday, 11 May 2002
Elland Road – 3pm
FA Barclaycard Premiership

'As we stand on the brink of an exciting new season, I can't help looking forward to our final game, against Middlesbrough next May, and hoping for a big celebration.' When writing the opening paragraph in his first programme notes of the season, David O'Leary could never have imagined the sorry state the club would be in when the Middlesbrough game came around.

The season had been anything but exciting. Leeds had been dull or disappointing for the most part, scoring fewer goals than George Graham's bargain-basement team had managed, despite boasting five top-class forwards in Mark Viduka, Robbie Fowler, Alan Smith, Robbie Keane and Harry Kewell (with Michael Bridges in the treatment room collecting a decent wage too). The fearlessness that O'Leary had wanted his team to play with had been shackled by the manager himself; now Leeds seemed more focused on not getting beat than winning matches. 'I have seen young coaches trying to change football, only to find the realities of the game changing them, which is always a shame.' Alex Ferguson's comments came four matches after O'Leary landed the Leeds job; four years later they sounded prophetic.

It feels wrong that I wasn't there to witness the final hoorah. Instead, I was busy living out O'Leary's prophesy by partaking in a big celebration, my brother's 21st birthday party in Florence, 1,000 miles from Elland Road. A 1-0 victory over Middlesbrough, coupled with Chelsea's final-day defeat to Aston Villa, secured another top-five finish for Leeds, their fifth in a row, and an 18th clean sheet – no team had kept more. That was scant consolation for a terribly disappointing season. Nevertheless, on the traditional end-of-season lap of honour the fans were in fine voice and gave generous support to the manager and his players. There was no expectation that they were waving goodbye to the O'Leary era.

Over the next six weeks David O'Leary unwittingly dug his own grave. Reports of player unrest were already rife when he labelled Danny Mills 'a liability' for his poor disciplinary record, on the day he was called up to England's World Cup squad (Mills had missed ten games through suspension over the

2001/02 season). Even outside of the now infamous book, this was not the first example of the manager publicly criticising his players and Mills hit back, comparing O'Leary unfavourably with other top managers who would apparently keep such comments in-house. It didn't help perceptions of a split camp when Lee Bowyer rejected a new contract and was placed back on the transfer list, although this could surely be traced back to the falling-out with Peter Ridsdale in the aftermath of the trial, rather than issues with the manager who had backed him so relentlessly.

O'Leary's relationship with his players was under the microscope, his relationship with the fans had become prickly, and his relationship with the board was stretched too. Their patience finally snapped at the end of June. Amid reports of Manchester United's interest in Rio Ferdinand, O'Leary claimed his employers could not expect Champions League qualification in the coming season if they sold his captain. It was the final straw. Later in the week, on Thursday, 27 June, it was announced that David O'Leary had left Leeds United by mutual consent. Just over an hour later it was confirmed that he had been sacked. It was huge news, and Sky Sports News talked about nothing else all day. I was stunned and upset, but also a little excited. It seemed a harsh decision but maybe it was the catalyst Leeds needed, and I presumed the club would have the pick of the world's top managers who would surely get this hugely talented squad back to its best. Finally, we might realise our potential.

O'Leary was left shocked and devastated by his sacking. He felt let down by his chairman, a man he considered a friend, and took the decision to heart, although these feelings were initially buried under dignified and magnanimous parting comments: 'I've tried to do the best I can to run the club and I've had great support. The fans were fantastic and I've tried to do my best for them. I went in to clear a few things up before I went on holiday and the chairman says I've got the sack.'

Peter Ridsdale too tried to remain respectful and would not talk about specific factors, namely the ramifications of *that* book. Instead, he pointed to 'the pressures of some of the off-field incidents' when explaining the board's decision, words which seemed to encourage sympathy towards the manager for everything he had to put up with. A little later Ridsdale would point to the simple fact that O'Leary had failed to meet the objectives of his job, and eventually he confirmed the widely reported story that the views of the players had been canvassed prior to the sacking, and their responses had convinced the board that O'Leary couldn't remain in the job. It was the allegations of a split camp that upset O'Leary the most, and drove an eternal wedge between the men who had taken Leeds to the brink of glory: 'He [Ridsdale] has stated that I will remain his friend, but I doubt that I will ever be able to speak to him again.'

It may have ended prematurely, and we would never know what might have become of the likely lads, but the O'Leary era had ultimately ended in failure. All that hope, all that expectation, all those enthralling occasions at Elland Road, all that adulation every time O'Leary headed out of the dugout: it had all come to nowt.

ACT V

What Became of the Likely Lads?

Season 2002/03 – The Crash

FOLLOWING DAVID O'Leary's sacking, everything unravelled spectacularly at Elland Road. His successor was Terry Venables, 'the best manager we could have possibly got' according to Peter Ridsdale. He turned out to be the worst.

Of the managers they couldn't have possibly got, Martin O'Neill was again top of Ridsdale's shortlist but this time rejected his advances with little fuss; his loyalties lay with Glasgow Celtic. Another high-calibre candidate was Guus Hiddink, who had just led South Korea to the semi-finals of the World Cup, but the former Real Madrid manager was already set on returning to PSV so was never a viable option. Nor was Argentina's revolutionary manager Marcelo Bielsa, who retained his job despite a shameful World Cup group-stage exit. So the job went to ITV's leading pundit, 'El Tel', whose managerial career had stalled since leading England in Euro '96. In fact, he hadn't completed a full season in club management since the birth of the Premier League.

Venables wasn't helped by the financial stress the club was under, but it really shouldn't have hindered him all that much either. Rio Ferdinand was sold to bitter rivals Manchester United for £30m two weeks into his tenure, and Robbie Keane joined Tottenham for £7m two weeks into the season, but Leeds already had an abundance of top-class centre-backs and an embarrassment of riches up front. There was also an unexpected boost when transfer-listed Lee Bowyer rejected a £9m move to Liverpool, sparing me the same emotions Gianni had felt when Fowler came to Leeds. 'It didn't feel right,' explained Bowyer, and just when I thought I couldn't love him more, I did.

You could even have argued that Venables's squad was the strongest Leeds had ever had. Having not kicked a ball in the previous season, the return of Michael Bridges and Lucas Radebe effectively replaced Keane and Ferdinand, and Stephen McPhail was back to bolster the midfield, along with England international Nick Barmby, who joined from Liverpool for £2.75m. Whether stronger or weaker, the squad certainly possessed enough quality and depth to mount a sustained challenge at the top of the league, and the new era got off to the perfect start with comprehensive three-goal victories over Manchester City and West Brom, with Leeds playing some marvellous football. In fact, they'd played so well that I took £100 out of a cash machine and marched into the bookies, to bet the lot on Leeds to beat Sunderland in the next game. Unbeknown to me, you couldn't make such a bet on a game that wasn't televised and the bookies refused to take my money. This let-off didn't stop me from spitting feathers after a dismal 1-0 defeat. Leeds had been so passive, I hated what I saw, but three games later, inside the hateful cauldron of Elland Road, Venables did what O'Leary could never do and kicked Alex Ferguson's butt. The only goal was headed home in the second half by Harry Kewell, made even sweeter as Rio Ferdinand could take a fair portion of the blame for leaving the Australian free in the box. It was a perfect afternoon, and Leeds United were back on top of the Premiership.

It proved to be a false dawn. An abrupt drop in form intensified the unrest in the camp and bewilderment on the terraces which had been lingering since the beginning of Venables's reign. One of the fundamental problems was the new manager's ethos, which contrasted with the characteristics that had made the team special. The 'up and at 'em' approach was thrown in the bin, replaced by a slow and patient 'continental' style. The plodding football and 4-5-1 formation narked the fans and players alike, but worse still was Venables's dishonourable man-management. Firstly, he had controversially axed the club's greatest ever goalkeeper, Nigel Martyn, who was punished for missing the pre-season tour of Australia in order to have a short break after World Cup duty with England. Venables froze out another club legend in David Batty, and started Olivier Dacourt just four times before famously telling the press he'd drive the Frenchman to Italy himself if it speeded up his protracted move to Roma. The man who had taken Dacourt's place in the team was Paul Okon, who had been released by Middlesbrough after failing to impress on loan at Watford.

By mid-December Leeds were stranded in the lower reaches of the Premiership, having collected just five points out of a possible 33 since beating Manchester United. They were knocked out of the UEFA Cup by Malaga, out of the League Cup by Sheffield United, and with Champions League qualification clearly out of the equation for the third year running, so began the fire sale. Leeds's plight wasn't helped by the introduction of the transfer window. With only a month available to sell players, Ridsdale couldn't afford to play for time and the stench of desperation emanating from the club was magnified. As a result, Robbie Fowler, Olivier Dacourt, Lee Bowyer and Jonathan Woodgate were sold for less than £20m combined, when six months earlier the club would have expected upwards of £50m for these players. Bad management had played a part too, of course; Dacourt had been turned into a leper by Venables, and Bowyer had only six months remaining on his contract. These departures depleted and demoralised the squad. There were still enough quality players to form a top team but Venables wasn't the man to mould them into one.

The sale of Woodgate to Newcastle was the final straw for the fans: they were furious. In the aftermath of the transfer Peter Ridsdale called a press conference, one for the ages. With Terry Venables sat beside him, doing his best to look bothered but clearly waiting to be pushed out of Elland Road himself, Ridsdale attempted to appease the supporters. 'Should we have spent so heavily in the past? Probably not.' *Probably* not? Bloody hell Peter! He was just about to deliver the line that would define the era for all eternity, but the way Ridsdale looked up from his notes and into the camera to deliver those two words, with the acceptance of wrongdoing plastered all over his face, was the highlight for me. 'But we lived the dream, we enjoyed the dream, and only by taking these steps can we rekindle the dream.' Ridsdale's words implied that the excessive spending had at least delivered some glorious times, but it masked a deeper truth: the excessive spending had ruined what Leeds United had built organically. The keepers of the club had trampled all over the flowers that blossomed so beautifully, ten years after the seeds had been planted by Howard Wilkinson.

It wasn't just the players who fled Elland Road. I headed off to Florence with Paul in what was supposed to be a gap year before university but ended up being a four-month jolly before returning to work in my dad's business. Would I have gone if Leeds had been doing well? Probably not. In the pre-digital age, I was only able to track Leeds's results by phoning my dad or visiting an internet café, but both of those cost money that I couldn't afford with a limited budget. The cheapest way was to steal a quick glance at the English papers, though they didn't arrive until two days after the match. I was completely cut adrift of the thing I had obsessed over my whole life, though it couldn't have happened at a better time. I hated Venables, and I hated what the directors had done to my club and our incredible young team.

By the middle of March Leeds were battling for their Premiership lives. They were on another stinking run and had collected only four points from a possible 24 when Venables was finally sacked. It was a parting gift from Ridsdale, who himself was sacked by the plc ten days later, with the club's debt reportedly standing at £103m.

Peter Reid was the man entrusted to save Leeds from relegation, a manager whose stock was still high after a successful period at Sunderland. Reid's first game ended in defeat at Anfield, but his first win was only days away, a stunning 6-1 victory at Charlton. Still, on the penultimate weekend of the season Leeds headed to Highbury tied with West Ham and Bolton on 41 points. One of the three would go down and Leeds were only above the relegation zone on goal difference. The game was just as big for Arsenal, who needed a win to keep the title race alive, and the match was screened live in our local Irish pub, The Fiddlers Elbow, only the second Leeds match I'd been able to watch since arriving in Florence. A classic, topsy-turvy battle was won in the 88th minute by Mark Viduka's stunning strike, the tenth of his 11 goals scored in Reid's eight matches in charge. Just like in 1999, Leeds had handed Manchester United the Premiership title, but at least this time it wasn't for nothing: it had secured their Premiership status.

Season 2003/04 – Into the Abyss

In the summer of 2003, the clear-out continued. Harry Kewell, Nigel Martyn and Danny Mills all left, while Michael Bridges and Stephen McPhail would follow them out of the door in the winter, bringing in the handsome sum of £5.5m for the lot. By now the squad had been decimated, but it still contained many of the players who had starred in the Champions League run – Robinson, Kelly, Harte, Radebe, Matteo, Batty, Bakke, Viduka and Smith – plus Barmby, Wilcox, Duberry and Johnson, and a new generation of exciting youngsters from the Thorp Arch academy: Scott Carson, Matthew Kilgallon, Frazer Richardson, Aaron Lennon and James Milner.

It was a good starting point for a season of consolidation, but the squad was contaminated by five useless loanees brought in from France, plus the disastrous Brazilian World Cup-winning loanee, Roque Junior. The only permanent signing was Jody Morris, a free transfer from Chelsea who was both useless and disastrous. Jermaine Pennant was an excellent signing on loan from Arsenal, but the squad would probably have been better off without any additions at all.

Leeds made a poor start, and by the beginning of November they had sunk to the bottom of the Premiership after a 6-1 humiliation at Portsmouth. It was no surprise that Peter Reid was immediately sacked: his team had lost seven of their last eight games, conceding 25 goals in the process. So, it was left to Eddie Gray to try and save Leeds; the man who had played such a prominent role in the realisation of Wilkinson's ten-year plan, the man who moulded 'O'Leary's babies' into the stars that shone so brightly that they lit up Europe.

Eddie went back to basics, the loanees rarely featured and there was an upturn in performances and results. The upturn coincided with my return to Elland Road, though not in the usual capacity. With Paul still in Florence, Lewis and Joe at university, and my dad in his second Elland Road exile, I had nobody to go to games with and, more significantly, nobody to drive me there. By the time Eddie took over I'd only been to two games all season, but the stars aligned as my new driving instructor was a turnstile monkey at Elland Road and informed me of some vacancies. I applied for a job, nailed the interview, and passed my driving test in time to take my place in the South Stand turnstiles for the visit of Chelsea at the start of December, a bottom vs top clash.

I was still counting up my ticket stubs when Leeds went ahead thanks to a wonder-goal by Jermaine Pennant, and when I finally made it into the Kop (25 minutes after kick-off) the atmosphere was as loud as I had ever heard it. Perhaps it only felt like that because it had been so long since I'd heard the old ground in full voice, but I was blown away as 'We are champions, champions of Europe' swept around the ground; it was incredible. Damien Duff eventually earned Chelsea a point, but Leeds were off the bottom and had proved they could still mix it with the top teams. The following week Leeds surrendered a 2-0 lead at home to Fulham but, in a stirring finish, newly appointed captain Dom Matteo headed an 88th-minute winner to send Elland Road into raptures. The victory took Leeds within a point of escaping the relegation zone and for the first time I felt confident that Eddie would steer us to safety.

With Viduka and Smith up front, Leeds always had a chance of scoring, but while Eddie's team lacked no heart, in midfield they were weak. An out-of-position Matteo was the only constant presence, partnered mainly by Seth Johnson, with injury restricting Batty, McPhail and Bakke to less than a dozen appearances each. The experience of Wilcox and Barmby would have been helpful out wide, but injury limited them to four starts combined. Instead, Leeds had 17-year-old James Milner on the right and 20-year-old Jermaine Pennant on the left, both lively and dangerous, but both very raw. The centre of defence was an even bigger problem. Michael Duberry played exactly half of the Premiership matches, making him the most-used centre-back by a distance. With 13 appearances Stephen Caldwell was next on the list, having only joined the club on loan in February. Injuries had taken their toll on Lucas Radebe, who would be 35 by the end of the season, while at 19, Matthew Kilgallon was too young to rely on in a relegation scrap. Gary Kelly was consistent at right-back, but Ian Harte's confidence had fallen off a cliff. This was not the left-back who almost fired Leeds to European glory, and he struggled to hold down a regular place in the team.

Following their mini-revival Leeds lost six games in a row after Christmas, but just when all hope was slipping away there came another uplift. Victories at Elland Road against relegation rivals Wolves, Man City and Leicester were as exhilarating as they were vital, and confidence was further boosted by draws against Manchester United and Liverpool. After winning another huge six-pointer at Blackburn Rovers, Leeds remained in the final relegation spot but were level on points with Blackburn and Portsmouth, and within two points of Manchester City, with just six games to go. Momentum was on their side and I truly believed Eddie was going to pull off the great escape, but in the next game Leeds were denied victory by a wonder-goal from 17-year-old Wayne Rooney, and a string of wonder-saves from none other than Nigel Martyn, on his first return to Elland Road since his free transfer to Everton. On the same night, unexpected wins for their relegation rivals put Leeds firmly back on the ropes, and after a 5-0 thrashing against Arsenal's invincibles, the next game was do or die, against Portsmouth at Elland Road.

The match was on *Super Sunday* and victory would draw Leeds level on points with 17th-placed Manchester City (they'd need to win 31-0 to overtake them on goal difference) and within two points of 16th-placed Portsmouth. The game was so critical that I couldn't bring myself to miss a big chunk of the first half counting ticket stubs. Instead, I skived off work and simply turned up at the gate minutes after kick-off, flashed my badge and took my place in the Kop just in time to see Yakubu open the scoring for Pompey. LuaLua made it 2-0 in the second half, and while Ian Harte's penalty set up a grandstand finale, Harry Redknapp's team held firm to secure their Premiership status for another season and send Leeds to the brink.

The following Sunday, Leeds headed to Bolton on the verge of relegation. Manchester City had beaten Newcastle the previous day to move six points clear of Leeds, who only had three games left and a much inferior goal difference. Mark Viduka's penalty put Leeds ahead, although my joy at the goal was overshadowed by my fury at the referee for failing to send off the defender who had bundled Smith to the floor when clean through. I just knew it would cost us. Six minutes later it was Leeds who were down to ten men, with Viduka sent off for a second bookable offence. So typical of Leeds's luck. The ten men crumbled to a 4-1 defeat and all hope was lost. Leeds United were relegated, three years after almost winning the Champions League.

And there was still more humiliation to come. After the final home game of the season, a 3-3 draw with Charlton, the Leeds fans invaded the Elland Road pitch, not in protest, but in adulation for their cult hero, Alan Smith. No player had ever been given such a send-off in the history of the club, but within a week Smith had stabbed us in the back. Before the Charlton game he had spoken of his preference to move abroad so that it would be easier to come back to Leeds once we were back in the Premiership, and a few years earlier he had told *Soccer AM* that the one club he'd never play for was Manchester United. It was all lies. It was soon revealed that Smith wanted to stay in England and had refused to sign for anybody not offering Champions League football. A move to Old Trafford was on the cards, the one move that would make it impossible for him to ever return to Leeds. In his final outing in a Leeds shirt – away to Chelsea – Smith flicked 'the Vs' at the same supporters who had paraded him around Elland Road on their shoulders a week earlier, in response to chants of, 'Sign for scum, you won't be back'. Smith duly signed for the enemy for £7m, although as a sign of goodwill he donated his £1m signing-on fee to the club he apparently still loved.

The End of Leeds United AFC

The Leeds fans had been through the wringer, and as they prepared for life outside the Premiership there was no surprise to see more players leaving. Robinson, Viduka, Harte, Matteo, Wilcox, Batty and Duberry brought in the paltry sum of £5.5m, and there was still time for a pinch more salt to be rubbed into the wounds as James Milner, the young star who Leeds were apparently building their promotion team around, was sold to Newcastle. In the end, £5m was too much to turn down for a club that hadn't raised close to what they had expected from selling off their assets, and who were still paying a large portion of their departed players' astronomical wages.

On the pitch, Leeds consolidated in the newly branded Coca-Cola Championship, but off the pitch the local consortium who bought the club in March 2004 had taken it to the brink of extinction by January 2005. Of all people it was Ken Bates who saved Leeds United with a £10m takeover, ironic as Bates was once quoted as saying, 'I shall not rest until Leeds United are kicked out of the Football League.' The club's debt was now around £25m and Bates fought fire with fire, spending handsomely to build a squad that came within 90 minutes of a return to the Premiership. Victory in the 2006 play-off final would have solved all their financial problems, but after a dismal 3-0 defeat to Watford, Leeds went into freefall.

A slow start to the 2006/07 season saw manager Kevin Blackwell replaced by Dennis Wise, a former Chelsea midfielder who was as unpopular with the Leeds fans as his children's godfather, Ken Bates. The new manager's confrontational style added to a toxic mood in the squad and on the terraces, culminating in relegation to the third tier of English football for the first time in the club's history. With unserviceable debts of around £35m, Ken Bates voluntarily put the club into administration, and Leeds United AFC was history.

The club were almost liquidated entirely, but after a summer of legal wrangling, Leeds United FC were granted their 'golden share' to compete in the Football League just a week before the new season began. The city still had a football club, but another decade would pass before the good times returned to Elland Road.

O'Leary's Likely Lads

Nigel Martyn
Never played for the club again after O'Leary left. Joined Everton after a year on the bench, and made 100 appearances for them before injury forced his retirement aged 38. Named by David Moyes as his greatest ever signing.

Gary Kelly
Retired at the tender age of 32 as a one-club man after Leeds were relegated to League One, having made 531 appearances for the club.

Ian Harte
Moved to Levante in Spain after Leeds's relegation from the Premiership. Never recaptured the form of his early 20s, spending the remainder of his career mostly in the English lower leagues.

Lucas Radebe
Remained at the club after relegation from the Premiership but suffered a serious injury in the third match of the Championship season which forced his retirement.

Jonathan Woodgate

Excelled at Newcastle before joining Real Madrid's Galacticos, where injury limited him to 14 appearances in two years. Scored the winning goal in the League Cup Final for Spurs but injuries blighted his career, which ended at his home-town club, Middlesbrough. Only received eight England caps.

Lee Bowyer

Continued to be a solid Premiership player for West Ham, Newcastle and Birmingham, but never reproduced the form from his early 20s. Only received one England cap (one assist).

David Batty

Retired after Leeds's relegation from the Premiership, withdrawing completely from the public eye.

Stephen McPhail

Never fully recovered from his early-career injuries. Never played another Premiership game after leaving Leeds in 2004, nor did he add to his 10 Ireland caps. Made 190 appearances for Cardiff City, captaining them in the 2008 FA Cup Final.

Harry Kewell

Left under a cloud when his agent took a huge chunk of the transfer fee from Liverpool, then caused outrage by joining Galatasaray. Won the FA Cup and Champions League at Anfield, though never recaptured the form he showed under O'Leary.

Alan Smith

Became back-up to Wayne Rooney at Old Trafford, before a horrific leg break ruined his career. Received a Premiership winners' medal despite falling one appearance short of the threshold, then moved to Newcastle as a midfielder and spent his later years in the lower leagues.

Paul Robinson
Possibly the closest of the Thorp Arch products to fulfilling their potential. Won 41 England caps, the League Cup at Spurs, and player of the year at Blackburn. Made 498 career appearances, scoring two goals.

Matthew Jones
Forced into retirement aged 24, with 13 Wales caps already to his name.

Eirik Bakke
Remained at Leeds after relegation, except for a short loan at Aston Villa. Injuries and contractual wrangling limited him to 13 appearances in three seasons, and he returned to Norway after relegation to League One.

Danny Mills
Won the League Cup while on loan at Middlesbrough as Leeds were being relegated. Joined Manchester City but injuries limited him to 54 appearances in five years. Retired at 32.

Michael Duberry
Left Leeds in 2004 for Championship rivals Stoke. Spent the rest of his career in the lower leagues, except for a brief stint in the Premiership with Reading.

Michael Bridges
Never fully recovered from his knee injury. Played for eight clubs in five years after leaving Leeds in 2004, mostly in the lower leagues. Moved to Australia in 2009 and remained there until retirement in 2015.

Darren Huckerby

Spent three seasons at Manchester City before settling at Norwich where he made almost 200 appearances. He suffered relegations and celebrated promotions at both clubs, but his best years were spent in the Championship.

Jason Wilcox

Moved to fellow relegated club Leicester in 2004, where he spent 18 months before a short stint at Blackpool brought the curtain down on his career.

Olivier Dacourt

Drove himself to Italy, where he enjoyed 18 months at Roma and won two Serie A titles with Inter Milan. Won two Confederation Cup titles with France.

Mark Viduka

Enjoyed three successful seasons at Middlesbrough after leaving Leeds in 2004, firing them to the UEFA Cup Final. Moved to Newcastle and retired two years later after suffering another relegation.

Dominic Matteo

Moved to Blackburn in 2004, but after a successful first season, injuries restricted him to just 32 appearances over the next four years. Retired after winning promotion to the Premiership with Stoke.

Rio Ferdinand

Went on to become a Manchester United legend, making over 300 appearances and winning more trophies than I'd care to count. With 81 caps to his name, he is considered one of England's greatest ever players.

Robbie Keane
Made over 300 appearances for Spurs, scoring 122 goals and winning the League Cup. Moved to LA Galaxy and scored another 100 goals, and won 146 caps for Ireland, scoring 68 goals. His country's greatest ever footballer.

Seth Johnson
Returned to Derby in 2005 and won the Championship play-off final in 2007. Cruelly, this was the last game of his career as a knee injury picked up at Wembley forced his retirement, aged 28.

Robbie Fowler
Three underwhelming seasons at Manchester City preceded a dream return to Liverpool as a bit-part player. Spent the final years of his career in Australia and Thailand.

David O'Leary
Appointed Aston Villa manager after a year out of the game. Finished sixth, tenth, then 16th, and was sacked. Four years later he returned to management in the UAE with Al-Ahli, but was sacked before the end of the season and has not worked in football since.

Peter Ridsdale
Continued to work in football, with roles as owner and/or chairman at Barnsley, Cardiff, Plymouth and Preston, all of whom suffered relegations and/or financial meltdowns. He was banned from being a company director by the Insolvency Service between 2012 and 2020, yet was appointed to the English Football League board of directors in 2021.

Roll Call

Player	98/99	99/00	00/01	01/02	Total
Nigel Martyn (32)	44	55	36	49	184
Gary Kelly (24)	0	47	38	25	110
Ian Harte (21)	44 (6)	49 (8)	48 (11)	47 (6)	188 (31)
Lucas Radebe (29)	36	40 (2)	33	0	109 (2)
Jonathan Woodgate (18)	33 (2)	49 (1)	21 (1)	15	118 (4)
Lee Bowyer (21)	45 (9)	48 (11)	54 (15)	30 (7)	177 (42)
David Batty (29)	10	22	26	44	102
Stephen McPhail (18)	20	38 (2)	10	4	72 (2)
Harry Kewell (20)	49 (9)	53 (17)	26 (2)	35 (11)	163 (39)
Alan Smith (17)	26 (9)	38 (6)	52 (18)	31 (5)	147 (38)
Paul Robinson (18)	6	0	24	0	30
Matthew Jones (18)	9	18	6	-	33
Eirik Bakke (21)	-	44 (8)	44 (3)	35 (4)	123 (15)
Danny Mills (21)	-	21 (2)	40	39 (1)	100 (3)
Michael Duberry (22)	-	16 (1)	8	7	31 (1)
Michael Bridges (20)	-	50 (21)	11	0	61 (21)
Darren Huckerby (22)	-	37 (2)	8 (2)	-	45 (4)
Jason Wilcox (27)	-	26 (4)	23 (1)	17	66 (5)
Olivier Dacourt (24)	-	-	48 (3)	25	73 (3)
Mark Viduka (22)	-	-	53 (22)	42 (16)	95 (38)
Dominic Matteo (24)	-	-	48 (2)	40	88 (2)
Rio Ferdinand (19)	-	-	32 (3)	41	73 (3)
Robbie Keane (18)	-	-	20 (9)	33 (9)	53 (18)
Seth Johnson (19)	-	-	-	14	14
Robbie Fowler (23)	-	-	-	23 (12)	23 (12)

- *Appearances in all competitions, including substitute appearances. Goals in brackets.*
- *Numbers in brackets after names are age of players when the O'Leary era began.*

League Record

	Pld	W	D	L	F	A	Pts	Pos
1998/99*	38	18	13	7	62	34	67	4th
1999/00	38	21	6	11	58	43	69	3rd
2000/01	38	20	8	10	64	43	68	4th
2001/02	38	18	12	8	53	37	66	5th

First seven games managed by George Graham: 2 wins, 5 draws, 8 scored, 4 conceded

Full List of Results

1998/99 Season

Leeds United 0-1 Leicester City
Nottingham Forest 1-1 Leeds United
Roma 1-0 Leeds United
Leeds United 0-0 Chelsea
Leeds United 1-0 Bradford City
Derby County 2-2 Leeds United
Leeds United 0-0 Roma
Leeds United 2-1 Sheffield Wednesday
Leicester City 2-1 Leeds United
Liverpool 1-3 Leeds United
Leeds United 4-1 Charlton Athletic
Manchester United 3-2 Leeds United
Leeds United 4-0 West Ham United
Leeds United 2-0 Coventry City
Arsenal 3-1 Leeds United
Newcastle United 0-3 Leeds United
Leeds United 2-2 Wimbledon
Rushden & Diamonds 0-0 Leeds United
Blackburn Rovers 1-0 Leeds United
Leeds United 3-1 Rushden & Diamonds
Leeds United 2-0 Middlesbrough
Portsmouth 1-5 Leeds United

Southampton 3-0 Leeds United
Leeds United 0-1 Newcastle United
Leeds United 1-1 Tottenham Hotspur
Aston Villa 1-2 Leeds United
Leeds United 1-0 Everton
Tottenham Hotspur 2-0 Leeds United
Leicester City 1-2 Leeds United
Leeds United 2-0 Tottenham Hotspur
Sheffield Wednesday 0-2 Leeds United
Leeds United 4-1 Derby County
Leeds United 3-1 Nottingham Forest
Leeds United 0-0 Liverpool
Charlton Athletic 1-1 Leeds United
Leeds United 1-1 Manchester United
West Ham United 1-5 Leeds United
Chelsea 1-0 Leeds United
Leeds United 1-0 Arsenal
Coventry City 2-2 Leeds United

1999/00 Season
Leeds United 0-0 Derby County
Southampton 0-3 Leeds United
Manchester United 2-0 Leeds United
Leeds United 2-1 Sunderland
Leeds United 1-2 Liverpool
Tottenham Hotspur 1-2 Leeds United
Coventry City 3-4 Leeds United
Partizan Belgrade 1-3 Leeds United
Leeds United 2-0 Middlesbrough
Leeds United 3-2 Newcastle United
Leeds United 1-0 Partizan Belgrade
Watford 1-2 Leeds United
Leeds United 1-0 Blackburn Rovers
Leeds United 2-0 Sheffield Wednesday

Leeds United 4-1 Lokomotiv Moscow
Everton 4-4 Leeds United
Leeds United 1-0 West Ham United
Lokomotiv Moscow 0-3 Leeds United
Wimbledon 2-0 Leeds United
Leeds United 2-1 Bradford City
Leeds United 1-0 Southampton
Spartak Moscow 2-1 Leeds United
Derby County 0-1 Leeds United
Leeds United 1-0 Spartak Moscow
Leeds United 2-0 Port Vale
Leicester City 0-0 Leeds United
Chelsea 0-2 Leeds United
Leeds United 2-1 Leicester City
Arsenal 2-0 Leeds United
Leeds United 1-2 Aston Villa
Manchester City 2-5 Leeds United
Sunderland 1-2 Leeds United
Aston Villa 3-2 Leeds United
Liverpool 3-1 Leeds United
Leeds United 1-0 Tottenham Hotspur
Leeds United 0-1 Manchester United
Middlesbrough 0-0 Leeds United
Roma 0-0 Leeds United
Leeds United 3-0 Coventry City
Leeds United 1-0 Roma
Bradford City 1-2 Leeds United
Leeds United 3-0 Slavia Prague
Leeds United 4-1 Wimbledon
Slavia Prague 2-1 Leeds United
Leicester City 2-1 Leeds United
Leeds United 0-1 Chelsea
Galatasaray 2-0 Leeds United
Aston Villa 1-0 Leeds United

Leeds United 0-4 Arsenal
Leeds United 2-2 Galatasaray
Newcastle United 2-2 Leeds United
Sheffield Wednesday 0-3 Leeds United
Leeds United 3-1 Watford
Leeds United 1-1 Everton
West Ham United 0-0 Leeds United

2000/01 Season
Leeds United 2-1 1860 Munich
Leeds United 2-0 Everton
1860 Munich 0-1 Leeds United
Middlesbrough 1-2 Leeds United
Leeds United 1-2 Manchester City
Coventry City 0-0 Leeds United
Barcelona 4-0 Leeds United
Leeds United 1-2 Ipswich Town
Leeds United 1-0 AC Milan
Derby County 1-1 Leeds United
Leeds United 6-0 Besiktas
Leeds United 4-3 Tottenham Hotspur
Leeds United 3-1 Charlton Athletic
Besiktas 0-0 Leeds United
Manchester United 3-0 Leeds United
Leeds United 1-1 Barcelona
Bradford City 1-1 Leeds United
Tranmere Rovers 3-2 Leeds United
Leeds United 4-3 Liverpool
AC Milan 1-1 Leeds United
Chelsea 1-1 Leeds United
Leeds United 0-1 West Ham United
Leeds United 0-2 Real Madrid
Leeds United 1-0 Arsenal
Leicester City 3-1 Leeds United

Lazio 0-1 Leeds United
Southampton 1-0 Leeds United
Leeds United 2-0 Sunderland
Leeds United 1-2 Aston Villa
Newcastle United 2-1 Leeds United
Leeds United 1-1 Middlesbrough
Leeds United 1-0 Barnsley
Manchester City 0-4 Leeds United
Leeds United 1-3 Newcastle United
Aston Villa 1-2 Leeds United
Leeds United 0-2 Liverpool
Leeds United 1-0 Coventry City
Ipswich Town 1-2 Leeds United
Everton 2-2 Leeds United
Leeds United 0-0 Derby County
Leeds United 2-1 Anderlecht
Anderlecht 1-4 Leeds United
Tottenham Hotspur 1-2 Leeds United
Leeds United 1-1 Manchester United
Real Madrid 3-2 Leeds United
Leeds United 3-3 Lazio
Charlton 1-2 Leeds United
Sunderland 0-2 Leeds United
Leeds United 3-0 Deportivo La Coruna
Leeds United 2-0 Southampton
Liverpool 1-2 Leeds United
Deportivo La Coruna 2-0 Leeds United
West Ham United 0-2 Leeds United
Leeds United 2-0 Chelsea
Leeds United 0-0 Valencia
Arsenal 2-1 Leeds United
Valencia 3-0 Leeds United
Leeds United 6-1 Bradford City
Leeds United 3-1 Leicester City

2001/02 Season
Leeds United 2-0 Southampton
Arsenal 1-2 Leeds United
West Ham United 0-0 Leeds United
Leeds United 0-0 Bolton Wanderers
Charlton Athletic 0-2 Leeds United
Maritimo 1-0 Leeds United
Leeds United 3-0 Derby County
Leeds United 3-0 Maritimo
Ipswich Town 1-2 Leeds United
Leicester City 0-6 Leeds United
Liverpool 1-1 Leeds United
Leeds United 4-2 Troyes
Leeds United 0-0 Chelsea
Manchester United 1-1 Leeds United
Troyes 3-2 Leeds United
Leeds United 2-1 Tottenham Hotspur
Sunderland 2-0 Leeds United
Grasshoppers 1-2 Leeds United
Leeds United 1-1 Aston Villa
Leeds United 0-2 Chelsea
Fulham 0-0 Leeds United
Leeds United 2-2 Grasshopper
Blackburn Rovers 1-2 Leeds United
Leeds United 2-2 Leicester City
Leeds United 3-2 Everton
Leeds United 3-4 Newcastle United
Bolton Wanderers 0-3 Leeds United
Southampton 0-1 Leeds United
Leeds United 3-0 West Ham United
Cardiff City 2-1 Leeds United
Newcastle United 3-1 Leeds United
Leeds United 1-1 Arsenal
Chelsea 2-0 Leeds United

Leeds United 0-4 Liverpool
Middlesbrough 2-2 Leeds United
PSV Eindhoven 0-0 Leeds United
Leeds United 0-0 Charlton Athletic
Leeds United 0-1 PSV Eindhoven
Everton 0-0 Leeds United
Leeds United 2-0 Ipswich Town
Leeds United 3-1 Blackburn Rovers
Leicester City 0-2 Leeds United
Leeds United 3-4 Manchester United
Tottenham Hotspur 2-1 Leeds United
Leeds United 2-0 Sunderland
Aston Villa 0-1 Leeds United
Leeds United 0-1 Fulham
Derby County 0-1 Leeds United
Leeds United 1-0 Middlesbrough
Cup games in italics

Full Record: All Competitions

Pld	W	D	L	F	A
203	101	47	55	320	217

EPILOGUE

Leeds United on Trial

IN MAY 2003, during my exile in Florence, Leeds had narrowly avoided relegation under Peter Reid and I wrote an analysis on what had gone wrong at Elland Road, scribbled on the back of my Italian homework. I found it while sifting through all my old Leeds stuff that had lived in various lofts for nearly 20 years. The real-time perspective of my 19-year-old self seems a fitting place to finish…

> 7.30pm on Tuesday, 5 May 2001. Leeds United players sat in the dressing room of the Mestalla Stadium, Valencia, just 90 minutes away from a European Cup Final in the San Siro. Two years later and Leeds United could well have been facing up to life in the Nationwide League. They were a club who had it all; great young British players, a great young manager with passion for the club, and a chairman who truly loved the club and would stop at nothing to bring success for the fans. Now they have nothing. Their best players have been sold off, they are on their third manager in a year, the chairman has gone, and they are heavily in debt.

247

Ask Peter Reid his hopes for next season and he may well tell you that they want to finish as high as possible, but the supporters know anything above 17th will be a plus. Last season the supporters expected nothing less than Champions League football: how fast things can change in the world of football. Instead of debating over which of the six international strikers should start on Saturday, Leeds fans are arguing over who is to blame for the most spectacular downfall ever seen in English football.

The man who has taken most of the blame is Peter Ridsdale, or Father Christmas as the press have nicknamed him. Yes, this man made mistakes, but I have a great deal of sympathy for him. He took over the club in 1997 and up until the 2000/01 season his performance was faultless. In four years, he took the club from bottom-half nobodies to the brink of European glory. From then the mistakes began. Spending £18m on Ferdinand was a shrewd move, getting Robbie Keane on loan was even shrewder, but with the amount of debt Leeds were in, surely buying Keane for £12m was a massive risk, especially for a squad player, and with Bridges returning from a long-term injury. The next season he spent £20m on Fowler and Johnson. Considering how much debt Leeds must have been in, buying a sixth striker and a reserve midfielder for that much money seems ridiculous.

On top of the financial mismanagement was Ridsdale's conduct in the aftermath of the trial. Fining Bowyer four weeks wages was so out of order it's untrue. He might as well have said to Bowyer, 'You may have got away with it, but we all think you're guilty, so take this fine you little bastard!'

Bowyer, quite rightly, refused to pay the fine and Ridsdale slapped him on the transfer list. Can you imagine how he felt? And what about Bowyer's mates, the players? Surely they lost respect for their chairman? As a result of Ridsdale's actions Leeds lost their most influential player for just £100k.

Now there is a defence to put forward. Firstly, let's not forget that Leeds United are a plc, spearheaded by Ridsdale. Every financial move made by Leeds United in this period was a joint decision. The board must take their share of the blame for over-spending, but they have hidden behind Mr Public Relations. Secondly, Leeds United were moving forward incredibly fast. O'Leary was doing a faultless job and Ridsdale put full faith in him. If O'Leary said Seth Johnson would be a great asset, why not believe him? If the board agreed that the finances were there, why not give the green light? Also, all the bold moves made by Ridsdale were done when Leeds looked certainties for a top-four finish. He wasn't spending to push Leeds into the top bracket, he was spending to secure Leeds as a European force. Leeds were top of the league when they bought Fowler. How could Ridsdale predict the awful second half of the season that threw Leeds into financial ruin? Yes, it was ridiculous to gamble the club's future, but this is not Ridsdale's fault only. Then, after finishing fifth Ridsdale sacked David O'Leary. Was this a mistake? Let's see.

David O'Leary took over a club which had finished fifth. George Graham had turned the club around and it was O'Leary's job to take Leeds further. Now, Leeds had some fantastic youngsters in the reserves – Robinson, Harte, Woodgate,

McPhail, Jones and Smith. O'Leary threw them into the team and they didn't let him down. Does this make him a great manager? Leeds finished third in 2000, the team was packed with players who had passion for the club, they were young, exciting and fearless. Then O'Leary spent £50m on a bunch of internationals, breaking up the team. However, at the end of 2000/01 Leeds had nearly won the European Cup. They finished fourth but had been the top team in England by seven points over the second half of the season. The squad was brimming with talent, but O'Leary wanted more. He spent £11m on Fowler, breaking up a strike partnership that had ripped apart the best teams in Europe just six months earlier. O'Leary should have known that Fowler and Viduka were too slow to play together, they provided no threat and now neither did Leeds.

Then, O'Leary wrote a book exposing personal details of players. He apparently lost the dressing room, but I suppose we'll never know. What is for certain is that Leeds were an awful team in 2002. They couldn't defend, they couldn't pass, they were awful. The players were playing terribly and Leeds scraped fifth place and were knocked out of all three cup competitions early. Can you blame O'Leary for the players' dip in form? Yes, I think you can. Even if the book didn't affect team spirit, I'm sure it affected morale when the manager started telling the press that Mills shouldn't play in the World Cup because he is a hot-head, or that Smith will be sold if he gets sent off again.

Perhaps O'Leary brought the youngsters in too soon? Take McPhail and Bakke. They were a magnificent midfield partnership that took Leeds to a third-place finish and a European semi-final. Now they are both rotting in the reserves. Kewell, Woodgate, Smith and Harte suffered huge drops in form for long periods, and Michael Bridges hasn't played for three years. George Graham didn't want to bring them in. Had he stayed the progress may have been slower but, with hindsight, this would have been for the best. I would love to have seen how he would have handled the Bowyer/ Woodgate incident.

Just like Ridsdale has his defence, so does O'Leary: luck. In David O'Leary's reign just about everything that could have gone wrong did go wrong. In his first full season they were top of the league in January when two of his best players were charged with GBH. This hung over the club for the next two years. This can't have been easy for a team as young as they were. What will have been even harder for O'Leary's 'babies' was seeing two fans stabbed to death the night before a UEFA Cup semi-final. That incident put an end to the season there and then. The next season was ruined by the most horrific injury curse imaginable up until January. Who knows what would have happened if Leeds's squad hadn't been on the treatment table until December. More serious were the long-term effects. Star player Harry Kewell didn't fully recover from injury until after O'Leary had gone. Top scorer Michael Bridges has hardly kicked a ball for three years, and playmaker McPhail has never been the same since his Achilles tendon injury. Then there was the Manchester United match. An injury-time winner was disallowed for offside even though it was an own goal. This robbed Leeds of the two extra points needed for Champions League qualification. Had they qualified they would not be in financial ruin, as they could have afforded the massive wage bill they had accumulated. What about the night in Valencia when Leeds only needed a draw to reach the Champions League Final? Sanchez punches the ball in the net and the goal stands. Going in for half-time at 0-0 would have made a gigantic difference in the second half.

Okay, so O'Leary was unlucky, but the bottom line is that Peter Ridsdale gave Leeds the best squad they probably will ever have and O'Leary failed to win any silverware and failed to qualify for the Champions League. On top of this the team weren't playing for him and his personality seemed to change. He was no longer 'young and naïve', he was bitter and totally stressed out. The public used to love him and now they didn't even like him. Leeds were moving backwards and change is exactly what they needed. One brownie point for Mr Ridsdale. But then Ridsdale appointed the next culprit for the club's downfall, Terry Venables, or Very Terribles as he should be known. Ridsdale praised Terry's 'great track record' at his press conference, so let's put that under the microscope, shall we?

Okay, prior to the 90s Terry had done well, and at Spurs he was doing quite well, but what about after that? Euro '96. Three good games, one against Scotland, one against a Dutch side split by racism, and one against Germany. Yes, Terry could have won Euro '96, but they needed penalty shoot-outs in the quarter-finals and semi-finals, plus England had home advantage. After England was Australia, where

Terry failed to get them to the World Cup, losing to Iran. Then came Crystal Palace. He put them in financial ruin and built an awful team. Finally came Middlesbrough. Venables did not keep them up. Robson collected one point less in the first half of the season than Tel did in the second half. So, in his 'fantastic' managerial career, Venables has only won one domestic trophy, the FA Cup.

Venables took over O'Leary's squad, fully fit for the first time ever, no trial hanging over them, nothing. His first move was to axe the best goalkeeper in Leeds's history, Nigel Martyn. He also axed another legend, David Batty. He brought in Paul Okon, released in the summer by Watford, to replace Batty. He played five in midfield even when Leeds were at home, he dropped the best midfielder in Dacourt, and he sold Robbie Keane when he could have got the same money for Fowler. These were radical changes and by December Leeds were out of Europe, out of the League Cup, and 16th in the league after losing six straight home games. Leeds should have been in the top three in January, and if they were then the players would not have been sold.

All in all, I think Peter Ridsdale deserved his sacking, as did O'Leary, as did Venables. What I can't understand about Ridsdale …

Sadly, I have lost what I believe to be the last page of my analysis. Unless this was an artistic ending, akin to *The Sopranos'* final scene (well ahead of time), portraying the fact that nobody will ever understand quite how Leeds fell so spectacularly.

The O'Leary years were a roller coaster; it's likely English football will never again see a group of youngsters rise so high so quickly, such is the direction football has taken. But it also took us to places beyond our darkest nightmares. It was the best of times, it was the worst of times.